DATE DUE

8/12/95	
DEC 31 1996	
DEC 5 1998	
OCT 24 1999	
OCT 19 2000 JAN 2 2001	
MAY 27 2002	

GAYLORD   PRINTED IN U.S.A.

100 Ways to Enhance Values and Morality in Schools and Youth Settings

Related Titles of Interest

Improving Social Competence: A Resource for Elementary School Teachers

Pam Campbell and Gary N. Siperstein
ISBN: 0-205-13757-1

101 Ways to Develop Student Self-Esteem and Responsibility

Jack Canfield and Frank Siccone
ISBN: 0-205-16884-1

100 Ways to Enhance Self-Concept in the Classroom, Second Edition
Jack Canfield and Harold Clive Wells
ISBN: 0-205-15415-8 Paper   0-205-15711-4 Cloth

Winners Without Losers: Structures and Strategies for Increasing Student Motivation to Learn

James P. Raffini
ISBN: 0-205-14008-4

Celebrating Diversity: Building Self-Esteem in Today's Multicultural Classrooms

Frank Siccone
ISBN: 0-205-16178-8 Paper   0-205-16390-4 Cloth

100 Ways to Enhance Values and Morality in Schools and Youth Settings

Howard Kirschenbaum

Allyn and Bacon
Boston • London • Toronto • Sydney • Tokyo • Singapore

LC
311
.K57
1995

Library of Congress Cataloging-in-Publication Data
Kirschenbaum, Howard
    100 ways to enhance values and morality in schools and youth
settings/Howard Kirschenbaum.
        p.   cm.
    Includes bibliographical references and index.
    ISBN 0-205-16411-0.—ISBN 0-205-15489-1 (pbk.)
    1. Moral education—United States.   2. Values—Study and teaching—
United States.   I. Title.   II. Title: One hundred ways to enhance
values and morality in schools and youth settings.
LC311.K57   1994
370.11´4—dc20   94-15335
                                                                CIP

Printed in the United States of America
10 9 8 7 6 5 4 3 2 1   98 97 96 95 94

Dedication

To the values educators
and moral educators
from whom I have learned so much.

Especially:

Abraham and Theone Kirschenbaum,
my parents;

Herb Goldstein,
my scoutmaster;

Sid Simon and Merrill Harmin,
my colleagues and friends;

Mary Rapp,
my wife;

Kimara Glaser-Kirschenbaum,
my daughter.

Contents

PART II   100 Ways to Enhance Values and Morality in Schools and Youth Settings   59

7   Facilitating Values and Morality   159

Preface

- Two dozen suburban high school athletes scored points for each of their sexual conquests, running up winning totals of 50 and 66, through seduction, date rape, group rape, and even having sex with a 10-year-old girl.
- Parents excused their sons' conduct, saying, "Nothing my boy did was anything any red-blooded American boy wouldn't do at his age," and "It's a testosterone thing." Fellow classmates cheered the boys on their return to school.[179]
- Sixty-five percent of high school students reported they would cheat on an important exam, if they had the opportunity.[36]
- Forty-eight percent of the high school class of 1990 admitted having taken illegal drugs at some time in their lives. One out of four 12- to 17-year-olds used alcohol within the past month.[195]
- In a large study by the Centers for Disease Control and Prevention, three out of four teenagers reported they had engaged in sex by the time they had finished high school. Forty percent said they were not virgins by the end of ninth grade.[26] In another study, 72 percent of teenagers said they had had intercourse by their senior year of high school, and 45 percent said they had not used a condom.[135]
- Racism, anti-Semitism, intolerance, and hate-related violence are on the rise among youth. In 1992, hate-inspired vandalism by all age groups rose 49 percent.[42]
- Teenage smoking has been increasing since 1988.[191]
- Only 36.2 percent of 18- to 24-year-olds voted in the 1988 presidential election.[50] Although the figure was better in 1992, analysts fear the

improvement was temporary and is still the lowest turnout compared to any Western democracy.

- One out of four children in the United States is now born out of wedlock, compared to about one in twenty in 1960. (It was one in ten in 1970, and one in five in 1980.)[133]
- While there is some variation among different groups, these statistical trends are strong in all geographic, economic, and racial groupings in the society.

As the popular songwriter Bob Dylan put it, "The times they are a-changin'." Indeed, they are.

Throughout history, adults have often bemoaned the decline in the younger generation's values and moral character. At no time, however, have changes in technology, personal lifestyles, geopolitics, and the global environment occurred with such rapidity. In times of accelerated social, political, and economic changes, nations and civilizations have come and gone. Today, many are concerned that the changing values of society, which these youth trends reflect, are both a symptom and a cause of a serious national decline.

Certainly these problems were not created by young people but are a reflection of an adult society which has often lost its own sense of values and its commitment to youth. Ours is a wealthy society which allows one out of four its children to live in poverty[51]; which fights a war on drugs while subsidizing the addictive drug tobacco, the nation's leading cause of premature death, which criticizes self-indulgent young people while running up a $5 trillion national debt to pay for its luxuries.

Faced with these statistics and realities, it would be understandable to feel despair when contemplating the future and to think that these trends are irreversible. There are many committed educators and youth workers who would like to help address youth problems in schools and other settings but feel powerless in the face of parent apathy, negative models in the media and in the sports industry, peer pressure, youth unemployment and violence, the decline in the influence of religion on society, political gridlock and corruption, and a general decline in social cohesiveness and a sense of community. On a more personal level, many feel powerless in their own lives to counteract these negative forces in raising their own children and teenagers.

Yet, despite the obstacles and the daunting challenges these trends represent, there is another spirit growing throughout the land. Increasing numbers of parents, teachers, clergy, and community and business leaders are saying "Enough!" and calling for a renewed commitment to our young people and, therefore, to our future. They are recognizing that involved parents and teachers already make an important difference in young people's lives every day. Millions of adults *do* exercise a steady, positive influence over the values and character of children and youth. In schools around the country, newly developed programs demonstrate daily that education in values and morality can succeed.[10,62] Young people *can* be taught to respect themselves and each other, to act responsibly, to respect and tolerate different ethnic and religious groups, to care for others and the planet, to participate in the body politic, to be effective thinkers and decision makers, and to take pride in their work.

The problem is not that we *can't* exert a positive influence, but that we haven't done it often enough. For many reasons, we have collectively stood by and allowed the problems among youth to grow worse. Rather than control the direction of change, we have allowed change to control us. Through lack of clarity, lack of consistency, and lack of resources (time, energy, and money), we have forfeited much of our ability to make a difference.

But that is changing. By regaining a clarity of purpose and commitment, mobilizing our energies, and working together for the common good, we, as a society, can rebuild the national character. Even as demographics change, we can remain united or become united in a sense of national purpose. This is more than soapbox rhetoric, reminiscent of the biannual ritual when politicians "rediscover" and advocate a return to traditional values. In recent decades, there has been much controversy about the best ways to address young people's needs and an equally vocal controversy about how schools can help teach values, morality, character, and citizenship to the next generation. The resulting discussion, experimentation, research, and cumulative experience have led to further insights about how schools can perform this crucial task.

This book offers a synthesis of that experience and insight. It presents a comprehensive approach to values education and moral education. It draws on the best of the approaches and the methods that have worked for centuries *and* that have been developed in recent decades to help young people grow up with clear values, good character, moral integrity, and the knowledge and skills to be good citizens. The comprehensive model utilizes traditional approaches for inculcating and modeling values, for teaching and demonstrating to young people the best values and moral traditions of their culture. At the same time, it utilizes new approaches to help students internalize these values and to develop the attitudes, beliefs, and skills to guide their own lives and make responsible, personal decisions in a changing world.

Above all, the approach set forth in these pages is meant to be practical. One hundred different methods for enhancing values and morality are described, with clear guidelines, examples, and suggestions for implementation. Teachers, administrators, school personnel, and youth workers—anyone who works with children and youth in and out of schools—can immediately begin using these methods to help reverse the tide of apathy, confusion, and moral decline. While no single book can provide all the answers to the enormous task of values education and moral education, this one provides an overview of the major components in a total program, as well as hundreds of practical suggestions for implementing such a plan.

The future of any nation depends on the values and character of its youth. The exciting thing is that today good programs in values education and moral education are succeeding in schools and districts around the country—in inner-cities, suburbs, and rural areas, alike. This is why many teachers and youth workers enter the profession—to make a difference in the lives of young people. There is no work more important. And there is no time to waste.

Acknowledgments

I want to express my appreciation to all those teachers, administrators, parents, graduate and undergraduate students, workshop participants, and colleagues it has been my privilege to know, teach, and work with over the past thirty years. Many of their ideas and practices fill these pages. Their example and dedication have motivated and inspired me.

I am extremely grateful to the secondary and elementary school students I have worked with over the years—as their teacher, workshop leader, counselor, or scout leader. Their optimism, resilience, courage, and frequent morality have kept me going and called upon me to do better.

Thanks again to those dear friends and relatives I identified in the dedication. Their personal example, guidance, and inspiration have contributed so much to who I am and what I have learned about values education.

Beyond these invaluable sources, there are many mentors, colleagues, and authors whose work has influenced and enlightened me, who certainly deserve and would receive special mention, if space allowed. Many of them are cited in references throughout the book. One, in particular, I must cite is Thomas Lickona, a leading values educator from whom I have learned a great deal and whose book, *Educating for Character*,[122] is of major importance to the values education field. Thanks also to Jacques Benninga, whose book of readings, *Moral, Character and Civic Education in the Elementary School*,[19] gave me valuable insights and ideas.

Finally, my appreciation to Hanoch McCarty and Gwen Fountain for their helpful comments on the manuscript and to Mylan Jaixen and Susan Hutchinson of Allyn and Bacon for all their support and encouragement throughout the publishing process.

About the Author

Howard Kirschenbaum has written, co-authored or co-edited twenty books in the fields of values education, professional development, psychology, and history. He serves as guest faculty at a number of institutions, including State University of New York at Brockport, and is an independent consultant to schools, businesses, and non-profit organizations. He holds a Doctor of Education degree in educational psychology from Temple University.

Dr. Kirschenbaum has lectured and conducted workshops on values education throughout the United States and Canada, as well as in Sweden, Israel, Venezuela, Philippines, and Australia. He has appeared on the former Phil Donahue segment of the *Today Show* and in many radio interviews.

Dr. Kirschenbaum is married (to a school principal) and has three children. He may be reached at 458 Whiting Road, Webster, New York 14580.

Part 1

Values Education and Moral Education: A Comprehensive Approach

Chapter 1

A Brief History
of Values Education

> *Politeness*
> I think it would be lots of fun
> To be polite to every one;
> A boy would doff his little hat,
>   A girl would curtsey, just like that!
>
> And both would use such words as these:
> *Excuse me, Sir*, and *If you please*;
> Not only just at home, you know,
> But everywhere that they should go.
> Gelett Burgess, *A Manual of Manners for Polite
> Infants Inculcating Many Juvenile Virtues Both
> By Precept and Example*, 1900.[28]

Parents, educators, religious institutions, and youth-serving organizations have always cared deeply about developing character, values, and morality in youth. For many centuries, in fact, these various teachers generally agreed on the basic values and moral standards they would pass on to the next generation. Even until the 1900s, in the United States and Canada, there was little argument over the goals and methods of values education and moral education.

For the past hundred years, however, there has been considerable controversy in education and in society over the best way to raise young people and to acculturate them into society's norms and values. More recently, there has also been serious controversy over whether our culturally diverse society *has* a coherent set of values agreeable to an increasingly pluralistic population.[136]

The values and goals of society, inevitably, are reflected in the schools, where educators are called upon to help achieve society's broader goals. When the society has a values conflict, the schools experience that conflict also, as they try to reconcile the conflicting demands placed upon them. It is not surprising, then, that the modern history of values education and moral education closely parallels American social history during this period.

Values Education Early in the Century

Early in the twentieth century, the public schools were seen as an essential means of socializing or "Americanizing" the millions of mostly working-class immigrants arriving each year. In addition to teaching language skills, academics, and citizenship, it was an important role of the schools to transmit the current Victorian standards for values and morality. Even if it was not always followed in personal and business practice, "middle class morality" was the only game in town, the only moral perspective worth speaking of in polite society, and the schools were expected to teach and reinforce it. The "Children's Morality Code" of that period was a popular code of conduct that schools, parents, and clubs employed to inculcate ten important values or character traits: self-control, good health, kindness, sportsmanship, self-reliance, duty, reliability, truth, good workmanship, and teamwork.[116] Scores of character education programs were available for schools to choose from to instill these virtues "by precept and example."

During Prohibition, character educators and youth-serving organizations attempted to counteract the permissive "Roaring Twenties," which many feared signaled the end of conventional morality. However, in the late twenties, landmark research by Hartshorne and May demonstrated that traditional character education programs were not working; repeated studies showed, for example, that products of traditional character education and scouting programs were no more honest than young people who did not participate in these programs.[81] This research lent credence to the growing "progressive education" movement with its program of teaching civic values through the project method and democratic participation. Progressive educators argued that by encouraging teamwork and group problem solving, schools taught respect, responsibility, tolerance, and concern for the common good—important character traits and civic virtues.

While progressive education demonstrated some positive results[33], like any new movement it was implemented inconsistently and, for a variety of reasons, eventually faded from prominence. Although formal character education programs were used less often in the thirties, it was still widely accepted that inculcating good character traits was important and that everyone—parents, religions, and schools—ought to be united in this endeavor.

Values Education Goes Underground

As the Great Depression and World War II came to dominate the national consciousness, there was no longer a conscious, concerted focus on teaching values, character, and morality in the schools. After the war, American education became more concerned with helping young people find their place in the rapidly expanding, post-war economy and, after Sputnik, keeping up with the Soviets in science and technology. Thus the late 1940s and 1950s became the so-called years of conformity, McCarthyism, and the "Organization Man." [198] Despite periodic expressions of concern about public and private morality (such as reactions to scandals in the Truman administration, the expulsion of ninety West Point cadets for cheating on examinations, and the unethical practices of television quiz shows and the "payola" industry[124]), there was a working consensus among parents, religion, and society regarding values and morality.

Values education and moral education during this period continued, in and out of school, to consist almost exclusively of the traditional methods of *inculcating* and *modeling* values. Children were occasionally exhorted to be prompt, neat, and polite; to work hard and succeed; to emulate venerated national heroes; to respect authority and other people's property, and to behave themselves. Not much time was spent explicitly teaching these values in school, nor were special courses or curricula developed to do it. Educators did not talk much about values or character education, nor organize workshops for teachers in this area. It was simply assumed that it was the school's role to expect young people to conform to social expectations and to do their work. The public schools had come to take their role in values education more or less for granted.

The New Approaches of the '60s and '70s

Then came the turbulent 1960s and 1970s, when traditional roles and values were seriously questioned—and in many cases rejected—by the younger generation. The status of blacks, women, students, and other minorities changed dramatically, in one of the fastest social revolutions in history. New attitudes about and experimentation with human sexuality, religion, career options, lifestyles, and personal values were widespread. The common thread underlying all these social changes could be summarized in the popular slogan, "Power to the people." Minority groups and individuals increasingly assumed greater decision-making power and control over their own lives.[159]

As might be expected, values education and moral education began to reflect these changes in society. Instead of simply inculcating and modeling traditional values, educators were now encouraged to help students *clarify their own values,* learn higher levels of *moral reasoning,* and learn the skills of *value analysis.*[110,130,137,154,185] Educators were counseled to avoid imposing their own values and morals on students—because, the argument went, in an increasingly pluralistic society, Whose values are the "right values?" A better course seemed to be to help young people learn the skills of moral reasoning and responsible decision making to enable them to make good decisions in the future. Just as some educators were arguing that it was less important to teach students isolated bits of information than to teach them *how to learn,* many values educators were arguing that it was less important to teach students particular values than to teach them *a valuing process* by which they could arrive at their own personally satisfying and socially responsible values. Teach young people how to analyze arguments and reason, morally, how to examine alternatives and the consequences, and how to integrate belief, feeling, and action, proponents maintained, and inevitably, they would make better and wiser decisions.

Sometimes parents and educators got caught between the inculcating methods of the past and the liberating philosophy of the present. One contemporary cartoon showed a long-haired, short-skirted mother standing over her teenage daughter saying, "Why should you grow up to be independent and think for yourself? Well . . . because I say so!"

Back to Basics in the '80s and '90s

Then times changed again. The relatively permissive, hopeful, idealistic 1960s and 1970s gave way to the more politically conservative, economically fearful, and socially disintegrating '80s. Ironically, the allegedly selfish "Me Generation" of the 1970s was supplanted by the allegedly selfish "Look-Out-for-Number-One" yuppie generation of the '80s. Many thoughtful analysts felt that, in emphasizing personal liberation, the 1970s had neglected the "communitarian values" that had previously held the country together.[183] While encouraging young people to take advantage of all the wonderful choices our wealthy society had to offer, we neglected to emphasize the basic values of hard work, family, education, and civic responsibility, which had helped create our prosperity and all those wonderful choices in the first place. One by one, social critics, groups of parents, religious leaders, and even the Republican and the Democratic parties, called upon society to return to the "traditional values"—respect, responsibility, self-discipline, pride in work, family, love of country, and service to others.

Once again, the world of education followed suit and went "back to the basics." This shift involved not only a renewed emphasis on academics, but a renewed faith in the basic, traditional morals and values of Judeo-Christian America. Enough of this moral relativism, many critics said. Enough of this let-each-child-decide-for-himself nonsense. The answer to the problems of America's youth was obvious: *Just say no!*

That phrase was initially a response to the problem of drug abuse among teenagers. It suggested that the answer to teen drug abuse was not teaching students how to make "their own responsible decisions" about illegal drugs, but to teach them *the only* responsible decision about drugs, which was to completely avoid them.[195] But the phrase "just say no" carried a meaning which went beyond the drug issue alone. It suggested that the newer approaches to values education and moral education were wrong, that the point was not to teach young people *how* to think about moral issues, but to teach them *what* to think about moral issues; not to teach them *a process* for determining what was right or wrong, but to *tell them* what was right and wrong; not to help them discover *their own values*, but to teach them *the best values*.

However, other educators soon pointed out that drug education was a bit more complicated than telling young people to "just say no." They also recognized that values education and moral education were more complicated than telling students how to think and behave and giving them noble role-models from American history who demonstrated those moral virtues. There were, in fact, more sophisticated approaches to the inculcation of values and morality. There were more interesting programs and curricula that employed a variety of techniques to help students understand, internalize, and act on such basic values as respect, caring, friendship, and cooperation.[19,34,88,120,187]

By the 1990s, then, good programs had been or were being developed to teach traditional values, and an almost universal concern for values and morality was being voiced by parents, the religious community, educators, and politicians of all persuasions.[37] This concern was spurred on by the country's apparent inability to control its drug problem, the growing dismay over crime, and the many indicators of social upheaval and collapse including violence, the disintegration of the family, teen pregnancy, teen suicide, a decline in civic responsibility, growing racial and ethnic antagonism, and an unprecedented number of scandals in the 1980s, which were symptomatic of a major ethical vacuum in government and business. For these and other reasons, parents, educators, and community leaders are now united in calling on the schools to become involved with educating our young people about values and morality. And well they should.

A Skeptical Look at Historical Trends

Yet those of us who lived through the last 20 or 30 years of educational innovation might understandably feel a certain weariness and wariness toward the current interest in dealing with values and morality in the schools. The brief history presented here describes a pendulum swinging back and forth, pushed by the winds of political and social change. Sometimes all it seems to take is a new administration in Washington and a change in the economy, and social and educational values begin to change. In the 1960s and 1970s the pendulum swung to the left again, as it had in the 1920s and 1930s. In the '80s and early '90s, it swung back to the right. Where will it swing in the late '90s and in the next century? Does American education learn from its previous experience, or is the current focus on values and morality in the schools another passing fad that will make little or no difference in the long run? Do we seriously believe that a return to the 1950s will meet the challenges of the 1990s and beyond?

American education has a problem with faddism. Behavioral objectives? Programmed learning? Oh, yes, they were big in the 1960s. Open education, grading reform, values clarification—we tried *those* in the 1970s. Back to the basics, shared decision making, critical thinking, school/business partnerships, cooperative learning, school restructuring . . . who knows which of the innovations and trends of the 1980s and 1990s will survive?

At best, promising new approaches and innovations can offer only partial solutions to education's problems. Yet we tout them and embrace them as panaceas. And when some prove to be potential improvements that require years of research and development; when the initial research proves ambiguous or debatable;

when the innovation fails to show dramatic results in the first years, we conclude we have been "had," once again, and look around for the next popular in-service approach, speaker, or consultant. Economists have noted American industry's obsession with short-term results, while other industrialized nations exhibit greater long-term commitment to research, development, and infrastructure. Similarly, our lack of long-range commitment to research, development, and training in educational innovation raises serious questions about the wisdom of a swinging pendulum as the basis for establishing programs in values and moral education.

The "Comprehensive" Model

This book suggests another approach. It is called "comprehensive values education" or "comprehensive moral education." (The distinction between the two terms is discussed in Chapter 2.) It is based on the assumption that there is a great deal of value in a number of *different* approaches to moral and values education. It is wise to emphasize traditional values and employ traditional methods of teaching them. Traditional values and methods of inculcating them have survived for hundreds and thousands of years, as civilization has made slow, inconsistent, but nonetheless forward progress. The advocates of new approaches to values education in the 1960s and 1970s, including the author, made a great mistake in devaluing and taking traditional values for granted. It was unwise philosophically, pedagogically, and as the subsequent backlash indicated, politically.

By the same token, the critics of the 1960s and 1970s run the risk of making an equally serious error if they dismiss and devalue the legitimate contributions of the values education and moral education innovations of that period. For the world *has* changed since the 1950s, and educators in the '60s and '70s developed some very valid insights, research, methods, and curricula to help young people deal with and prepare for that changing world. These programs would not have lasted for over twenty years—many are still being used successfully today—if they did not have value. The new programs of the 1960s and 1970s re-legitimized the school's role in dealing explicitly with values and morality.[162] They developed many activities and methods for involving and motivating the students to thoughtfully grapple with serious moral and values issues. Initial research results in many of the programs demonstrated promise. Others succeeded marginally but were dropped before they could be improved. Many current writers go to great lengths to distance themselves from some of the values education innovations of the 1960s and 1970s, lest they seem passé or controversial; yet many of the methods and insights of those decades reappear in some of the better programs today.

If we can free ourselves from the ever-present tendency of "my approach is better than yours," we will recognize that both traditional *and* newer approaches are needed. We *should* do a much better job of inculcating certain traditional values in our young people. The current thrust in values education and moral education is very valuable in calling us back to that important task. But, sooner or later, our young people are going to encounter situations that require them to make decisions on their own. It is wonderful when our inculcation and modeling nurture and teach them to be caring and respectful persons; but look around. Caring, respectful, and otherwise moral persons are both pro-life *and* pro-choice. Otherwise caring and respectful persons refrain from *and* engage in premarital sex. Caring and respectful persons anguish over religious and spiritual questions. Caring and respectful persons do *and* don't smoke cigarettes and marijuana. Caring and respectful persons struggle with difficult choices over vulnerable marriages, career dilemmas, and the meaning of personal success.

Many similar examples could be given. Unless we are completely cloistered from the pluralistic and changing world around us, the most successful inculcation does not free us from many difficult life decisions that we, and we alone, must resolve. These choices do not begin when we leave home. Value choices and moral dilemmas over friends, family, dating, sex, drugs, school, sports, competition, work, and money, confront elementary and secondary students as well. All the good inculcating and modeling in the world may not make difficult choices much easier when the time to choose arrives. Young people need *roots*, so that they know where they come from, *and wings*, so that they can fly on their own.

So what is a parent or a values educator to do? The solution is not to return to the past—neither to the permissive '60s and '70s nor to the conservative '50s and '80s. Nor is the solution to discard past experience and search for yet another new method for tackling old problems. As others have suggested, there is value in both the traditional approaches and the new approaches to values education and moral education.[8,76,77] Why not take the best elements of each, synthesize them, and improve from there? That is the comprehensive values education approach. It is comprehensive in four respects.

First, it is comprehensive in its *content*. It includes all value-related issues—from choice of personal values to ethical questions to moral issues.

Second, comprehensive values education is comprehensive in its *methodology*. It includes inculcating and modeling values, as well as prepares young people for independence by teaching and facilitating responsible decision-making and other life skills. *All these approaches are necessary*. Young people deserve to be exposed to the inculcation of values by adults who care: family members, teachers, and the community. They deserve to see adult role models with integrity and a joy for living. And they deserve to have opportunities that encourage them to think for themselves and to learn the skills for guiding their own lives.

Third, comprehensive values education is comprehensive in that it takes place *throughout the school*—in the classroom, in extracurricular activities, in career education and counseling, in awards ceremonies, in all aspects of school life. Examples include the elementary principal who, during morning announcements, thanks the student who turned in a lost wallet; the tenth grade teacher who uses cooperative groups in class; the second-grade teachers who spend a whole month centering their students' reading, writing, and other activities on the value of "kindness"; the school counselor who uses values clarification activities in career counseling; the social studies teacher who discusses moral dilemmas in conjunction with the Civil War; the teachers who are seen smoking or not smoking; the principal who has the courage to cancel the rest of the football season because his school started a serious fight at the last game. Collectively, these examples begin to suggest the meaning of comprehensive values education in schools.

Finally, comprehensive values education takes place *throughout the community*. Parents, religious institutions, civic leaders, police, youth workers, and community agencies all participate. To the extent that these sources are consistent in their expectations, their rules, and their personal behavior, there is a greater likelihood of succeeding in influencing community values and morals in youth.[86]

Comprehensive values education, in a sense, goes "back to the future." It is both conservative and progressive. It is conservative in that no new methods or experimental techniques are proposed that have not been around for many years, some for many centuries. It is conservative in that the traditional approaches of inculcating and modeling values and morality are given validity and prominence within the overall model. It is conservative in its claims: no quick fixes for youth's alienation or for winning the war on drugs are promised.

At the same time, comprehensive values education is also progressive. In the past, a great deal of energy has been wasted as educators, parents, and community groups have attacked one another while defending themselves over values education programs. Particularly in the late 1970s and early 1980s, many programs were attacked—some still are—for undermining traditional values. Today, many programs trying to inculcate traditional values are criticized as over-simplified, unrealistic, head-in-the-sand approaches to complex problems. This academic and political squabbling has delayed progress in values education and moral education. A comprehensive approach offers the opportunity to reduce misunderstanding and improve communication, to recognize common goals and, yes, common values. A spirit of cooperation frees time and energy for the more important task of implementing effective programs in schools and communities.

Comprehensive values education is also progressive because it forces us to make progress in an area that has been almost totally neglected in the history of values education. We have spent so much time arguing whether it is better to instill the right values in young people or to teach them to think for themselves that we have avoided the more difficult question of *when is each approach appropriate?* The comprehensive approach suggests that there is a time to moralize to our children and a time to listen to *their* wisdom; a time to model and a time to ask clarifying questions; a time to reward and a time to be neutral; a time to intervene and a time to overlook; a time to say "no" and a time to let go.

When is the time and place for each, and how does one choose the right method? How should values education be different for young people of different ages and developmental stages? Must all parents and educators be inculcators, role models, and facilitators of values development, or can we specialize, with some being better inculcators and others more effective facilitators? These are but a few of the questions we might explore and, in the process, we might see the field of values education progress in new and more effective directions.

Finally, comprehensive values education is a progressive model in that it actually offers hope for success. Several studies on the effectiveness of drug education and character education programs suggest that more comprehensive approaches offer the best hope for the war on drugs.[13,186,190,201] We have already seen positive results in the area of smoking, where the combination of educational efforts and changing social norms and laws have helped reduce smoking in some segments of the population, unfortunately not among young people.[191] What alternative is there? Piecemeal approaches and superficial applications only produce limited results.

Hopefully, the next decades of American education will be a period when we begin to implement a truly comprehensive approach to values education and moral education in schools, a period when we are less concerned with the labels of the past and more concerned with the challenges of the present and future, a period of building on over four decades of experience in values and moral education. No doubt controversy will continue. Principals and superintendents can expect to hear periodically from concerned parents who will ask, "Why are you teaching my child morals when he should be learning reading?"; "Are you using values clarification?"; and "Whose values are you teaching, anyway?" But this is the dawn of a new millennium, and the principal and the superintendent will have the confidence and the historical perspective to respond:

"Of course we still emphasize academics. At the same time, we believe it is essential for us to support the family in teaching our students civic and moral values and character traits that most parents, educators, and community members agree are essential. Just as important, we teach our young people the skills to solve problems, to think for themselves, and to make their own responsible decisions. Anything less would not be worthy of an educational system in a democracy and in a changing world."

If the [educational] system works . . . it provides students with the skills and desire to learn and to keep on learning through life. It prepares them for a rewarding career in a field of their choice. It gives them the ability to make wise decisions about their personal life and to participate responsibly in the democratic processes of our society. Most of all—and I think this is too often overlooked—education should teach young people how to enjoy life, how to get a kick out of it. Life is a great experience if you're trained and confident and know where you're going. An education that meets all these requirements is by far the greatest gift that America can bestow upon its young people.

TERRELL H. BELL
FORMER U.S. COMMISSIONER OF EDUCATION[16]

Chapter *2*

An Overview of Values Education Approaches

The problem with a field like values education is that it relates to almost every-thing. There are so many different ways to approach it. Educators, parents and public officials speak of:

- Character education
- Ethics
- Law-related education
- Critical thinking
- Moral education
- Values clarification
- Empathy training
- Cooperation skills
- Citizenship education
- Decision-making skills
- Moral reasoning
- Life skills
- Sex education
- Drug education
- Religious education

For each of these "fields," there are books, research studies, curricula, organi-zations, consultants, and training programs which advocate a particular peda-gogical approach. Proponents of each of these approaches would say that they are engaged in the task of values education and/or moral education. And they would probably be right, for values and moral education is a very multifaceted and complex undertaking. It has been defined differently by people, usually emphasizing the particular approach an individual advocates. Taking the *comprehensive* view, however, we can define the field of values education and moral education in its broadest terms:

Values Education and Moral Education

The conscious attempt to help others acquire
the knowledge, skills, attitudes and values
that contribute to more personally satisfying
and socially constructive lives

This definition describes values education and moral education as *one endeavor with two goals*. The first goal is to help people—young people in this case—to live more personally satisfying lives, which have meaning, joy, and satisfaction. This is not to suggest that it is a realistic goal to always be "happy," but that we experience a reasonable degree of satisfaction and success as we meet life's many challenges, opportunities, and even tragedies. It means that we are living vitally, experiencing the richness of ourselves, others, and the world around us, as we move toward self-selected, meaningful goals.

The second goal of values education and moral education is to help people live more socially constructive lives; which contribute to the good of the community; which are based on care and compassion for fellow humans and other living things, and which do not interfere with the rights of others to pursue *their* legitimate values. To be socially constructive is to act in a way that supports the values of "life, liberty, and the pursuit of happiness," not just for ourselves but for all people.

It is tempting to separate the overall endeavor into two distinct fields, thinking of "values education" as the attempt to help young people develop values which serve as the foundation for a personally satisfying life, and "moral education" as the attempt to help young people learn the moral attitudes and behavior to care for and respect the rights of others. This fits with a widely accepted distinction between *values* and *morals*, values being the domain of what is preferred and desirable, morals being the domain of what is right and wrong.

This distinction, though, breaks down in actual practice. Moral educators believe they are teaching *values*—moral and civic values; and values educators believe that people who have the life skills to make good choices for themselves will also be more productive, positive members of society. Most moral educators believe that "good people" will find greater satisfaction in life; while most values educators believe that people who have greater satisfaction in life are more likely to be good to others. Which comes first? Some prefer to approach the target from one side and some from the other. Either way, it is hard to separate the two sides of values education and moral education.

The comprehensive values education approach considers values education and moral education to be *one* endeavor. If we as parents, educators, and a community neglect to help our young people learn to develop either personally satisfying values *or* moral and civic values, then we have not completed our task.

Because values education and moral education are like two sides of a coin, for simplicity's sake, both sides are often described in these pages by the single term "values education." (This is consistent with the conceptual relationship between values and morality, in which moral values are a subset within the larger universe of all values.) At other times, however, both terms are used together, to emphasize the two goals of a comprehensive values education.

Like many areas in life, there is more than one way to reach a set of goals. This is especially true of values education, where numerous methods, programs, and curricula have been developed to help young people lead more personally satisfying and socially constructive lives. These many different approaches fall into four major *movements* in the overall field of values education:

- Values Realization
- Character Education
- Citizenship Education
- Moral Education

These four movements are illustrated in Figure 2-1. The hope is to make sense of a sometimes confusing field, because it is so all-encompassing, and to highlight the major approaches.

However, any attempt to analyze and synthesize the major movements and approaches of a complex field will not satisfy everyone. For example, a proponent of "law-related education" might prefer to see that approach described as a major category, rather than an example in the broader movement of "citizenship education." There are certainly other ways to piece together the puzzle of dozens of approaches to values education and moral education. The goal of *this* particular organization is to be as comprehensive as is feasible and to include and honor the many different approaches for accomplishing this important educational mission.

Some of the same objectives are intentionally listed in more than one column. For example, critical thinking skills are described as an ingredient of both Values Realization and Citizenship Education programs. Compassion is included as an aspect of both Character Education and Moral Education. Some of the same skills and attitudes serve several goals of values education and moral education, illustrating, again, that it is difficult to separate values education and moral education and that the two sides of the field are complimentary.

Values Realization

Values Realization, a term coined by Sidney B. Simon in 1980, perhaps comes closest to accurately summing up the first major movement in the values education field.[193] It encompasses all those approaches that help individuals determine, recognize, implement, act upon, and achieve their values in life. It is the process of moving toward a life that is personally satisfying—one of the dual goals of values education and moral education.

FIGURE 2-1   Comprehensive Values Education

Values Realization	*Character Education*
Knowing Oneself—one's feelings, beliefs, priorities	Respect—for others, for oneself, for property for environment
Self-Esteem	Responsibility—reliable, honest, trust-worthy
Goal-Setting Ability	
Thinking Skills—critical thinking, creative thinking	Compassion—kind, helpful, friendly, empathic, humane, tolerant
Decision-Making Skills	Self-Discipline—perseverance, thrift
Communication Skills	Loyalty
Social Skills	Courage
Knowledge of the World	Work Ethic
	Etc.

This same thrust has also been described as "life skills education"—learning the skills and knowledge which help young people guide their lives in a complex, changing world. Whatever one calls it, many educational methods and curricula have been developed to help young people develop skills to realize their values, to be effective people in all situations, and to find meaning in life. The most prominent are described briefly below.

Knowing Oneself

To know oneself requires an important set of life skills. These include being aware of one's feelings, beliefs, priorities, and values; knowing one's strengths and weaknesses; recognizing one's behavior patterns, and being honest with oneself. The values clarification approach, popular in the late 1960s through the early 1980s, was probably the most widely-used technique for helping people recognize, clarify and act upon their feelings, beliefs, and values.[103,154,176] Many other approaches were also developed to help people understand their inner experience, their patterns of thinking, and their behavior in group settings.[54,67,80,90]

Self-Esteem

Self-esteem includes both accepting oneself and appreciating oneself. There have been many programs and activities developed to help young people feel a greater sense of self-esteem.[31,32,194]

The connection of self-esteem with values education and moral education may initially not be apparent, but it is important. The lower a person's self-esteem, the less worthy a person feels, and therefore, the less likely a person will be

FIGURE 2-1   *(Continued)*

Citizenship Education	*Moral Education*
Knowledge—understanding history, democratic system	Moral Knowledge—understanding moral tradition, justice, fairness, ethics
Appreciation—heritage, rights and responsibilities, cultural diversity	Moral Reasoning—higher level reasoning, reversing roles, examining consequences. etc.
Critical Thinking Skills	
Communication Skills	Compassion and Altruism
Cooperation Skills	Moral Tendencies—conscience, loving the good, self-control, humility, moral habit
Conflict Resolution Skills	

to take charge of his* life, set appropriate goals, or get out of an abusive situation. If we devalue ourselves, the less likely we will be to realize our values and find satisfaction and meaning in our lives.

Also, how we feel about ourselves influences how we feel about and act toward others. Students who feel better about themselves are more likely to act thoughtfully toward others.[182] We know this on a common sense level. Who is more likely to cruelly tease another child about his appearance—one who feels secure in himself or one who feels insecure? Who is more likely to bully another person—one who likes himself or one with low-self esteem? Who is more likely to abuse others—one who has been emotionally supported and feels good about himself or one who has been abused?

The connections between self-esteem and school achievement are well-documented; although there is disagreement about which comes first and leads to the other.[15] The connection between self-esteem and moral behavior is clearly reciprocal. Feeling good increases the likelihood of doing good; and doing good feels good.

Goal-Setting Ability

Part of developing and achieving one's values involves setting clear and realistic goals. The "achievement motivation" approach of the early 1970s did some pioneering work in helping people learn to set appropriate goals, that is, goals that are neither too easy to be challenging nor too difficult to achieve.[3] Educational approaches and techniques which help young people learn to be better goal-setters

---

*Every author must resolve the pronoun problem. One solution, consistent with this author's values, is to use the male pronoun in the first half of the book, while using the female pronoun in the second half of the book. Hopefully, this approach avoids awkward, distracting phrasing ("he or she," "him or her") and inefficient circumlocutions, while achieving gender equity.

are contributing to values education. Successful goal-setters are going to be more effective in their personal lives and contribute more to their work setting and community.

Thinking Skills

There is a lot of discussion about the need for critical and creative thinkers in our society. Employers are often quoted saying they need more employees who know how to think and solve problems, rather than workers who just do what they are told. Career counselors and planners point out that, in a rapidly changing work environment where jobs and job descriptions continually change, it is not *how much information* one has that is critical for success but *the ability to think,* which enables one to learn new information. Consequently, critical thinking skills and, to a lesser degree, creativity skills made a great comeback in education in the late 1980s. Numerous books and organizations offer curricula and training programs in thinking and creativity skills.[40,41,128,138,143,144,166]

Enhancing students' thinking skills is an important part of values education. Intelligent life decisions require taking in, analyzing, synthesizing, and evaluating a great deal of information. We cannot control our own lives and get where we want and need to go, if we are at the mercy of others who manipulate the information we receive. To be effective consumers or effective decision-makers, we must be able to distinguish fact from opinion, recognize persuasion techniques, and evaluate arguments logically.

Similarly, when our alternatives seem limited or the obstacles in our path seem difficult to overcome, it is our creative thinking that enables us to generate new and better solutions to personal and professional problems. There is more than one way to achieve goals and values. The ability to be creative—which we all possess but may need to nurture—helps us find those better ways.

> *A passionate drive for clarity, accuracy and fair-mindedness, a fervor for getting to the bottom of things, to the deepest root issues, for listening sympathetically to opposite points of view, a compelling drive to seek out evidence, an intense aversion to contradiction, sloppy thinking, inconsistent application of standards, a devotion to truth as against self-interest—these are essential components of the rational person.*
>
> RICHARD W. PAUL[142]

Decision-Making Skills

Many different programs have been developed to teach decision-making skills.[66,170] They incorporate life skills, such as goal-setting and thinking skills; but they set these and other skills in a structured, sequential process designed to increase the likelihood of achieving a good decision—one which achieves the goal. Steps in most decision-making skills curricula include defining the problem, setting a goal, gathering information, generating alternatives, considering consequences, making a decision, and evaluating the outcome.

With so many decisions to make in life, a skilled and thoughtful decision maker is more likely to realize his values than the person who chooses thoughtlessly, irrationally, or inconsistently. In groups, the participant or leader with good decision-making skills is also more likely to help the group make effective decisions.

Communication Skills

Essential for values realization are the human relations skills of communicating one's thoughts and feelings clearly, listening well to others, and resolving conflicts effectively. One does not simply develop values in a vacuum. Being able to truly listen to other people—parents, teachers, friends, people with different views and experiences than our own—can be one of the most enriching means for learning, growing, and developing values. Then, knowing what we believe and want from life, we need other people to help us get what we want; unless we are hermits. Being able to communicate our ideas, feelings, values, and needs clearly with others increases the likelihood that we will realize our values. Finally, because some conflict is inevitable whenever people with different values and needs are together, our ability to resolve conflict successfully is also essential in order to fully realize our values. Programs and methods which teach these communication skills contribute directly to values realization.[22,47,70]

Social Skills

Beyond the generic communication skills described so far, there are many social skills that young people need to learn to achieve personal success, however they might define success. "Please" and "Thank you" may rightfully be viewed as part and parcel of the moral virtue of "respect for others," but they also are social *skills* which help one succeed in life. Knowing when to say "Yeah" and when to say "Yes," when to arrive on time for an appointment and when to be fashionably late for a party, when it's cool to be cool and when it's appropriate to be sophisticated, when "black vernacular English" is alright and when "white standard English" is required—these are a few examples of social skills that are essential for realizing one's goals and values. Some people would call them "survival skills."

Schools, which have a lot to do already, do not often teach social skills, per se. Yet employer surveys repeatedly indicate that one of the main reasons employees fail at their jobs is not lack of knowledge and work skills, but inappropriate attitudes and behaviors, which includes not knowing how to behave in a work setting, how to get along with supervisors and coworkers, and how to follow norms about time, attire, and social comportment.[89] This is true both on the assembly line and in the office. If we want to prepare young people to realize their values and succeed in life, teaching social skills is important.[45,126]

Academic and Worldly Knowledge

Values realization programs generally focus on life skills, but *knowledge* is also important for achieving one's values in life. This includes the academic knowledge taught from elementary school through college. When we separate out the trivial, irrelevant, and outdated information that many schools still teach, what remains is a great deal of useful, meaningful and important information, concepts, and skills that are also taught in schools. Young people need to know how the human body works; to be competent in math, science, and technology; to communicate through written and oral language; the history of their nation and communities, and a great deal more to master the complex world they live in.

Beyond academic learning, knowledge of how the "real world" works is also essential to achieving one's values. If you don't understand the legal system, you are more likely to be overwhelmed by it and less likely to use it to reach your goals. The same could be said for the economic system, the political system, the health care system, organizations, work, life on the street, and myriad of other realms that people have to understand in order to realize their values.

Knowledge, then, is an important part of values education. Unfortunately, it has often been the *only* part of the task which schools have taken seriously; but that appears to be changing.

Transcendental Knowledge

Many people believe finding satisfaction and meaning in life can only be partially achieved through the skills and knowledge described above. They contend real meaning and true contentment can only come from recognizing and relating to another dimension of life beyond worldly, day-to-day reality. Some call this additional dimension God, Elohim, Allah, the transcendent, the universe, Brahma, nature, or The Way. They suggest that true values realization comes not only from psychological health, rational thinking, good decision making, and positive human relationships, but also from an intuitive, non-rational, spiritual dimension of living. They might even say there is no way to true enlightenment but through a particular religious faith, leader, or approach.

Transcendental knowledge is not widely regarded as within the province of the public schools, and it is not being suggested here to make it so. However, values education and moral education take place in many settings outside of public schools—in parochial and private schools, homes, youth groups, and religious institutions. No discussion of a comprehensive values education would be complete without acknowledging this important dimension of values realization. Those who work in these settings may want to incorporate additional skills, knowledge, experiences, and training in their values education programs to foster this transcendental knowledge and belief.

Character Education

The second major movement in the field of values education and moral education has the goal of teaching certain "traditional values," values which are widely regarded as the cornerstones of virtuous and responsible conduct. These values have also been described as "moral virtues." When people say "We need to teach kids values," they typically mean traditional values or moral virtues.

However, because "values education," "teaching values," "traditional values," and "moral virtues," are ambiguous terms, with different and sometimes controversial meanings, some educators prefer to describe teaching traditional values or moral virtues as "character education." It is an old-fashioned concept—*character*—yet an apt one, which evokes a set of internal qualities that have always been admired as hallmarks of goodness, virtue, and moral maturity.

What are these character traits, these values, and these virtues? Again, they are described differently by different people, yet when various lists are compared, there is a great deal of similarity. The differences are mainly in which of the several, almost-synonymous terms is selected to describe a particular character trait and how many traits the author decided to list before feeling that the list was getting too long and cumbersome. The most commonly cited character traits and goals of character education include the following:

Respect

There are several levels of respect—*respect for oneself, respect for others, respect for property,* and *respect for the environment.* A person with respect recognizes that others have rights too. A person with respect will be more likely to treat others fairly, courteously, and considerately. A person with respect recognizes the inherent worth in living things—people, animals, and the global environment.

Responsibility

This character trait is also described or defined as being *reliable, trustworthy,* and *honest* (to others and oneself). Responsible people can be counted on and trusted. They do what they say and mean what they say. A responsible person accepts responsibility for his actions. A responsible person has integrity.

Compassion

Compassion is an even stronger feeling than respect; it involves truly *caring.* Other synonyms, descriptors, and behavioral correlates of compassion include being *kind, helpful, friendly, empathic, humane,* and *tolerant.* To feel compassion for others is to be concerned about them and their welfare. From compassion, respectful and responsible behavior naturally flow. Some people regard compassion as the most important of all moral virtues.

Self-Discipline

This is the "true grit" of character. *Perseverance, hard work, thrift,* the ability to delay gratification, *prudence,* and *moderation* are all associated with self-discipline. It is self-discipline, perseverance, and hard work that we admire in star athletes, scientists, and others who spend years working hard to achieve excellence and success. It is these same character traits, combined with compassion, that enable many parents to work hard so their children will have a better life than they do.

Loyalty

Loyalty is the readiness to stand by in times of need, to remain in the relationship when it is difficult and work to improve it, to keep confidences, to protect, and to hold dear someone or something. While loyalty to *friends* is an almost-universally admired character trait, it is loyalty to *family* and to *country* that are most often cited as "traditional values." There is not a single political candidate these days who does not cite his or her love of family and country as a qualification for office. Indeed, family loyalty and patriotism are litmus tests for public office. In public life and in many people's personal value systems, it is assumed that a person with good character is loyal to his family and country and, even when disagreeing or working to improve the situation, remains faithful and devoted to their well-being.

Other Character Traits

There are additional character traits which have often been suggested as worthy goals of values education.

Courage is one. Bravery on the battlefield typically comes to mind, but the courage to follow one's convictions, to be oneself, is equally important and more easily achieved by the average person than acts of extraordinary heroism.

Tolerance or respect for diversity is another trait which is often cited as basic to living in a democracy.[27] Tolerance means more than a grudging acceptance of those who are different, but an attitude rooted in true respect and appreciation for all persons. It is easy to respect people who think and act as we do. Tolerance enables us to treat people with respect even when we disagree with them. Thus, tolerance, in a broader sense, implies the related character trait of being *fair* or *open-minded*. The fair and open-minded person is committed to seeking the truth, is able and willing to consider other perspectives, and can look beyond his own self-interest. This character virtue is the opposite of being narrow-minded and prejudiced.

The *work ethic* is another character trait that many people feel is too often lacking today and one that should be more explicitly taught and encouraged in schools, homes, and society. The work ethic includes both the willingness to work hard (self-discipline) and the commitment to excellence and high quality in all of one's work.

Reverence is a character trait that, again, goes beyond the realm of public education. But in many private schools, religious institutions, homes, and other private settings, reverence—a belief in and love of God and a cherishing of one's religious faith and traditions—is considered an important aspect of a person's character. In those settings, development of this value or characteristic is an appropriate educational objective.

Recently, in U.S. politics there has been a great deal of discussion about, and lip service paid to, "American values" and "family values." When pressed for more specific examples, politicians invariably cite the values of *hard work, family, love of country, faith,* and *respect for diversity.* Politics aside, these probably *are* the values that most Americans (and citizens of many other nations) have aspired to, if not always achieved. Advocates of character education argue that if these values are truly important, then we ought to be consciously teaching them in the nation's schools. It is in the character of our young people that these personal and shared values will be nurtured.

Based on this belief, two impressive national coalitions were formed in 1992 and 1993 to promulgate character education programs on the broadest possible scale. The Character Education Partnership (1250 N. Pitt St., Alexandria, VA 22315, 703-739-9515) includes many leading professional associations and organizations dedicated to "developing civic virtue and moral character in our youth for a more compassionate and responsible society." The Character Counts Coalition (4640 Admiralty Way, Suite 1001, Marina del Rey, CA 90292) numbers over 40 organizations, from the American Red Cross to 4-H to the YMCA of the USA, reaching over 30 million young people, parents, and youth leaders.

> *Only a virtuous people are capable of freedom.*
> BENJAMIN FRANKLIN

Citizenship Education

A third major movement in values education and moral education is devoted to teaching the "civic values" on which the country was founded and from which its legal and political principles were derived. A recent, major curriculum project identified the following "Fundamental Values" as central to the American political system:

1. The public good
2. Individual rights
3. Justice
4. Equality
5. Diversity
6. Truth
7. Patriotism[152]

Learning civic values means acquiring the knowledge, attitudes, beliefs, and behaviors consistent with the country's political and legal system. Other terms for this effort are "civics," "civics education," and "law-related education." [25,30,56,65]

Traditionally, citizenship education took place almost exclusively in history and social studies classes and lessons. In a comprehensive values education program, citizenship education takes places in more facets of the school day. The major aspects of citizenship education include the following:

Knowledge

In a democracy, young people need to learn a great deal to be good citizens. They should know the country's history, the laws and rules of society, the diversity of its citizenry, and what the aforementioned curriculum project called its "fundamental principles," such as popular sovereignty and constitutional government (including separation of powers and checks and balances, separation of church and state, federalism, etc.).[152] Educators might argue over which facts and concepts are necessary for "cultural literacy," but there is no argument that a basic knowledge of the country's history and political and legal systems is essential for an effective citizenry.

Appreciation

Learning and knowing the country's history and political system is a cognitive, intellectual accomplishment. *Appreciating and valuing* one's country, its democratic system, and its civic values is quite another matter; but it is an important goal of citizenship education. We want our students to appreciate their country, to value their democratic heritage, to appreciate the essential connection between citizens' rights and responsibilities, and to treat different groups with tolerance and respect. These are emotional attitudes which go beyond intellectual knowledge. Such appreciation can exist even while recognizing the country's flaws and the more shameful chapters in its history.

Critical Thinking Skills

Democracy is predicated not only on an informed citizenry, but on citizens who can think for themselves. The images of fascist mobs, willing to blindly follow their leaders into an immoral abyss, is the opposite of the Athenian or Jeffersonian ideal of the thinking populace. The importance of a citizenry that would exercise informed, independent judgment was so important to the Founding Fathers that they instituted the Bill of Rights' first amendment protections of free speech, free assembly, and free press. Therefore, an essential part of citizenship education is developing a students' ability to think logically, to analyze arguments, to distinguish fact from opinion, to recognize logical fallacies, to understand propaganda techniques, and to analyze stereotypical thinking—in short, to think for themselves.

"I expect you all to be independent, innovative, critical thinkers who will do exactly as I say."

Reprinted by permission.

Communication Skills

To be an effective citizen requires good communication skills. By expressing our attitudes, beliefs, and values effectively, we are more likely to influence others and have our values become part of the larger group's values. By listening well to others, we gain important insights—insights that enhance our own thinking, enable us to respect others and their viewpoints, and allow us to more effectively voice our own viewpoint. Thus the many methods and programs that teach young people to communicate clearly and to listen well not only help them to achieve their personal values, but also to be more effective members of society.

Cooperation Skills

We can rarely attain our own values without the help of others. We need to work together to achieve the common good. Competition has a legitimate role in helping us achieve individual and collective goals, as many former communist countries discovered, but so does cooperation. To use a classic example, it is appropriate for the Harvard football team to compete with the Yale team or for IBM to compete with AT&T. It is not appropriate for the Harvard or IBM team to be competing with team members within their own ranks.

One of the most popular pedagogical movements in education in the 1980s and '90s has been "cooperative learning"—one or more approaches that teach students how to work together as they pursue their academic learning tasks.[91,94,177] When done effectively—and there is voluminous research to demonstrate this—both academic learning and social learning is enhanced. Students learn respect and tolerance for teammates who are different from them (in ethnicity, class, or disability), they learn to work more effectively with others, and they learn more academic material and skills.[92,95] Thus cooperative learning helps teach and reinforce several key civic values.

Conflict Resolution Skills

The flip side of learning to work together is learning to work through conflict. Whenever people live and work together there *will* be conflict—especially in a society like ours that tolerates individual differences and in a world with such different cultures and political systems. Whether by teaching students conflict resolution skills in the classroom, creating peer mediation programs to reduce intergroup tensions, utilizing "peace education" curricula K–12, or employing other methods, conflict resolution is an important ingredient of citizenship education and values and moral education.[98,148] To resolve disputes by force and violence—"Might makes right"—is an essentially amoral or immoral approach. Ultimately both sides, winners and losers, attain fewer of their real values. For both individuals and societies, conflict resolution skills help everyone realize more of their values in a more just resolution of the conflict.

> *Mankind's Ten Sins*
>
> Life without goals
> Love without devotion
> Pleasure without conscience
> Wealth without work
> Commerce without morality
> Knowledge without character
> Science without humanity
> Politics without principles
> Friendship without trust
> Promises without fulfillment
> MOHANDAS GANDHI

Moral Education

The fourth major movement in values education and moral education can be explicitly labeled "moral education." Moral education includes the approaches and methods that teach young people the knowledge, attitudes, beliefs, skills, and behaviors to be good, fair, kind—in a word, "moral"—people. Many of these approaches can be viewed as teaching "moral literacy."[21] One task force agreed that the goal of moral education is "to produce autonomous individuals who know those moral values and are committed to acting in a manner consistent with them." [8]

Moral education has a number of related components:

Knowledge of the Moral Tradition

A starting point of moral education is getting students to understand the concept of *morality*. We hear the word often, but what does it mean? Inevitably, to answer that question, we must also discuss the concepts of "justice," "fairness," and "ethics." In other words, a part of moral education involves helping young people to understand our society's and our civilization's moral tradition, to develop a moral vocabulary. As part of citizenship education, we might help them understand the political and legal tradition. Moral education goes a step further, exploring more abstract concepts like justice, fairness, decency, right, and wrong—concepts which are the foundation for specific laws of the land. It is also appropriate to explore the contributions that world religions have played historically in developing our moral tradition.

Moral Reasoning

For years, it was taken for granted that morality was synonymous with following society's moral rules, such as "Thou shalt not steal," or practicing the traditional moral virtues, such as hard work, thrift, and moderation. Recently, educators have become interested in the phenomena of "moral development" and "moral reasoning" and the complex interactions of psychological development, social context, and educational interventions, which produce moral thought and action.[118,150] Certain approaches have been developed to specifically teach the skills and processes of moral reasoning.

Lawrence Kohlberg and his students have studied and taught the process by which young people progress through the levels of moral reasoning. Students' first concept of what is right is based on what they can get away with and what's in it for them. As they mature, their moral reasoning becomes based on wanting to be well-liked, following the social rules, understanding mutual rights and responsibilities, and finally, appreciating the universal principles of justice and fairness.[110,168] Other approaches involve teaching particular "moral skills," such as reversing roles, examining the consequences of one's actions on others, and applying "moral filter questions," such as "Would I feel the same way if I did not have a personal interest in the matter?" or "Would the world be a better place if everyone followed that course of action?" [64]

Compassion and Altruism

By definition, moral knowledge and moral reasoning are intellectual processes. Many people point out that true morality comes as much from the heart as it does from the head.[68] The admonition to "Love thy neighbor as thyself," which appears in almost all of the world's great religions, is not an intellectual dictum, but an emotional one.

Therefore, other approaches to moral education emphasize techniques designed to increase young people's levels of compassion and altruism.[34,181] "Empathy training" utilizes methods that help students understand and appreciate how the world appears and feels to others.[102] "Service projects" give young people the opportunity to experience the satisfaction of giving to others, of helping. Readings, films, and resource people can be used to help students to appreciate cultural diversity and the shared human condition.

Moral Tendencies

Beyond moral knowledge, the skills of moral reasoning, and the feelings of compassion and altruism, there are other attitudes and predilections which constitute moral maturity. These might be termed "moral tendencies." Thomas Likona describes some of these tendencies as including: *conscience*—recognizing moral and ethical standards and being concerned when one is not living up to them; *loving the good*—a passionate commitment to truth and doing right; *self-control*—the ability to control impulses and forgo immediate gratification and focus on doing the right thing; *humility*—knowing one's own limitations and recognizing the capacity to rationalize and deceive oneself; *moral habit*—developing the patterns of kind, considerate, and fair behavior until these ways feel natural and normal; and *will*—the internal commitment and determination to do the right thing, even when it is difficult.[122] Programs and methods which nurture these and similar tendencies play an important role in moral education.

I was in a class of third graders yesterday. It is a group with five physically disabled children "included" for part of the day. One of the included children is a terminally ill youngster, paralyzed, with breathing tubes. Many of his classmates have known him since he was well, back in their pre-school days.

While I read a story, one little boy motioned to me that he was going to sit next to the boy in the wheelchair. As I read, I glanced over to see them holding hands and making eye contact during the humorous parts. When our included friend left, the little boy returned to his seat. This is what inclusion is all about— compassion, being able to be true friends no matter what.

WENDY O'ROURKE
SUBSTITUTE TEACHER, ROCHESTER, NY

Integrating the Many Approaches

This is a tall order. Just to implement *one* character education program or conflict resolution skills program or law-related education program could easily involve a two-year or three-year commitment to teacher training, program implementation, and evaluation. Try to employ *all* these approaches to values realization, character education, citizenship education, and moral education, and there would be little time for anything else.

Therefore, some schools have chosen to implement one or more packaged programs or curricula that they believe do a good job of addressing *some* of the goals of values education and moral education.[88,151] That is fine, often excellent, as far as it goes; but, typically, only a few teachers on staff receive the training and implement the program—for example, the fifth grade teachers in elementary schools or the social studies or health education teachers in secondary schools. *Other* teachers, the principal, the guidance counselors, the teachers' aides, the coaches, and other school staff receive no special training or encouragement to get involved in values education. Also teachers who *are* using the packaged curriculum often "do" values education when they are teaching that curriculum and "don't do" values education the rest of the time, at least not consciously. Even when the entire faculty, administration, and school staff receives the training, no one program fits everyone's style or role.

The comprehensive approach described in this book takes a different direction. It is based on the premise that teachers are professionals who are capable of adopting useful methods from many sources and combining them to fit their particular goals, their community, and the needs of their students. Therefore, instead of advocating one particular program or method, it suggests that there are "100 Ways," that is, one hundred methods, strategies, techniques, and activities that can be used to accomplish the goals of values education and moral education. (Actually, when the additional ideas, examples, and variations in each section are included in the count, there are really *several hundred* suggestions, methods, and activities to use.) Of course, there are many more ways than these; but the book is long enough already, and 100 methods are more than enough to begin with. They are all practical strategies, which teachers in all disciplines and at all grade levels, administrators, youth group leaders, and other youth-serving professionals can use "on Monday," that is, right now, to accomplish the goals of values education and moral education.

The 100 ways are drawn from all the approaches described earlier. They include both traditional and innovative methods for values realization, character education, citizenship education, and moral education. They have all been tried and used for decades, and, in many cases, for centuries. Collectively, the 100 ways are a synthesis of many approaches, intended to be combined into a comprehensive approach to values education.

Chapter 3

Comprehensive
Values Education

As previously described, a comprehensive values education utilizes many of the methods and activities from the values realization, character education, citizenship education, and moral education movements to help young people lead personally satisfying and socially constructive lives. This book describes 100 of those methods.

However, the 100 methods are not listed randomly. They are organized under the headings of:

- Inculcating Values and Morality
- Modeling Values and Morality
- Facilitating Values and Morality
- Skills for Value Development and Moral Literacy
- Implementing a Values Education Program

The first four categories illustrate one important aspect of comprehensive values education. The comprehensive approach utilizes the traditional, more direct methods of teaching values through inculcating and modeling, but it also employs the more contemporary (albeit with roots back to Socrates), indirect approaches of encouraging values and moral development by giving young people the opportunities and skills to become autonomous, constructive, and effective decision-makers and citizens. The categories of inculcating, modeling, facilitating, and skill-building all emphasize the comprehensive nature of the task. Many teachers and youth leaders find these categories helpful in conceptualizing and carrying out the broad task of values education.

Inculcating Values and Morality

Inculcating is a powerful word. Some colleagues have suggested it is too strong a word, conjuring up images of *indoctrination*. They recommend *instilling, imbuing,* or just plain *teaching* values and morality as more acceptable terms. Indeed, while *The American Heritage Dictionary*'s definition of inculcate is "to teach or impress by urging or frequent repetition; to instill," its Latin derivative meanings include "to force upon" and "to trample." Some educators prefer the term "direct instruction" as an alternative that avoids the harsh connotations of inculcation, while reflecting the traditional mission of schools—to instruct.

Debate over the meaning of terms like educate, teach, train, inculcate, instruct, and indoctrinate has long occupied philosophers of education, and will not be repeated or resolved here. Yet, after considering all the ramifications, the word inculcate still seems the most useful and accurate term to describe the 34 specific methods and ideas included in Chapter 5. "Teaching" is not an acceptable substitute, because *all one hundred* methods and ideas in this book are ways of teaching or aiding the teaching of values and morality. "Direct instruction" does not suffice either, because the ten skill-building approaches to teaching values and morality in Chapter 8 also employ direct instruction, and these ten approaches are very different from the previous 34. The point of the comprehensive model is to acknowledge that there *are* very different approaches to teaching values and morality, and that many of them can and should be combined.

So rather than retreat from a term that accurately describes one of the more direct approaches to values education, it is more useful to explore and understand its meaning. This may be done by contrasting inculcation and the related concept of indoctrination, as shown in Figure 3-1 on the following page.

As you see, the distinction between inculcation and indoctrination is both qualitative and quantitative. For example, treating a skeptic with respect or scorn is a qualitative distinction. There is no fine line between respect and scorn; they are quite different. The system of rules, rewards, and punishments, however, is a matter of degree. For example, a school citizenship award is a moderate way of inculcating values associated with good citizenship. But if rewards and punishments become so pervasive or powerful that they leave a person very little choice (such as "Accept our way or die," then it is indoctrination. When the intensity of inculcation virtually eliminates a person's free will to choose his own beliefs or actions, as in brainwashing, or when inculcation becomes so total as to be "totalitarian," then inculcation has become indoctrination.

The distinction raises provocative philosophical and practical questions, such as "How can one recognize or measure the precise point at which inculcation becomes indoctrination? Can a particular values education program combine inculcation and indoctrination methods, and then what is it called? Is it appropriate when children are very young to exert total control over their environment and influences and, later, decrease the control and structure to the level of inculcation? At what point in their development should the transition begin?"

FIGURE 3-1. Inculcation Versus Indoctrination

Inculcation	*Indoctrination*
Communicate what you believe and the reasons why you believe it	Communicate what you believe solely on the basis of authority
Treat other views fairly	Treat other views unfairly
Accord respect to those with other views	Vilify, dehumanize those with other views
Answer doubt with reason and respect	Answer doubt with rigidity and scorn
Partially structure the environment to increase likelihood of exposure to desired values and decrease likelihood of exposure to undesirable values	Totally control the environment to increase likelihood of exposure to desired values and decreased likelihood of exposure to undesirable values
Create positive social, emotional, learning experiences around the desired values—within limits	Create positive social, emotional, learning experiences around the desired values—to an extreme
Provide rules, rewards and consequences—within reason	Provide rules, rewards and consequences—to the extreme
If someone disagrees, keep open lines of communication	If someone disagrees, cut off communication
Allow a certain latitude for divergent behavior; if beyond acceptable level, leave open possibility of change	Allow no latitude for divergent behavior; if beyond acceptable level, ostracize totally and/or permanently

Some of these questions are specifically addressed in the book. However, the purpose in distinguishing between inculcation and indoctrination here is to make it very clear that *inculcation can and should be a humane and respectful approach to values education.* It is *not* the same as indoctrination. Teachers and principals should feel comfortable about the appropriateness of inculcating values and morality. It is a noble and necessary endeavor. Historically, every generation has done it. We can be thankful that we are learning to do it better—more effectively, with more awareness, and more humanely. That is what the 34 methods of inculcation described in Chapter 5 are all about.

Many educators in the 1960s and 1970s were embarrassed or uncomfortable with the idea that we might have values we wished to inculcate in our youth. We have matured since then. As teachers, principals, and youth leaders, we *do* have deeply felt values and moral beliefs we wish to impart to young people. For many of us, this is why we entered teaching. There is nothing to be embarrassed about. Once we acknowledge the importance of teaching values and morality, then it follows we would want to teach them effectively and deliberately, not leaving the matter to chance, or occasional games, or the "hidden curriculum," (the values which inevitably are communicated by how we operate the school, teach, comport ourselves, and react to various situations). Once we are clear on the "target values" we hope our students will internalize and live by, which are discussed in Idea #1, then we should ask, "What can we do to increase the likelihood that these values will actually be acquired?"

Modeling Values and Morality

It is commonplace to make two assertions about modeling in values education and moral education. First, teachers should be good role models for their students; second, students should learn about the virtuous role models of the past. Both of these truisms have a long history. In Plato's *Meno*, Anytus tells Socrates that the youth learn virtue by following the example of the city's elders and the great men of the city's past.[184] The expectation is that if: (a) teachers act in a kind, caring, fair, tolerant, and morally responsible manner—or, as one writer put it, if they "work diligently; are obedient to school rules and policies; display goodwill and consideration toward colleagues, pupils, and parents; are basically optimistic about their work, and take pride in the school and their community,"[99] and (b) the historical or literary figures that students are exposed to similarly demonstrate courage, perseverance, loyalty, self-discipline, and other character virtues, then it follows that young people will learn from these good examples. Conversely, teachers should avoid demonstrating immature, self-destructive, or immoral behavior that would set a bad example for impressionable youth.

All this is true, of course, and imperative. It is surprising, however, that on a subject of such importance, very little else is typically said about the process of modeling values and morality in educational settings. For example, one neglected question is why does modeling work?, What motivates young people to model themselves after parents, teachers, peers, or other figures? An understanding of why and how modeling works can improve the effectiveness of modeling as a tool for values education.

Depending on the situation, any or all of at least six distinct motives or processes may be involved in modeling. In all six instances, the younger a person is, or the less certain or secure of his identity, the stronger the motive to model after someone will be.

1. *Patterning*. Like the duckling who waddles and models after the first living object it sees, whether that is a mother duck, a dog, or a person, we humans often pattern our behavior after those around us. What do *we* know? Not much at first. So we look around and assume that the way we see other people do things is the way they are supposed to be done. This is possibly the major reason why it is so difficult to change how teachers teach. If we experience a similar model of teaching for twelve years of elementary and secondary school and most of college, it is difficult to escape from this pattern when an education professor suggests we do things differently (especially if the professor is teaching by the old model while advocating the new one). Patterning, and the "habit formation" associated with it, can be a most potent form of values acquisition.

2. *To gain love and approval.* Experience quickly demonstrates to us as children that when we behave as others want us to, when we become like they want us to be, they often appear to like us, approve of us, or respect us more. We all need love and approval, so we conform. We model ourselves after others to gain their affection and esteem.

3. *To avoid fear or punishment.* We will take on characteristics of a stronger person to avoid punishment or to reduce our fear of punishment, anger, or reprisal. This is the other side of the love and affection motive. If we model ourselves after the leader, he will like us better, and we will be less likely to incur his disapproval or wrath.

4. *To gain other rewards.* When we behave, believe, and become like our parents, teachers, employers, and others, this often results in our gaining toys, grades, money, or status; so we behave, believe, and become like them to achieve these rewards. George Bernard Shaw suggested, it's not a question of *whether* we will sell ourselves, but what our price is. Hopefully, we will eventually develop our own identity, values, and unshakable moral integrity that cannot be bought at any price. Meanwhile, we follow the example of those around us to achieve the rewards that conformity brings.

5. *Positive associations; identification.* By "identifying" with a stronger person who appears secure, by taking on that person's characteristics, we may feel stronger and more secure ourselves. By identifying with the "Pepsi Generation" television models who appear so attractive and happy, we hope that by drinking Pepsi ourselves, we will be attractive and happy, too.

6. *Consciously choosing an alternative.* Little children, teenagers, and adults—we are all continually looking around for deeper understanding, more effective solutions to life's problems, and better ways to live and feel good about ourselves. When other people present a model of greater wisdom, peace of mind, genuine enthusiasm, or admirable behavior, it makes sense to attend to that person's example and consider following it. It is reasonable to say, *"That's an intelligent viewpoint. It makes more sense than any I've heard. I will adopt it as my viewpoint,"* or to conclude, *"That was a courageous thing for her to do. I admire that. I have the same beliefs, yet I have not stood up for them the way she just did. I will try to do so from now on."* Role models present an example which we may freely and consciously choose to follow.

There are many reasons, then, why modeling works. At first, it would appear that teachers and youth leaders want to be role models for the reasons stated in ways students pattern themselves unconsciously after a model of positive values) and six (students consciously choose the wiser and better viewpoints and example). We certainly would not want students to embrace our values and morality out of fear of punishment, would we?

Or wouldn't we? What if it worked? Why not use fear as a tool for values education? It's a tempting thought; but on further examination, we see there is a contradiction in terms. If students adopt our beliefs, behaviors, or stated values because of our *power* over them (the power to give failing grades, ridicule, criticize, or withdraw care), what have they learned? We have modeled for them the value of power, of winning by force; you get people to do what you want by power, force, and intimidation. This is hardly the morality we wish to teach.

While the third motive for modeling (to avoid fear or punishment) is not consistent with most people's view of values education and moral education, the second (to gain love and approval), fourth (to gain other rewards) and fifth (identification) motives may be—at least within reason, because these motives for modeling can easily be exploited and abused. We know that students look up to us and seek our love and approval, and we can use or abuse that knowledge. Use versus abuse is much like the previous discussion of inculcation versus indoctrination. It is honest and humane to say "That's just great," or "I am disappointed in you," and hope that by saying this we inculcate our values on the student who cares very much how we feel toward him. But to take this to an extreme and communicate, verbally or nonverbally, "I will only love and care about you if you model yourself after me and believe thus-and-so and follow my rules and meet all my expectations" would be the equivalent of indoctrination. It would be exploiting the teacher's powerful role as a model and modeling *disrespect* for other people's integrity.

With different forms of modeling happening simultaneously in a typical classroom, then, it follows that there are different ways a teacher can be an effective model. Surprisingly, little has been written about how a teacher actually does this. "Go forth and be a good model" is about as far as most discussions go. It is assumed that modeling simply happens. A teacher "does his thing," hopefully a good thing, and the students model after him. This description assumes that the teacher has no choice in the matter. He is who he is; his values or lack of values will be apparent, and that's what students will witness. But a teacher *does* have a choice here. In fact, he has hundreds of choices as to which beliefs, feelings, experiences, skills, and interests he will share with his students. He can also choose when and how often he will share them, where he will share them, and to what extent he will involve himself in his students' lives.

In other words, a teacher wishing to be an influential model of values and morality does not simply ask himself, "How will I use readings, films, service projects, class meetings, decision-making activities, and the like to teach my students values and morality?" He also considers, *"How will I use myself?* I am an important force in the classroom. I am a major resource here. Who I am, what I believe, what I care about, what I know, what I have learned from my life, who I know—I have all this and more to bring to the task of values education. How shall I use *me?"*

Stated another way, the teacher asks, "How can I best use my personal resources to establish the kind of relationship with my students that is most conducive to influencing their values?" Amitai Etzioni asserted: "Only when you build a relationship can you transmit values." [60] If this is true, what sort of relationship works best for a values educator?

Chapter 6 provides many concrete and practical answers to this question. It presents and explores a dozen different ways that you, the teacher or group leader, can have a relationship with your students in which you are *consciously* a model of values and morality. You can do more than just "be yourself." You can also use yourself and your personal resources to the fullest. If this idea makes you uncomfortable or embarrassed, that is understandable; teachers have self-esteem issues like everyone else. But it's a fact. *You* have a lot to offer. Chapter 6 describes many ways you can use your gifts and personal strengths to be, not so much a "better" model (because, it's true, you are who you are), but a more active, visible, and effective model for your students.

Beyond the teacher's personal role in modeling values and morality, the teacher is also a "gatekeeper," who can bring other models—historical, literary, and contemporary—to the attention of his students. The efficacy of using current models was demonstrated when "Magic" Johnson, arguably the most popular basketball player of his time, announced that he had contracted the AIDS virus and began a national media campaign to alert young people to the danger of AIDS. Visits to health clinics for blood testing purportedly skyrocketed, and irresponsible sexual behavior decreased, at least temporarily, because of Johnson's educational efforts. So Chapter 6 includes a number of ways to use contemporary models, as well as historical and literary figures, in the service of values education and moral education.

> *I want to remind you of . . . the incredible influence you have on young people. You really do! You remember the classic study of the one thousand successful adults who were asked to look back over their lives and identify the single influence that was most responsible for their success. There were no limits on what they could say. Nine hundred of these one thousand identified one single adult when they were growing up. Nine hundred! They could have said anything. But nine hundred thought of one, single adult influence. A teacher, a parent, a pastor, a counselor, a next door neighbor, an aunt, an uncle. One person!*
>
> RICK LITTLE, PRESIDENT
> INTERNATIONAL YOUTH FOUNDATION[123]

Facilitating Values and Moral Development

If inculcation and modeling help teach and demonstrate to students *our* best answers to life's value and moral dilemmas, facilitation helps them find *their* best answers. At the same time, in the context of comprehensive values education, facilitating students' autonomous thinking and decision making can also foster the traditional moral values we are teaching.

The use of facilitation activities in values education is most apparent in the area of personal values development. There are many choices and decisions in life—careers, relationships, leisure time, politics, health, use of money, life balance, spirituality, to name a few—which involve personal value decisions. There may be moral issues involved also, but not necessarily. Making personally satisfying choices may be solely a matter of having enough information and sorting through one's goals, preferences, feelings, priorities, and personal values. Values clarification and other facilitation activities can be useful tools to help young people and older people make better personal choices in life and learn how to make such choices. Many of the ideas in Chapter 7 are particularly helpful toward the goal of personal values realization.

But what about choices, decisions, and issues in life that *do* involve morality, fairness, ethics, character, and good citizenship? Are these matters to be handled by the teaching methods of inculcation and modeling only, or does facilitation have a role here as well? Indeed, it does.

Imagine a training course in map and compass reading. You teach students to read maps, to use the compass, to orient themselves, and to set and follow a compass bearing. Beyond skills and knowledge, you inculcate rules and principles associated with map and compass work—rules of safety, what to do if you get lost, the ethics of respecting private property, and the like. Perhaps you take students out in the field and demonstrate or model how to do it, so they can learn from your good example. Then, if this is a school course, you probably give them a classroom test and go on to the next topic. But if it's life, if you really want them to be able to use this skill, you know what you have to do. *The students must be given the opportunity to go out in the field and try it themselves.* Maybe you will first accompany them, to help if and when they have problems; that's good, responsible teaching. But, eventually, students will need the opportunity to try it all by themselves, and later, they can return to the classroom and report on how it went, how some groups had no problems, how some got lost, how one was stopped by a property owner, or how one never achieved the objective. Then you teach some more—analyzing the successes and the mistakes; repeating some of your training; moralizing and supporting, and giving students another opportunity to try it on their own.

This is what values education is or should be like. In addition to inculcation and modeling, in addition to training in skills, students need the opportunity to put their learnings to practice in the real world. Inside or outside the classroom, this means creating occasions for students to determine their own opinions and conclusions, to make choices for themselves, to develop their own rules, and to experience a sense of autonomy and empowerment. The 30 activity ideas for facilitating values and moral development presented in Chapter 7 are ways to give students those opportunities.

Some would say creating such opportunities is not the role of the school: "Students will have ample opportunities after graduation and when they are older, to make their own choices and decisions. They also have plenty of opportunities now in their private lives, after school and on weekends. Values education in school should consist only of "training" experiences—inculcation, modeling, and skill training. We certainly don't want to give students the idea that it's alright to make decisions about values, morals, and ethics in school. They can think for themselves on their own time."

The main problem with this viewpoint is that it is not consistent with the principles of effective teaching. As in the map and compass reading example, we can't simply "teach the stuff" and assume that students have learned it. They must be given the opportunity to use and practice their learnings under direct supervision, with the chance to review and learn from the experience. In values education this means creating learning activities in which students can clarify and discuss their beliefs, debate moral questions, and make value choices. Students do not do this in a vacuum. The teacher is there to urge them to consult their sources of inculcation and their positive models. The teacher is there to insert his own values and morality and to represent the collective values and morality of the culture. This is a very different situation from the playground or "the street," where students make their own choices, but where sloppy thinking typically goes unchecked, where decisions are made without careful thought of the consequences, and where voices offering a moral counterpoint are often absent.

Giving students the right and the opportunity to discuss their own opinions, feelings, or choices and to make some of their own decisions does not mean halting our inculcating and modeling values. For example, when students are discussing a problem such as peer teasing or drugs, and are being encouraged to express their own, evolving ideas, while the teacher holds back for the moment from stating his own views, the teacher is also creating a "moral context" for the discussion. He is saying in words, nonverbally, and in how he structures the discussion:

- It is worth caring about this subject, because some people are being hurt by teasing or by drugs, and *we care about people.*
- *Your choices are important,* both for your future and for everyone's future. So it's important that you *choose responsibly* and that you *take responsibility* for your choices.
- As we engage in this search for values, *we must respect one another.* We will listen and not interrupt. Even if we disagree with someone, we will not scoff at them but will show them respect. Regardless of race, religion, economic class or other background, we will show respect.
- *Every one of you has worthwhile ideas.* You have something to contribute to this group discussion.
- *Everyone of you is capable of being trustworthy and responsible and thoughtful toward others.* I expect no less of you.
- In the following discussion, whatever you say, if you're serious, your answer will be respected. I am not going to tell you that you are right or wrong; I want you to think for yourself. But that does not mean there is no such thing as right or wrong. *There is right and wrong; there* are *better and worse choices.* Our job is to become wise enough to understand the difference.
- Now what do you have to say about this subject?

This concept of a moral context is one answer to the dilemma, How do we encourage young people to think for themselves while teaching them moral values? Experience demonstrates that in class discussions on serious values issues and moral topics students are capable of saying some very wise things when given the chance. Because they are young, they also sometimes say some foolish or immature things. But wise or foolish, their positions are not fixed. Students are growing and changing all the time. The important thing is that they are given opportunities to think and decide for themselves, they operate in a moral context—both the moral context of the activity itself and the context of inculcation, modeling, and skill development taking place in class, throughout school, and, hopefully, at home and in the community.

In addition to providing a moral context for reflection and discussion, facilitative methods can aid and support the inculcation of values and morality in another way—by providing opportunities for students to *internalize* the values you have been teaching. There is a big difference between students listening to your moral thinking and thinking that way themselves. There is an equally big difference between students knowing what is the right thing to do and doing it, or doing it consistently. Facilitation activities give students opportunities to recognize and verbalize the wisdom of the values they have been taught and to make personal choices and commitments to live according to those values.

To illustrate this point, let us say you have just taught a unit on drug and alcohol education. You discussed the dangers of drugs and the importance of saying no. You showed the class a film, with celebrities and athletes talking about their past drug and alcohol problems and parents who lost their children because of drugs. You taught skills for resisting negative peer pressure and had students practice them. All excellent strategies for inculcating, modeling, and skill development.

With great teaching like that, none of your students are going to have problems with smoking, alcohol, or illegal drugs, right? Of course not. You know there are no guarantees. Your good teaching most assuredly will help, but it's a tough world out there, and many of your students may be in for a rough time ahead. Even if you do a good job conveying information, inculcating values, modeling, and teaching relevant skills, in any classroom there will be students who fall into several different categories:

- Those who accept the values you teach and will act consistently upon them.
- Those who accept the values you teach intellectually but will not act consistently upon them.
- Those who are on the verge of accepting the values you teach but are not quite there yet.
- Those who tuned you out or never tuned in or who disagree more than they agree with you.

There are really more categories, but these suffice to demonstrate the dilemma. Inculcation, modeling, and skill development are successful to a point. Facilitation can help take values education a few important steps further.

The following are examples of facilitative questions and activities on the issue of drugs and alcohol—a difficult values and moral issue.

"How many of you agree with what I just said about marijuana being a dangerous drug?"

"You know where I stand on this subject. Now I'd like to hear what *you* think and believe. I'm going to just listen right now."

"If you found yourself at a party where the friend who drove you drank two beers and now it was time to go home, which of the following three choices would you be most likely, next most likely, and least likely to make? Which choice should you make? Are there better choices than the three I gave you?"

"Make an inventory of all the drugs we discussed. Put an "N" next to those you believe you will *never* take. Put an "M" next to those you *might* take. Put a "W" next to those you think you *will* take. . . Now let's poll the class, anonymously, to see how people answered, and then we'll discuss the results."

Remember, you have already done a good deal of inculcating, modeling, and skill development on this topic. What more does facilitation have to add? Many things.

1. Facilitation activities can significantly enhance your rapport with students. *If you listen well to students, it is more likely that they will listen well to you.* Students appreciate very much being given the real respect of having their views and opinions heard and understood. This, in turn, greatly increases your credibility as a values inculcator and role model.

2. Facilitation activities help all students clarify their thoughts and feelings on a subject, which is useful in itself. For example, they were just exposed to a lot of information about drugs. Facilitation activities give them a chance to organize their thoughts, remind themselves of what they heard, and clarify any confusion they may have.

3. Facilitation activities help students in the second category, those who accept values taught but act inconsistently, to move from an intellectual understanding to a commitment to action. Moral action requires not only moral knowledge but feeling, purpose, and will. As Likona points out, "Values clarification encourages people to close the gap between espoused values and personal action." [122]

4. Facilitation activities help students in the third category, those whom you haven't quite reached yet, to think further about the subject, to achieve insight themselves, to learn from other students in the first and second categories who accept the values taught, and to finally recognize the merit of what you are trying to communicate. Facilitation activities help them say, in effect, "Okay, I've heard *you* say it, but now *I'm saying* it. *I believe* this value is important or this viewpoint is correct."

5. Facilitation activities help some of the students in the last category, those who previously tuned out, to tune back in. Almost everyone likes to be asked what they think and to be listened to. Once the students tune back in, you have a chance of reaching them again. Many hard-to-reach and at-risk students respond particularly well to facilitation activities and, as a result, become more involved in other classroom activities.

6. Facilitation activities help some of the students in the last category, the skeptics, the ones who were tuned in but disagreed with you, to voice their doubt, disagreement, or problem. Now you have a chance to engage those students to address their concerns, and to succeed in communicating your message and values.

7. Facilitation activities give you, the teacher, a much deeper understanding of how your students think and feel. Open-ended discussions on values issues and more structured facilitation activities can lead to insights about your students and their needs that you never would have gained otherwise. This knowledge is helpful to you both as a values educator and in all other aspects of teaching.

8. Facilitation activities are motivating activities which help students make the connection between the values issues or the academic subjects being discussed and their own lives, beliefs, and feelings. Because students get personally involved, the study of any subject area becomes more interesting—from history to science to ethics to careers.

The 30 facilitation ideas and methods in Chapter 7, then, have three main purposes:

1. to help students learn to think for themselves and make personally satisfying decisions in their lives, that is, *values realization.*
2. to teach or inculcate a *moral context* for decision making and values realization.
3. to give students the opportunity to *internalize the moral, character,* and *civic values* to which they were previously exposed.

Ironically, when doing facilitative activities, students frequently recognize that their own best answers are the same ones their parents and teachers have been inculcating and modeling all along. Used in a moral context as described, and in the context of a comprehensive values education, facilitation activities are practical and enjoyable ways to help students learn to guide their lives in increasingly responsible and constructive ways.

Skill Development for Values and Morality

As previously suggested in Chapter 2, there are necessary skills for getting along in this world that are directly related to realizing one's own values and behaving in a constructive, moral fashion within society. Suggestions for teaching ten of those skills are presented in Chapter 8.

Teaching students these skills could be considered a form of inculcating *or* facilitating values and moral development. For example, we might consider teaching conflict resolution skills a facilitative endeavor, because those skills will help students get along with people more effectively and, therefore, get more of whatever they want out of life—realize their values. Or we might consider teaching conflict resolution skills an inculcating activity, because the conflict resolution process we teach is an inherently moral and fair process. To teach conflict resolution skills *is* to teach morality.

To use another example, we may view critical thinking skills as insurance to prevent people from blindly following peer group pressure and authoritarian pressure into immoral behavior. In fact, we can teach critical thinking skills with that in mind, emphasizing how to use thinking skills to evaluate the morality of particular assertions or courses of action. In this sense, teaching critical thinking skills helps inculcate morality. On the other hand, to the extent we regard critical thinking skills as a way of helping people make their own decisions, based on personal values and moral beliefs, teaching thinking skills is a way of facilitating personal value development, of helping use their rational capacities to get more out of life, to help them control own lives and not be manipulated by others, to realize their own values. This type of teaching would be facilitative in nature.

The point here is not to belabor the distinction between the modes of inculcation and facilitation, but to emphasize that teaching the ten skills for values and morality described in Chapter 8 is a way to accomplish *both goals* of a comprehensive values education—helping young people lead both more personally satisfying and socially constructive lives.

A Semantic Aside

It can be argued that everything in this comprehensive values education approach is a form of inculcation. By saying, "You should experience your life as satisfying and meaningful and you should behave morally," we are saying that satisfaction and morality are two of our target values. All one hundred ideas in this book, then, are ways to inculcate those two values. In this sense, we can think of direct inculcation, modeling, facilitating, and skill development as being four ways of inculcating the two major goals of a comprehensive values education—helping people lead personally satisfying and socially constructive lives. Nevertheless, in actual practice, the four modes of values education are very different and remain as useful categories for organizing the various methods of values education.

Chapter 4

Implementing the Comprehensive Approach

Integrating the Four Modes

So much of the literature on values education has been occupied with arguing that one approach is better than another that little attention has been paid to the problem of how to integrate the various approaches. One reason this problem has probably received so little attention is that it is possibly the most difficult question to answer about values education.

Parents know this. As your children grow, you want to protect them, provide structure, set rules, influence, and guide them. Yet inevitably and appropriately as children get older, they will begin to make more choices for themselves. You want them to grow up, yet you fear they are not ready for the responsibility of making their own decisions. But time does not stand still, and as you ponder this parenting dilemma, your children stand before you, saying they want to wear their hair differently, or choose their own clothes, or get their ears pierced (boys, too), or begin dating, or borrow the car, or stay out until 1:00 A.M., or go to a different church, or not go to church at all. You believe in both inculcating values *and* facilitating their values development, so what do you do? Do you give them the car keys or not? Are they ready for the next stage of responsibility? How do you know?

Part of the dilemma of conducting values education in a school setting is much the same: When do we use the different approaches? When should we employ the different ideas this book and other sources offer for inculcating, modeling, facilitating, and teaching skills for values and moral development? *Where* should we use the different approaches, *when* should we use them, and *who* should use them?

> *My best teacher [was] my father. Although he had never read a book on teaching values (he dropped out of school in 6th grade), he somehow knew when to be noncommittal. We children had no doubts about what he believed. He could have shoveled a few extra bushels of corn from the landlord's bin to his own, but that was out of the question; his honor was his most precious possession. He was never ambiguous about that.*
>
> *Even so, he seldom criticized when, at the supper table or while milking the cows, we told him about our exploits. But a few days later—maybe Saturday morning when we were cleaning out the barn or fixing fence—he might refer, very indirectly, to something we had said and start a conversation about the right thing to do.*
>
> *Advocates of values clarification have been attacked because they advise teachers sometimes to remain nonjudgmental in order to encourage young people to express their real views. Parents and teachers must never be neutral, these critics say; it sends the wrong message. But when my father chose not to take a stand, he was not being wishy-washy; he was being a sensitive moral educator. Like Mark Twain, when I look back on what my father "learned" as I grew up, I am impressed by his uncommon common sense.*
>
> RON BRANDT[24]
>
> ---
>
> Reprinted with permission from *Educational Leadership* (May 1988) Copyright by ASCD.

Where

Values education takes place everywhere, whether we consciously work at it or not. Every adult the students encounter is a role model—good, bad, or ambiguous. How students are treated and encouraged to treat each other in the classroom, on the bus, on the sports field, and on the playground is a part of their values education. The textbooks, assignments, and grading system—almost every aspect of the curriculum and instruction embodies values, implicitly or explicitly. Special units or courses on drug education, sex education, career education, or religious education inculcate values and raise values issues and moral issues at every turn; but values are present in all the traditional subjects as well. There is simply no escaping values education.

The ubiquitousness of values education may be viewed not only as inevitable, but also as a great opportunity. That is the perspective of the comprehensive values education model described in this book. The 100 ideas for enhancing values and morality are meant to be used in the classroom, during morning announcements, with students informally in the hallway, during extracurricular activities, in the lunchroom, on the school bus, in cooperation with parents and the community, in short, wherever and with whomever the school has the opportunity to influence young people.

You can undertake values education in your own classroom today. Even if no other teacher, counselor, or administrator has attended a workshop or read a book or is consciously trying to use values education, *you* can do it, and you can accomplish a good deal. But it is a far cry from one classroom to the whole school and community. *Everywhere* should be the ideal. Until then, the more teachers who recognize the importance of comprehensive values education and begin implementing it, the better.

Who

If, ideally, comprehensive values education takes place everywhere, then presumably it would be undertaken by everybody, that is, everyone connected with the education enterprise. Some schools have tried to follow the model of enlisting and training all teachers, administrators, teacher aides, bus drivers, cafeteria workers, and other staff as values educators; but typically, it is primarily the professional staff who become involved.

Recognizing the diversity of teachers and their different skills and personalities in a typical school, the question arises: *Should* every teacher try to be a values educator? Is everyone cut out for the task? Moreover, should everyone try to be a *comprehensive* values educator, employing a combination of inculcating, modeling, facilitating, and skill-building techniques? Might some teachers be better at inculcating, for example, and others at facilitating? Should they be encouraged to specialize?

There is no hard research to shed light on these questions. A controlled study that compares the outcomes of two similar faculties—one with the teachers all trying to be comprehensive values educators, and a second with teachers specializing as inculcators, role models, facilitators and skill developers—is intriguing to contemplate. However, it will probably be a long time, if ever, before such a study is undertaken. Meanwhile, the experience of values educators who have worked with many teachers over the years will have to suffice when considering who should undertake values education and how comprehensive they should try to be.

Some teachers tend to moralize in a harsh way that turns young people off, while others facilitate in a "loosey-goosey" way that conveys the wrong message about moral relativism. It is tempting to say, in these cases, it would be better to leave the task of values education to colleagues who can carry it off more effectively. However, many teachers can learn to modify and to moderate their behavior. Their heart is probably in the right place, that is, they really do want to show young people the right path or help them discover it for themselves; they just go too far toward authoritarianism or permissiveness. Good training can help them move toward a happier middle ground. With a little help, almost all teachers can make a helpful contribution to values education and moral education. If a teacher is authoritarian or permissive to the extreme, he should not engage in explicit values education.

It is unrealistic, however, to expect every teacher to be completely comprehensive, using all four modes of values education with equal skill and integrating them with balance and grace. Some teachers are better at inculcating, modeling, facilitating, or skill training and should be allowed, even encouraged, to go with their strengths. On the other hand, their strengths will only be enhanced by being flexibly comprehensive to some degree.

For example, picture a teacher who is skillful in setting high expectations and standards, instilling concepts of right and wrong, creating clear rules and structures in which students develop good habits, and otherwise doing a fine job of inculcating values. That teacher will benefit from being able to ask students questions about how *they* think and feel, from time to time, if for no other reason, because the students appreciate this act of respect and will therefore attend even more carefully to the teacher's inculcation. Similarly, the teacher who has won his students's trust by engaging them in discussions and activities to help them develop their own beliefs, skills, and values is a teacher whose occasional inculcation or modeling of traditional values will have a powerful impact on students.

In a typical school faculty, there are going to be teachers with different fortes as values educators. It is inevitable and desirable that they will capitalize on their diverse strengths. However, the dual goals of values education are best served if all teachers who engage in it are at least moderately comprehensive in utilizing inculcating, modeling, facilitating and skill-building approaches.

When—The Developmental Issue

Former Secretary of Education William Bennett has no doubts on the subject of when to inculcate, when to model, when to facilitate, and when to teach skills for values and morality:

> And we need not get into issues like nuclear war, abortion, creationism, or euthanasia. This may come as a disappointment to some people, but the fact is that the formation of character in young people is educationally a task different from, and prior to, the discussion of the great, difficult controversies of the day. First things first. We should teach values the same way we teach other things: one step at a time. We should not use the fact that there are many difficult and controversial moral questions as an argument against basic instruction in the subject. After all, we do not argue against teaching physics because laser physics is difficult, against teaching biology or chemistry because gene splicing and cloning are complex and controversial; against teaching American history because there are heated disputes about the Founders' intent. Every field has its complexities and its controversies. And every field has its basics, its fundamentals. So too with forming character and achieving moral literacy.[18]

The "developmental" perspective is persuasive. Elementary children are quite different from teenagers, and there are great differences even within each group. Students are different intellectually, emotionally, in interests, and in experience. Because of these developmental differences, much of Bennett's statement makes a great deal of sense. Children should be taught and should know that hurting people is bad and that caring for and respecting other people is good, long before they begin to debate whether premarital sex can be caring and respectful or whether it is by nature selfish, hurtful, and disrespectful. They should know that stealing is basically wrong, before they entertain the moral dilemma of whether stealing under some circumstances can be justified. They must understand the meaning and importance of laws, before being expected to understand complex, constitutional issues.

Does this mean, in effect, that in a comprehensive values education system, we begin by exclusively inculcating and modeling values and morality and, only later, say in high school, begin to facilitate values development as well? To put it bluntly, do we teach kids what to think and how to think in elementary school, and only start encouraging and teaching them to think for themselves in secondary school? The question is not meant to be coy or to imply a correct answer. This is a very difficult question for values eduction and moral education.

There are elementary teachers who will readily agree with the previous proposition. They would say that it is enough of a challenge to teach students a few basic values. Even if it were appropriate, they do not feel they have the time to engage students in discussions of values issues, to conduct class meetings, or to employ other facilitative activities like those described in Chapter 7. Other elementary teachers will say just the opposite. They feel that having their students develop class rules, solve problems in class meetings, and engage in thoughtful discussions of values and moral issues are *the very settings in which they can teach students basic values and skills* like respect, responsibility, good listening, democracy, self-esteem, and conflict resolution. They have difficulty separating the processes of inculcating and facilitating values development.

Again, we have an apparent paradox here, that upon closer examination is resolved by thinking in terms of "and," rather than "or." Students of all ages, from elementary to high school, can benefit from a *combination* of values education approaches. However, the younger students are, the greater the *emphasis* should be on direct instruction or inculcating values and morals. "Emphasis" might mean: devoting more time to directly teaching, explaining, and repeating concepts and rules regarding values and morals; using readings and audiovisuals that present a clear "moral" rather than a moral dilemma; or using more frequent rewards, posters, slogans, and other methods for inculcating values. At the same time, the teacher can continue to use class meetings, discussions, and other facilitative experiences to enhance students' thinking skills, self-confidence, personal values, and moral maturity.

There may be one exception to the rule that all students will benefit from a combination of values education methods, with different emphases on inculcation and facilitation based on age and maturity. The exception applies to those children who are so retarded in their social and intellectual development or so lacking in any sense of right, wrong, and appropriate behavior that they require an environment of absolute control and indoctrination. A controlled environment enables these students to settle down and begin to become socialized, so they can begin to engage in a normal, comprehensive values education with its combination of inculcation, facilitation, and other elements. This exception is offered with some hesitation. Too often, teachers see an individual or group of unruly students and conclude they are beyond help or too untrustworthy or too emotionally handicapped to live up to normal expectations, when in fact, a good, comprehensive values education is exactly what is needed—firm rules, expectations, rewards, consequences, and other inculcation activities combined with the trust, respect, and opportunities to learn responsible autonomy that comes from facilitated experiences.

When—The Instructional Issue

Assuming a teacher wishes to be comprehensive and use inculcating, modeling, facilitating, and skill-building techniques, when should each take place? Is there a particular order in which it is done—for example, inculcating, then modeling, then facilitating?

In practice, the teacher utilizes several modes simultaneously or in quick succession. While explaining and moralizing, he stops and says, "Is this getting through to you? Do you buy what I'm saying?" and gives the students an opportunity to express their thoughts. While engaged in a facilitative discussion on any values issue, the teacher is inculcating the values of respect and responsibility in how he conducts the discussion. While teaching communication skills, the teacher is modeling his own use of these skills and other values as well. While conducting a class meeting, the teacher may be inculcating, modeling, facilitating, and skill building simultaneously—establishing rules for responsible participation and good listening, modeling respect for others, and encouraging students to speak their own minds. In presenting a hypothetical choice situation to students, the teacher may begin by asking, "What *should* you do?" (an inculcating question) and later shift to "What *would* you do?" (a facilitating question), or vice versa. After a class discussion in which students expressed themselves freely, the teacher may say, "I think one of the views that several people expressed was wrong, and I'd like to tell you why I think so." A day after explaining the importance of honesty to students, the teacher may ask students to complete the sentence stems "I think honesty is important because _____ ," and "I find it hardest to be honest when _____."

In other words, a teacher employing comprehensive values education moves in and out of inculcating, modeling, facilitating, and skill-building activities all the time. The precise sequence and the time devoted to each vary according to the subject, the activity, the teacher's goals, and the students's responses. There is no formula, alas. It comes down to an individual teacher or leader, with many goals, doing his best to choose the right activity or intervention, at the right time, to accomplish a particular objective. It comes down to good teaching.

Additional ideas and suggestions on how to both distinguish and integrate the modes of inculcating, modeling, facilitating, and skill building can be found in the introduction to Chapter 7 and throughout 100 methods.

Where—Sex Education, Drug Education, Religious Education, and Other Special Areas

Integrating the different modes of values education is just as important in special subject areas as it is throughout the regular academic curriculum and the life of the school. (In many cases, these special areas are part of the standard curriculum.) Areas like sex education, drug education, career education, multicultural education, environmental education, and, in appropriate settings, religious education all lend themselves to inculcation, modeling, facilitation, and skill development.

In all these areas, there are attitudes, values, and moral positions the teacher and school wishes to inculcate. The sex education teacher may want to inculcate the value of respecting the other person or the benefits of abstinence. The drug education teacher may want to inculcate the value of healthy living and the importance of never riding with someone who has been drinking. The career educator may want to inculcate the value of hard work and the importance of planning ahead. The environmental educator may want to inculcate the attitude of respect for nature. The religious educator may want to inculcate his faith.

Similarly, in all these areas, the teacher has the opportunity to model desired values and morality. The male sex education teacher can model how to be truly respectful of women, and the female sex education teacher can model self-respect and setting clear limits (and vice versa). The drug education teacher can model good health habits and a variety of ways to get high naturally. The career education instructor can model an adult who is enthusiastic about his work. The teacher of a multicultural curriculum can invite positive role models from different ethnic groups to speak to the class. The environmental educator can demonstrate the energy efficient practices he employs in his own life.

Each of these teachers can also facilitate students's values and moral development in these areas. The sex education teacher who has inculcated the value of abstinence can ask students whether they agree with his viewpoint. He can also draw a continuum or line on the board with "No talking or dancing with the other sex" at one end and "Sexual intercourse" at the other end, and point out that saying no to intercourse is but one choice, then ask students to privately consider the other choices they might have to make about drawing the line on sexual behavior. The drug education teacher can ask his students when they personally find it difficult to say no to peer pressure and have them role play alternative solutions. The career education teacher can ask students to inventory their likes and values and relate these to different careers. The religious education teacher, after having students memorize the Lord's Prayer, can ask, "What does the Lord's Prayer mean *to you*?"[53,115]

Finally, each of these special subject teachers might spend some time teaching students various skills for values and morality that pertain to their particular area. Many students will benefit from critical thinking skills to help them evaluate the great deal of information, and sometimes conflicting information, about sexually transmitted diseases, drugs, generalizations about ethnic groups, and careers. Skills for cooperation and conflict resolution will help students in careers, intimate relationships, and intergroup conflicts. And in each special area there are other, particular skills—such as saying no to peer pressure, safe sex (that's a controversial one), and interview skills—which can help students live more personally satisfying and socially responsible lives.

Where—The Home and Neighborhood Issue

Let's face it, students come to school from many different economic, racial, religious, ethnic, class, and geographic backgrounds. Some students come from homes that teach them to work hard, respect others, and never talk back to a teacher. Others come from homes that do not value education and teach their children to fight back if anyone pushes them around. Others come from homes where there is little or no parental guidance or support, or they come from homes or neighborhoods filled with drugs, explicit sex, or violence. One inner-city, middle school teacher speaks of some of his students who come to school with what he calls "church values," and others who come with "street values"—children from the same neighborhood with vastly different values.

In any classroom or school, then, you will find some students who are more predisposed to accept values and moral education than others. Their parents or community have already begun to instill respect, responsibility, compassion, tolerance, critical thinking, the work ethic, and other positive values and character virtues. It is a pleasure to support, reinforce, and build upon the good teaching and example of their parents—the primary teachers of values and morality.

Meanwhile, other students' backgrounds create a formidable challenge to values educators. You want to teach them how to control their anger and respectfully work out conflicts, while their prior training has taught them that the only way to gain respect is to fight for it. You want to teach them to appreciate others who are different, and their previous training has taught them prejudice, stereotypes, and ethnocentrism. You want to help them be responsible and successful in school, yet they have few role models in their lives who demonstrate and teach them to value perseverance, responsibility, and academic achievement. You want to teach them that good citizenship, altruism, and positive relationships are ideals to live for, and they seem hopelessly caught up in a material culture that values immediate and personal gratification above all. Their idea of a good time is going to a mall, and their greatest aspiration is to be wealthy.

Some classes or schools seem to have so many students with apparently no values or negative values, that being successful in values education can appear as a hopeless, idealistic goal. In many other cases, students come to school with contradictory values, attitudes and behaviors, having been exposed to both good and bad influences in the home, street, and media. Some days it seems like you can really help influence their values and character for the good; other days it seems like a futile endeavor. It is easy to become discouraged when we set our sights on a goal so important as values education or moral education. And, on bad days, it may be tempting to conclude that children from families where values education is deficient or nonexistent or children from violent, dysfunctional communities are lost causes—to feel that the good you can do as a teacher or youth leader is overwhelmed by the lack of support or countervailing forces in the students' back-home reality.

Well, there are no guarantees, but the good news is children are remarkably resilient. Many succeed in spite of almost overwhelming odds.[17] And values education programs are succeeding, too—in tough, inner-city schools, poor rural schools, and wealthy suburban schools alike. Many of the references in the bibliography contain examples of schools that are making a real difference in the lives and values of their students. Some are struggling perhaps, but they are making real progress. Every school can become a healthy environment—for academic learning and character education. Just because you may not succeed with every student does not mean you won't succeed with some or many students. It doesn't require 100 percent success to reverse the values deficits, ethical decay, and moral confusion of our time; it just takes a critical mass. Every parent, every teacher, every school, and every youth-serving agency can contribute to achieving that critical mass. That's all anyone can ask.

When—The Limited Time Issue

One of the most frequently heard objections to adding any new programs or activities to a curriculum is that teachers have such limited time to accomplish so many objectives. The last thing they need or want is a whole new set of objectives and activities that would take valuable time away from academic learning.

A major point made throughout this book is that values education already is or can easily become an integral part of subject matter learning and the day-to-day life of the school. From morning announcements to extracurricular activities to classroom subjects, values education can be integrated into teachers' existing routines and academic program. In fact, there are numerous ways that comprehensive values education will help teachers accomplish their academic objectives more effectively—by setting high expectations (#5), introducing students to positive role models (#47), helping students clarify their purposes (#56), relating the subject matter to values issues (#2, #67), using cooperative learning (#92), involving the parents (#98), to name just a few of the methods for integrating values education and academic education described in these pages. A teacher can implement an excellent values education program without taking significant additional time away from other activities and objectives.

However, this does not mean continuing business as usual. It is one thing to recognize that values education is taking place all the time, whether we are aware of it or not. It is another thing to consciously, deliberately, and consistently build values education into all aspects of the classroom and the school. The haphazard, intermittent, and inconsistent application of values education will produce fewer and more short-lived positive results. What has been learned about other aspects of education applies also to values education.

Research has shown consistently that the one constant in explaining how much students learn in virtually any situation is "time on task," defined as how much time a student spends actively attending to the learning task at hand. This factor seems to hold for teaching first-graders to read, army recruits to fire a rifle, quarterbacks to throw a football, or auto mechanics to tune an engine. No matter what skill or understanding is being taught, and no matter to whom, the one abiding factor crucial to the success of the process is time on task.[188]

Why should we expect values education and moral education to be any different? If we really want to enhance values and morality in schools (or at home or in society), we shall have to spend a significant amount of time at that task. Unless we do, it just won't happen.

Getting Started

Before delving into the activity ideas that follow, there are a number of factors related to using this book and employing comprehensive values education in the schools that should be considered.

Parent and Community Involvement

The importance of the parents' and the community's involvement in a school's values education program is stressed throughout this book. Therefore, one of the first things to do in getting started in values education is to inform and involve the parents and, when appropriate, the community. Ideas #1 and #96–#98 discuss why this is so important and describe very explicitly how to accomplish it. Be sure to read these sections before getting started, and use these ideas for parent and community involvement as you implement your values education program.

Selection of Activities

DO NOT TRY *ALL* THESE IDEAS AT HOME!

This book offers an array of possibilities for values education in the schools and other youth settings. It is not intended to suggest a fixed sequence of activities, in which you begin at Idea #1 and proceed step by step to Idea #100. Some of the ideas are described as being essential, like establishing target values (#1), setting high expectations (#5), respecting students' right to pass on certain activities (#66), and actively involving parents in the process (#96-#98). Others are strongly recommended; but most of the ideas in this book are optional. You do not possibly have the time to do them all, so don't even try. Select those that appeal to you from each group—those which make sense to you and which appear appropriate for your students.

Age Level

Most ideas in this book are appropriate for both elementary and secondary students. In many cases, explicit examples are provided for the different age levels. Only a few of the activities are geared to one level only, and these are described accordingly. There are many ideas that, with a small adaptation or a different example, are applicable to a higher or lower grade level. For primary age children, there are many opportunities to have students speak or draw their responses, where older students would write their answers.

Counselors, Youth Group Leaders, and Other Helping Professionals

For simplicity's sake, the word "teacher" is used throughout the book to describe the person leading the activities and implementing ideas. However, the comprehensive values education model and almost all the ideas in this book are also applicable to individual counseling, group counseling, scouting groups, church groups, day-care centers, and other youth settings. If your role is that of counselor, youth leader, social worker, minister, or other helping professional, please look beyond the focus on teachers and schools and recognize the many applications of comprehensive values education to your own work situation. By changing the words "teacher," "classroom," and "student" to "leader," "group," and "young person," you will find that most of these ideas translate directly to other youth settings.

Categories

Don't be overly concerned as to whether a particular activity you are using is in the inculcating, modeling, facilitating, or skill-building mode, as those categories have been defined here. Sometimes it is hard to classify an activity or intervention. The same method can be used for different purposes. For example, the question "What did you learn from that?" can come across as a moralizing reprimand or an open-ended clarifying question, depending on the timing and the tone of voice used. A values-clarifying facilitative activity can also be used to inculcate values. It is often the teacher's *intent* in using a particular activity that ultimately determines whether it is an inculcating, modeling, or facilitating activity. The main point is to recognize that there are several modes for conducting values education and to try to incorporate all or most of them in your teaching or group leadership.

An Idea Is an Idea Is an Idea?

All the ideas in this book are not comparable in terms of their potential for achieving the goals of values education. For example, slogans (#25), the personal bulletin board (#41), and the board of directors strategy (#84) are excellent activities, but most likely they will be used once or twice and, by themselves, will have only a limited impact. On the other hand, readings (#2), sharing your beliefs and reasons (#36), three-level teaching (#67), and class meetings (#76) are profoundly effective activities that can be used repeatedly to achieve the goals of values education. In other words, some of these methods are more important and profound than others.

The 100 ideas are not comparable in another way. In many cases, the entire idea is explained in this book. If you do the activity, you've gone about as far as you can go with it; what you read is all there is. In other instances, particularly the skill-building activities, like listening, cooperative learning, and conflict resolution, there is much, much more to the ideas than what is described in the few pages devoted to them. One could build an entire course of study or a curriculum around some of these ideas or approaches, like teaching values through literature or using class meetings for group problem solving. The treatment in the book is intended to introduce the idea; give a few specific examples and suggestions so you can actually begin to use the idea, and to provide an additional source or sources to consult for further understanding.

Further Training

Almost all the activities and ideas described in this book are fairly straightforward. They are not esoteric. It is possible to use most of them immediately, without any specialized training. However, there are two qualifications to be made here.

First, if a teacher has not attained a basic level of teaching and classroom management skills, these 100 ideas won't work much better than any other instructional activities that that teacher might employ. A teacher who walks into the classroom and begins laying down rules (#11) or asking students voting questions (#57), without explaining or framing the activity or without establishing a context or purpose, is going to see a lot of passive or confused faces looking back at him. A teacher who expects these activities or ideas to work, when his classroom is out of control to begin with, is going to be disappointed. In some cases, further training in teaching and classroom management techniques may be in order before one goes too far with values education.

Second, while most of these ideas may be relatively easy to use initially, further training can only help to deepen the effectiveness of the implementation. Particularly with regard to the ten skill-building ideas for values and moral development, further training would be very useful. For example, entire courses and workshops are offered on thinking skills, creativity, communication skills, and conflict resolution. Your principal, teacher center, intermediate unit, office of curriculum and instruction, or other source of support regularly receives notices of professional development workshops. In many cases, additional training can make the difference between fair and good, or between good and excellent, in how well well the teacher implements comprehensive values education.

Terminology

A certain amount of terminology has been explained and discussed so far. To summarize briefly:

Values Education is used as the shorthand term for the field of values education and moral education.

Values Education and Moral Education is described as an educational field or endeavor with two complementary goals—helping students lead personally satisfying and socially constructive lies.

Values Realization, Character Education, Citizenship Education, and *Moral Education* are described as the four major "movements" within the values education field. Within these four movements, dozens of particular "approaches" are discussed, such as law-related education, empathy training, values clarification, and cooperative learning. Many of the various "techniques," "methods," and "activities" that these approaches employ, as well as some of the approaches themselves, constitute the 100 strategies included in this book.

Inculcation, Modeling, Facilitating, and *Skill Development* are described as the four main delivery "modes" within the values education field. The various techniques, methods, and activities of the different values education approaches can be organized into these four delivery modes, which is how this book is organized.

However, some readers may note that, in an entire book devoted to values education and moral education, the terms "values" and "morality" have not been defined, at least not yet. They are discussed, described, and detailed but never defined. This is intentional. Philosophers have long debated the meanings of and subtle distinctions between terms like values and morality—or morality, moral, morals, immoral and amoral, for that matter. It would be an impossible task without also including and defining related terms like just, fair, right, wrong, and ethical to name a few. It would be an interesting pursuit, but would hardly make the more practical task of values education much easier.

Defining terms can also quickly lead to divisive political debate. For example, the dictionary might define a value as "a principle, standard, or quality considered worthwhile or desirable." A philosopher might define a value as "a belief, grounded in feeling, which predisposes one to act in a certain way" (or as this author prefers: "a quality or aspect of life that one believes is important, feels strongly about, and acts upon"). A psychologist might define a value as "an enduring belief that a specific model of conduct or end-state of existence is personally or socially preferable to an opposite or converse mode of conduct or end-state of existence." [162]

Immediately someone objects that such definitions of a value are "value-free," that is, independent of the *content* of a person's values. They point out some evil person like a Hitler, for example, might believe that a particular race or religion is inferior. He might feel strongly about his belief, and even act on it in a hateful or violent manner. They would argue that calling "race superiority" a value, like the values of respect and compassion, is an oxymoron. When some people ask, "Does this person have values?" they mean does he have respect, responsibility, compassion, and comparable moral virtues. They cannot easily accept that people can have destructive or evil values. In other words, one's beliefs about what constitutes "good values" often colors one's definition of the very term "values."

Problems with definitions like these have often caused gridlock among those who might otherwise agree on a set of goals for values education. Ironically, even those who disagree over the meaning of the *term* values can usually agree on the values they want their children and students to learn. In the end, it is not a definition of a single word that unites a community around values education but a set of commonly shared goals for its young people. Such goals or "target values" are described at the beginning of Chapter 5 and throughout this book.

Part 2

*One Hundred Ways
to Enhance Values and Morality
in Schools and Youth Settings*

Chapter 5

Inculcating Values
and Morality

1

Target Values

A logical starting point for any endeavor is to clearly identify the goal. Accordingly, many teachers, schools and, especially, school districts begin values education or moral education programs by clearly identifying the values they wish to instill in their students. Typically, the result is a list of "target values" that the educators aim to achieve in their program.

For example, the Baltimore County Public Schools identified the following "common core values" for their elementary schools:

- courtesy
- honesty
- responsibility
- responsible citizenship
- tolerance
- patriotism
- compassion

The Ontario, Canada Ministry of Education set these values for the primary and junior high levels of their provincial schools:

- compassion
- cooperation

- patience
- peace

- courtesy
- freedom
- generosity
- honesty
- justice
- loyalty
- moderation

- respect for the environment
- respect for others
- respect for self
- responsibility
- self-discipline
- sensitivity
- tolerance

It is no accident that most of those values sound like the Boy Scout motto, which helped inculcate values in tens of millions of young males throughout this century (see box below). As the Ontario Ministry put it, these values are "important for developing a society in which citizens can maximize their own potential and fulfill their commitments" and "which are consistent with the teaching of the world's great religions."[196]

Other districts, however, have gone beyond the "traditional values" in listing desirable values to inculcate in their students. The Rochester, New York City School District, for example, in their list of target values for both elementary and secondary students, includes many of the "process values" and social values which were emphasized in the 1960s and 1970s. Rochester's 22 value goals are:

- justice
- equality
- legitimate authority
- respect for the rule of law
- participation
- obligation to the public good
- respect for others
- kindness and caring
- cooperation
- reasoned discourse
- advocacy

- due process
- personal freedom
- privacy
- patriotism
- giving your best effort
- responsibility for oneself
- honesty
- imagination
- inquiry
- diversity
- personal empowerment

The Boy Scout Motto

A scout is:

trustworthy	obedient
loyal	cheerful
helpful	thrifty
friendly	brave
courteous	clean
kind	reverent

If some of these lists seem like they were written by a committee, with each member's pet values included to achieve a group consensus, they were. There is always the danger that a list of target values becomes so long and cumbersome that it becomes almost impossible to accomplish. If we try to hit too many targets at once, we may miss all of them, spreading ourselves so thin as to render our efforts so superficial they are practically meaningless. It is often wiser to compromise on a shorter list of target values and then move on to the even more difficult task of developing a program to actually achieve them.

The Fort Washington Elementary School in the Clovis Unified School District in California tried to solve this problem by grouping twenty-six desired "character qualities" under seven umbrella values:[180]

Honest
- Trustworthy
- Truthful
- Ethical

Responsible
- Dependable
- Accountable
- Conservation-minded

Respectful
- Courteous
- Obedient to legitimate authority
- Patriotic

Dedicated
- Courageous
- Involved
- Faithful

Perseverant
- Industrious
- Self-disciplined
- Diligent
- Resourceful

Self-Respecting
- Self-accepting
- Confident
- Resilient
- Health-minded

Concerned for Others
- Friendly
- Helpful
- Considerate
- Fair
- Cooperative
- Civic-minded

Some values education committees (#96) may be tempted to adopt another district's target values if that list seems to accurately reflect their own goals. But there is much to be gained by going through the exercise and generating one's own list. It is an important way to build a real commitment to a values education and moral education program among all constituencies represented on the committee. If people feel their own ideas went into establishing the very goals of the program, they will have a much larger stake in implementing and supporting it. On the other hand, seeing what other districts have come up with may help the committee get started more efficiently, rather than totally reinventing the wheel.

The good news is that, in the past decade, schools and communities who attempted to identify a list of target values usually succeeded in doing so. As it turns out, parents and community members, even those from different political, racial, religious, and ethnic backgrounds, *do* share many common goals for their children. In the annual, Phi Delta Kappa/Gallop Poll national survey of the public's attitudes toward education, 69 percent of the adult respondents thought local communities could agree on a set of basic values to be taught in the public schools, while 27 percent thought it was not possible. When asked about what values they thought should be taught, there was, in fact, *overwhelming agreement*, with the following values achieving a broad consensus: honesty (97%), democracy (93%), diversity—acceptance of people of different races and cultures (93%), patriotism (91%), caring for friends and family members (91%), moral courage (91%), and the Golden Rule (90%).[52]

In July 1992, 29 national leaders in values, moral, character, and citizenship education came together in Aspen, Colorado and drafted a joint declaration, including six "core ethical values." Further descriptions and behavioral correlates of these six core values have been developed by the Josephson Institute of Ethics, the sponsor of the Aspen conference.[97]

All these values, virtues, and character traits, and those on the half-dozen lists given as examples, are either "universal values" or "traditional American values" or both. Even when groups disagree on specific applications of these values, the values listed are an excellent starting point for building a consensus that enables a values education program to begin and to achieve broad community support.

Aspen Declaration on Character Education

1. The next generation will be the stewards of our communities, nation, and planet in extraordinarily critical times.
2. In such times, the well-being of our society requires an involved, caring citizenry with good moral character.
3. People do not automatically develop good moral character; therefore, conscientious efforts must be made to instruct young people in the values and abilities necessary for moral decision making and conduct.
4. Effective character education is based on core ethical values rooted in democratic society, in particular:

    - respect
    - responsibility
    - trustworthiness
    - caring
    - justice and fairness
    - civic virtue and citizenship

5. These core ethical values transcend cultural, religious, and socio-economic differences.
6. Character education is, first and foremost, an obligation of families and faith communities, but schools and youth service organizations also have responsibility to help develop the character of young people.

Continued

7. These responsibilities are best achieved when these groups work in concert.
8. The character and conduct of our youth reflect the character and conduct of society; therefore, every adult has the responsibility to teach and model the core ethical values and every social institution has the responsibility to promote the development of good character.

Reprinted with permission from the Josephson Institute of Ethics © 1992–1994.

2

Literature and Non-Fiction

One teacher in an urban high school recently taught an elective, social studies course on "American Values." He thought it would be interesting to have his students read one of Horatio Alger, Jr.'s books, which had been popular among young readers at the turn of the century. Prowling through antiquarian bookstores, he managed to find about 20 copies of Alger's work like *Strong and Steady*, *Mark Mason's Victory*, *Shifting for Himself*, and *Andy Grant's Pluck*. Surprisingly to him and his students, about half of the old books were personally inscribed: "To Foster, from Aunt Hannah and Uncle Frank, Dec. 25, '07." "Merry Christmas to Lauren from Grandma and Grandpa, 1909." Apparently, over a period of two decades, millions of adults had given their children, grandchildren, nieces, and nephews these books as presents. Why? The reason was obvious—to improve their character and to influence their values and moral development.

Horatio Alger's young heroes all exhibited the same values and character traits: honesty, friendliness, loyalty (toward their invariably widowed mothers), perseverance, a work ethic, and courage. By each novels' end, all the heroes (alas, there was nary a heroine) had arrived at or were well on their way to achieving wealth, success, and happiness. While Alger's version of the "American Dream" might seem unrealistic to some today, the story nevertheless illustrates the potential of reading to affect the values of a generation. In fact, some of the teacher's most cynical high school students admitted enjoying the Alger books and asked to read more of them. Even while they were resisting the obvious "good-will-be-rewarded" and "hard-work-pays-off" inculcation, they were still being captivated by it. They liked the moral universe that Alger created and wanted to remain there. This example illustrates how reading can be one of the most powerful ways of transmitting values and morality.

On the primary level, books like *The Little Engine That Could* and *Little Toot* demonstrate the values of perseverance, courage, and caring for others. Aesop's fables teach the values of prudence, moderation, and hard work. Many schools have collected some of the finest children's literature available and made these books and stories the heart of their values education programs.[48,119] The Heartwood Project (155 Cherrington Drive, Pittsburgh, PA 15237) disseminates one such literature-based "ethics curriculum." Critical Thinking Press has published another.[165] There are many excellent biographical series for young readers that portray the contributions of women and minorities in history, and teach the values of diversity and tolerance, as well as the traditional values of self-discipline, belief in oneself, and getting a good education.[96,157] In appropriate settings, Bible stories, sometimes modified for younger readers, inculcate the importance of faith, righteousness, and other traditional values. The excellent Newberry and Caldecott Award classics are filled with moral and value lessons for older children.

For secondary students, longer and more complex biographies of noteworthy men and women demonstrate the same moral virtues of perseverance, belief in oneself, honesty, and courage that ultimately account for the hero or heroine's success. Important documents from American history—the Declaration of Independence, the Gettysburg Address, Martin Luther King's "Letter from a Birmingham Jail"—teach many of the values the country was founded upon: the dignity of each person, the preciousness of life, and the common good, to name several. Works of literature—from *The Book of Job* (righteousness, humility) to *Hamlet* (courage, honesty) to *The Good Earth* (family, hard work, respecting nature) to *To Kill a Mockingbird* (family, respect, tolerance) are filled with value lessons, especially when the teacher helps elucidate these sometimes implicit themes. *King Arthur and His Knights* demonstrates the values of courage and courtesy. Anne Frank's *Diary of a Young Girl* inculcates a powerful moral lesson of compassion and tolerance. The list is endless and the opportunities legion for teachers and students to learn to identify and explore the moral and ethical issues present in literature.[100,141]

Edward Wynne and Kevin Ryan argue that encounters with good literature and narratives can enhance moral education by helping students learn:

- "to have both an intellectual and emotional understanding of the lives of good and evil people and what drove them to do what they did,
- to acquire an incarnate sense of justice and compassion and of greed and cruelty, learned through the study of the narrative's characters,
- to be emotionally touched by some lives and repelled by others,
- to continually be deepening their understanding of and feeling for moral facts of life and ideals by seeing them lived out in the narrative's heroes and villains,
- to enhance their moral imagination and moral sensibility as they vicariously experience the lives of characters,
- to have greater insight into the lives and stories depicted in literature and history,
- to have a storehouse of moral models to guide them when they act."[200]

Because reading can be so influential on one's developing values, it is not surprising that parents and religious groups sometimes have problems with the selection of reading materials given to their children in schools. They may object to Salinger's *Catcher in the Rye* because of certain profanity or to Shakespeare's *Merchant of Venice* for its anti-Semitism. One group may object to a novel because it shows women in subservient roles, while another may protest a different novel because it shows men and women in equal roles! In cases like these, the school is placed in the difficult position of balancing the legitimate right of parents to influence their children's values, the legitimate right of the schools to teach common civic values, and the legitimate right of the students to learn and to read. There are a number of good sources, including those developed by The American Library Association and the National Council of Teachers of English, which help schools learn how to balance these various interests.[5,104,134,156]

However, most reading materials you select for your students will not be controversial. Most parents appreciate the school's assistance in the task of teaching values and morality to their children. Once the school or district has identified the "target values" it wishes to focus upon (#1), it is actually quite an enjoyable task to find readings that illustrate and reinforce target values. As a teacher you can ask other teachers for suggestions; ask the librarian, or ask your students' parents. Giving your students good books, stories, and articles to read is an easy and important way to enhance values and morality, while simultaneously accomplishing your academic learning objectives.

Every beautiful sentiment implanted in the fertile mind of youth is a seed of truth that will yield a perennial harvest of good thoughts developed into worthy acts.

J. WILLIS WESTLAKE,
COMMON SCHOOL LITERATURE, 1878

3

Stories

How many stories have you heard in your life? Hundreds? Thousands? Alright, here's a test: In what story were there *wicked step-sisters*?

You got it right, didn't you? It was Cinderella who had the wicked step-sisters. Next question: In what way were they wicked?

They were wicked because they were *jealous* and *mean* to Cinderella. You knew that, too, more or less. Okay, one last question: How do you feel about Cinderella's wicked step-sisters? Do you like them?

No, you don't like them. In fact, you probably *dislike* them. Do you feel sorry for them, because after all, they didn't have Cinderella's good looks, and they were probably teased at school, so they had low self-esteem; and that's why they were mean to Cinderella, so it really wasn't all their fault? Nonsense. If you are like most people, you have little sympathy for those mean young women, and you'll *never* forgive them for how they treated poor Cinderella.

Such is the efficacy of storytelling. After all these years, you remember the story, the characters, their moral virtues or lack thereof, and the feelings of love of the good and contempt for the bad that you felt when you were young and impressionable. Stories contain powerful images and symbols and operate on both conscious and unconscious levels, conveying intellectual and emotional meaning.

Storytelling begins at home. Whether one tells family stories of how ancestors came to this country and overcame many obstacles; or Bible stories like Joseph and his brothers, or the multiplication of the fishes; or fairy tales and children's stories like "Goldilocks and The Three Bears" or "The Little Engine That Could," or the proverbial tale of how the parent as a child trudged six miles through the snow to attend school, such stories are designed to pass on the culture's collective wisdom, values, and morality to succeeding generations.

The stories may be absolutely accurate from a historical perspective. They may be mostly accurate, with some embellishments, additions, or omissions to enhance their meaning. Or they may be myths, fairy tales, or obvious fiction. In any case, their purpose is the same—to inculcate the desirable values, moral beliefs, and character traits in the youthful listeners.

Storytelling is an equally effective tool for inculcating values in school. To begin with, there are stories with an obvious "moral," or moral lesson, such as Grimm's fairy tales, Aesop's fables, and the story of athlete Len Bais's death from taking drugs. Many such stories contain a moral warning or admonition. "The Three Little Pigs" warns its audience to do their work well, to use bricks rather than straw as they go through life. "The Grasshopper and the Ant" admonishes one to forgo immediate gratification and plan for the future. "The Tortoise and the Hare" teaches that "slow and steady wins the race," that moderation and perseverance will succeed in the end, that pride leads to an inevitable fall.

There are stories of heroic models from history—George Washington chopping down the cherry tree, Abraham Lincoln walking miles to return the few pennies, Harriet Tubman and her numerous trips south to help slaves escape to freedom—stories that illustrate the values of honesty, courage, and dedication to an ideal. (The use of positive role models is discussed further in #46.)

There are stories about good and evil—"Aladdin and his Wonderful Lamp," "How the Grinch Stole Christmas," "The Devil and Daniel Webster," stories of African slavery, stories of the Holocaust—stories which help develop the moral predisposition to love the good and despise the bad.

There are stories of scientists, inventors, social change agents and the values—*perseverance, dedication, desire to help others*—that motivated and sustained them and ultimately led to their discoveries and important contributions. Spencer

Johnson's "Value Tales" books (*Louis Pasteur: The Value of Believing in Yourself, Helen Keller: The Value of Determination, Eleanor Roosevelt: The Value of Empathy*), written for the elementary level, include many value-laden stories.

There are stories of individual and collective accomplishment and success—her story as well as *history*—which give nations, cultures, and genders pride in their past and in themselves. Teachers whose students are primarily African American, Hispanic, Asian, or from other specific ethnic, cultural, or geographic backgrounds will do well to learn the stories of individual and group accomplishments from that specific background to help instill values in their students.

There are stories about the dedication of real people, people known to the teacher or the students, who persevered, worked hard, and succeeded. Their examples of how they achieved success in sports, or learned a foreign language, or learned to read, or achieved excellence inculcates important values and suggests that such values and the success they foster are within each person's reach.

There are stories that humanize other cultures—stories of different nationalities, religions, and ethnic groups, stories that impress the listeners with the universal truths about the human condition and encourage the values of mutual tolerance, respect, and appreciation.

Both elementary and second students love hearing a good story. Whether you read a story aloud, play a recording, or tell it as you remember it, you will reach your students in a very different way than any other form of instruction or communication. Storytelling is a unique medium. In addition to storytelling's efficacy to convey *academic* knowledge to all age levels, "Let me tell you a story" is an excellent introduction to and opportunity for values education.[14,101]

4

Audio-Visuals

It's a "media generation" out there, for better *and* worse. As many critics have argued, most of the fare coming from Hollywood is not representative of the professed values of the vast majority of the population; yet there it is, proffering irresponsible sex, violence, intolerance, selfishness, and rampant materialism as though these are the normal expectations and values of society.[129] The same can be said of the programs seen and heard on television, in music videos, and on tapes, records, and compact disks. No wonder many parents, ministers, and other adults feel desperate and determined to protest against, boycott, and oppose the products of the media industry.

Parents certainly have a personal right and responsibility to exercise some control over the viewing habits of their children, to try to influence what and how much of the media culture is seen and heard. Teachers have a different role here and a special opportunity, which is *to use the media for the purposes of values education.* Because, in addition to all the depressing, anti-social, self-destructive, and frivolous models and behavior shown in the media, there are also positive models, true heroes and heroines, traditional values, and moral courage to be found. Maybe not in the majority of releases, but they are there, waiting to be used for the purposes of instilling values and morality in young people.

1. *Movies and videotapes.* Take advantage of timely contemporary movies, such as Spike Lee's *Malcolm X,* which took the country by storm. Among other things, the movie strongly affirmed the values of family, self-discipline, education, sobriety, courtesy, self-respect, and by the end of the movie, the value of universal brotherhood and sisterhood. A year later, this movie had faded from the limelight; but while the box office was packed, and young people everywhere were wearing "X" hats, and the paperback of *The Autobiography of Malcolm X* was seen on every bookseller's display rack, it was the perfect time for high school teachers to have their students see and discuss the film. No doubt, there is another popular movie showing today, filled with values and moral issues and lessons for your students.

Beyond current movie releases, the videotape rental industry has made thousands of films available on demand. Surely you have your favorite films—movies that inspire you, stand for values you cherish, have characters whose *character* you admire, and illustrate valuable lessons in values and morality to show your students. In addition to your personal favorites, there are many others, including animated movies for younger children, which present healthy values, moral perspectives, and heroes and heroines who are role models of the traditional virtues. Use them in conjunction with your curriculum. You will get your students' attention.

Most movies, though, are longer than a typical, secondary school class period. To cope with the problem of available time, teachers can use a variety of strategies. One common approach is not to show the whole movie, but to show a key segment. If it is important enough to see the entire movie, you can show it over two or three periods throughout the week. The videotape can also be circulated among the students, for example, with groups of five getting together at one group members' home to watch the movie. Students can be given a set period of time to rent the movie themselves, especially if it's easily available in video stores or the library. Some teachers arrange special showings—at a school assembly, after school, or at their own home or a student's home.

Incidentally, an excellent videotape *for teachers* on the subject of values and moral education, called "See Dick & Jane Lie, Cheat & Steal," is available from Pyramid Films.[62]

2. *Television.* If you asked elementary and secondary school students throughout the 1980s what person they would most like to be like when they grow up, or what family represents their image of a healthy family, the names of Clifford and Claire Huxtable would inevitably head the list. Like "Father Knows Best" and "Ozzie and Harriet" did for previous generations, "The Cosby Show" demonstrated an idealized portrait of contemporary American values—a cohesive family; hard-working, successful adults; the importance of education; love combined with firm, humane discipline; responsibility; men and women in equal roles and mutually respectful relationships; respect among races, religions and nationalities. So there *are* positive values to be learned from television, at least from some of the programming.

The *TV Guide* or its equivalents, then, are among the best teacher resources for values education and moral education. "I would like you to plan to watch the following program on Wednesday night on Channel 5 at 8 P.M." is a perfectly feasible homework assignment. You can also videotape the show and bring it to class to show the next day or whenever it best fits (obtaining permission when required). Between the major networks, public television, and the cable channels (if enough students' families or friends subscribe), there are series, specials, made-for-TV movies, movie reruns, educational TV programs, news events, and other programs that can be used for values education. From Mr. Rogers specials to documentaries on drug abuse to situation comedies, there is much to learn. By regularly watching the television listings for programs that illustrate and explore the values and subjects you want to teach, you will probably be surprised at television's many possibilities for teaching values.

However, watching a movie or video or television show alone will not accomplish a great deal. The real goals of values education are achieved when the viewing experience is integrated into a more comprehensive lesson plan or unit. Therefore, when using movies and television for educational purposes, it is important to:

- Introduce the values issues or moral issues *before* the students see the video or program. Get students interested in and motivated about the subject.
- Give them specific questions or things to look for as they watch the film or program.
- Follow up their viewing with further discussion and activities to help accomplish your values education goals.

3. *Audio tapes, compact disks, records.* You probably own some tapes, disks, or some of those antique objects known as "records" that can help illustrate and inculcate the values you wish to teach. Another excellent resource is your students' music collections. Music is a major part of most young people's lives. (Were *we* like that?) Bringing their music into the classroom is an effective way to gain their interest and get them involved.

You might say to students, "We have been talking about the importance of getting along with people who are different from us, about working out our differences, not by fighting, but by talking and understanding. I'd like you to look in your music collections and try to find one song that illustrates this moral way of living with others." Some teachers use a variation of this assignment on an on-going basis, setting aside a few minutes each week for a different student to play a song for the class that illustrates the value the teacher has selected. (To *facilitate* values development, other teachers have adapted this activity, assigning students to: "Bring in a piece of music to class that demonstrates or embodies a value or belief which is important *to you*" or "which says something *to you* about this value.")

Whenever you or your students bring in songs to play for the class, you or they should clearly write or type out the lyrics ahead of time and duplicate them, so that *each student can read the words as the music is being played.* Providing the lyrics is very important. The point of the activity is not to enjoy the music, although that helps, but to derive values from the meaning in the words. Since popular song lyrics are often hard to understand (that's an understatement), being able to understand the words is essential for the activity to have any value.

There are other audio-visual aids—older tools like fine art or film-strips and new multimedia technology which is being developed all the time—that also can be employed to teach values and morality. The combination of literature and nonfiction (#2), stories (#3), and audio-visuals (#4) begin to comprise a rich body of content material for values education.

5

Expectations

> *"Good morning students. Please be seated. I am Miss Stacy, your new teacher. I wish to begin by saying that I believe it's very unfair for the teacher to ask all the questions, so I'm hoping that you will be excited enough about my classes that you will ask me lots of questions. But I warn you, I am extremely strict about punctuality and attention in class. However, I think that the teacher should serve as a guide, and I give you my promise, that if you will entrust yourself to my guidance, I will do my very best to help you develop strong ideals—ideals that will serve as a foundation for the rest of your lives. I hope to think back on your class as the brightest, the most creative, and the most committed students on Prince Edward Island."*
>
> FROM THE MOVIE "ANNE OF GREEN GABLES"
> (PARAPHRASED)

Expectations are one of the most powerful tools for inculcating values. If we hold high, but realistic expectations for students, they will come to hold high expectations of themselves. This is true in terms of academic accomplishment,[17,38] and it is also true with values and morality. If we expect all students to act responsibly, respectfully, and diligently, and we convey this expectation to them, they will be more likely to do so. Why is this so?

Because young people's self-concepts are still in a formative, uncertain state, even the seemingly most assured and macho of them, they are vulnerable to believing what parents, teachers, peers, and significant others tell them about who they are. This works in both positive and negative ways. If we communicate to students that they are lovable, capable, and responsible people and we expect them to act that way, then they will entertain the idea that they are or might be, in fact, loveable, capable, and responsible and will try to act in a manner consistent with that self-concept. If, on the other hand, we consistently communicate to students that we expect them to act in an incompetent, untrustworthy, and thoughtless manner, they will probably internalize the message and fulfill that expectation as well.

Self-concept formation aside, many students will try to fulfill the teacher's positive expectations of them, because they like or respect the teacher and do not want to disappoint him. This is a step on the road to values and moral maturity. For now, it is alright that they fulfill the teacher's expectation of virtuous behavior because they believe this will maintain the teacher's liking and respect. At least they are learning what the moral expectation is—in effect, developing a conscience—and are practicing the moral behavior. If their values education and moral education is comprehensive and doesn't stop there, in the future they will come to expect moral behavior of themselves because *they* believe it is the right way to live.

> *Education should bring its subjects to the perfection of their moral, intellectual, physical nature in order that they may be of the greatest possible use to themselves and others.*
>
> EMMA WILLARD, 1814

Almost two hundred years ago, Emma Willard founded a school for girls in Troy, New York, based on the premise that girls, as well as boys, could be expected to achieve their full intellectual, moral, and physical potential. Today that high school still exists, and continues to instill in its students the expectation that they have great talents and abilities to offer society. The expectation is pervasive that these young women are to do their best, to be responsible and caring persons, and to contribute to the wider world. One teacher's belief in and expectations for his students can be an important force for values education. As the Emma Willard example illustrates, *an entire school's* belief in its students and their ability to demonstrate good character and moral behavior is an even more potent force for the good.

In describing the essence of conveying high expectations, Merrill Harmin wrote, ". . . by word and deed, we tell them that we know they *can* do it, that we trust they *will* do it, and most significantly, that we care that they *do*."[77] It works like this:

1. *Hold high expectations.* Believe in the students' potential, set high standards, and expect to see results. At our best, we know, in the words of Father Flanagan of Boys Town, "There's no such thing as a bad kid," that even the most troubled and anti-social youngster can be turned to the right path. But, fortunately, faith in miracle cures is not required to maintain high expectations (although it helps). The hypothesis that holding high expectations pays off is supported by experience—by the many schools, of all types, who have instituted values education programs and have succeed in changing an obviously unruly and disrespectful student body into a visibly purposeful, responsible, caring group of students. *The students in those successful schools were no different from your students.* It can be done. Your students can do it.

2. *Believe in yourself.* This is the flip side of believing in your students. For values education to succeed, you need to not only have high expectations of your students but of yourself as well. You are not powerless. While it is natural to sometimes be discouraged at the large task of values education, it is feasible. Others have done it and are doing it. You can, too, if you believe in yourself and work at it.

3. *Communicate those expectations.* One way to do this is through words, and it is very important to say the words. "I believe in you." "You can do it." "In spite of what just happened, I know that you are not like that." "You can be trusted." "I know you won't let me down." "You can control your temper." "I know that you care, and I know a part of you feels badly about what you did." "You're a great bunch of kids." "I believe you can learn from this mistake."

Another way to communicate expectations is through behavior. By periodically entrusting students with responsibilities and choices, you convey your expectation that they can and will handle their freedom responsibly. By giving them challenging work—appropriate to their ability, but also requiring them to stretch their abilities—you convey the expectation that they are intelligent and capable—not only capable intellectually, but also able to set goals for themselves, to persevere and work hard, to take pride in their work, and to succeed.

4. *Repeat those expectations.* Again and again. They may not be believed or internalized by students at first, but when backed up by your actions and by their initial successes in fulfilling your expectations, the students will come to have higher expectations of themselves.

5. *Affirm positive effort and success.* The positive effort is probably even more important to affirm than the initial success. Continuing effort leads almost inevitably to success.

6. *Respond to discouragement and failure.* Respond with understanding, support, concrete help, and reaffirmation of your positive expectations.

7. *Respond to transgressions* or failure to live up to high but fair expectations (for example, you trusted them alone for a minute and when you returned the class was in chaos) with: (a) disappointment, correction, feedback, moralizing, or whatever other response you feel is appropriate at the time, (b) plans or goals for the future so they can learn from their mistake, and (c) reaffirmation of your positive expectations.

One may be tempted to lower expectations following a failure to achieve them. But we would not want a student to give up believing in himself because of one or more failures; so we shouldn't give up on them when they don't fulfil our positive expectations for thoughtful, responsible behavior.

6

Explanation, Moralizing, and Admonition

Three of the most direct ways of inculcating values and morality are to explain, admonish, and moralize, that is, *to convey a clear message about the beliefs, behaviors, choices, and values that you regard as desirable and undesirable, or right and wrong.* Related terms for these activities include advice, persuasion, exhortation, preaching, or sermonizing.

Explanation

Explanation involves helping students understand your values, expectations, and rules. The Baltimore County Schools, for example, give students several behavioral descriptions for each of the core values taught. Among other things, *courtesy* means "refraining from 'booing' at assemblies and competitive activities." *Compassion* means "helping children who are new to the school." *Integrity* means "keeping a promise made." *Responsibility* means "completing homework and assignments on time." Such detailed explanations help students understand the meaning of these core values and how they might implement them in their daily lives.187

Explanation also includes the rational presentation of the *reasons* for one's values, expectations and rules. Here are some abbreviated examples of teachers explaining the reasons for various moral and value positions.

"One reason honesty is so important is that, without it, none of us could ever trust one another."

"You can't run in the halls, because someone could get hurt. In fact, there were two serious accidents last year when . . . ."

"We believe that democracy is the best form of government, because . . . ."

"Why should you never drive with alcohol in your system? Let me tell you about some of the research on drinking and reaction time . . . ."

"It would be a mistake to become sexually involved at your age, because teenagers are not ready to handle the commitment and emotional complexity of such a relationship."

As the last example indicates, your explanation may or may not be persuasive to the recipient. One of the challenges of teaching *any* subject is to make our explanations clear, persuasive, and effective, so that students in fact learn, in this case, the moral or value we wish to instill.

We often assume that young people know the reasons for our values, rules, and expectations. They often do not or need to be reminded. By helping students understand the reasons for our values, expectations, rules, advice, admonition, and moralizing, the effectiveness of all these methods for inculcating values is enhanced.

Moralizing and Admonition

While explanation relies on rational argument, moralizing and admonition rely on moral persuasion and authority. Sometimes there is a fine line between moralizing and explanation and, as the following examples indicate, they often work together.

An excellent example of admonition occurs in the movie *Witness*, when Harrison Ford's character finds the young boy he is protecting handling his revolver. The lad, who respects and looks up to Ford, is amazed at the vehemence with which he is told, "Never, *ever*, play with a loaded gun!" Ford goes on to explain how guns are not toys and how dangerous they are. The viewer senses this admonishment will stay with the boy for the rest of his life.

In another example, in an elementary classroom, students have been discussing a value-laden story about a mischievous bunny. The teacher summarizes the discussion as follows:

> You know something, boys and girls? This was really a good discussion. Sometimes, life is complicated, and we have to face problems in dealing with others. And sometimes, that means that we have to take a stand. In some cases, it could mean that we'll get hurt in the process. If we try to avoid the hurt, if we run away from our problems, they usually have a way of coming back again. It takes courage for all of us to face hard choices. But, sometimes facing a problem helps us find solutions. We must all respect the rights of others to what is theirs. These are things we do and value as adults as well as children. This is part of our responsibility as citizens no matter whether we are adults or children.[19]

Clearly the teacher is delivering a mini-sermon on the values of courage, respect, and responsibility. Similarly, in a high school biology class, the teacher is giving advice and moralizing on the values of hard work and self-discipline when she tells her students, "It's important that you take this assignment seriously, and don't leave it until the last minute. You know, when you go on to college, no one is going to hold your hand. You are going to have to work independently and get your lab experiments done on time. You need to develop these work habits now, so they become second nature to you when you get to college."

Admonitions and moralizing are among the most effective ways of communicating to young people your own and society's values and morality. As award-winning football coach and motivational speaker Lou Holtz says, "If you preach something long enough, they're going to believe it."[84]

In most cases, however, it takes more than admonitions and moralizing to get young people to *internalize* these values and morals. We might say that moralizing is a very helpful, but not a sufficient means of values education and moral education. Moralizing helps develop in young people an awareness of what society regards as desirable or undesirable, right or wrong, which is an essential foundation for any value or moral system. Moralizing leads them to the moral waters, so to speak, but does not insure that they will drink.

One caution here. Explanation, advice, admonition, moralizing, preaching, and sermonizing are important in helping develop a moral awareness, sensitivity, or conscience in young people, but these methods can be overdone. Repetition works to emphasize a communication, *to a point*, after which it begins to diffuse and devalue the communication. In most cases, if people, young or old, are moralized to too frequently, too intensely, too repetitively, or too harshly, they will begin to tune out the message. With moralizing, the point of diminishing returns is reached when young people cease to listen or to care and begin to resent the communication and to retreat psychologically or physically. Therefore, it is important to combine moralizing with other methods for inculcating, modeling, and facilitating values development.

> *Train up a child in the way he should go: and when he is old, he will not depart from it.*
>
> PROVERBS, 22:6

7

Quotations

Quotations and aphorisms are an effective means of inculcating values and morals. Particularly when they are repeated or posted on a classroom wall for the students to see over time, they become short, memorable lessons in moral and cultural literacy.

Some teachers place one or more quotations on the wall as a permanent part of the classroom decor. Every day, week in and week out, the students see:

> *Do unto others as you would have others do unto you.*
>   THE GOLDEN RULE
>
> *This above all: to thine own self be true,*
> *And it must follow, as the night the day,*
>   *Thou canst not then be false to any man.*
>   SHAKESPEARE
>
> *It is never too late to be what you might have been.*
>   GEORGE ELLIOTT

Some teachers post a different quotation on the chalkboard or wall *each week*. One social studies teacher, for example, has 40 quotations, each of them nicely lettered, on posterboard. She uses them every year, rotating them once a week. Included among her "Quotations-of-the-Week" are:

> *Ask not what your country can do for you, but what you can do for your country.*
>   JOHN FITZGERALD KENNEDY
>
> *Never doubt that a small group of thoughtful, committed citizens can change the world. Indeed, it is the only thing that ever has.*
>   MARGARET MEAD
>
> *We hold these truths to be self-evident, that all men are created equal, that they are endowed by their Creator with certain inalienable rights, that among these are life, liberty, and the pursuit of happiness.*
>   DECLARATION OF INDEPENDENCE

Other teachers use quotations daily. Still others use them on an ad hoc basis, whenever quotes fit into a particular unit or lesson plan.

Repeated use of a quotation or a saying increases its impact. One teacher frequently quotes his former scoutmaster, who would always say, "Leave your campsite a little better than you found it." He never forgot that statement and later came to see that it applied to much more than campsite cleanliness. By sharing the quotation with his students more than once, this teacher hopes that, just as he did when he was younger, his students will never forget this important moral guideline about responsibility.

Making a file of quotations, integrating them into your teaching, and posting them on the classroom wall is a simple, enjoyable, and effective strategy for values education. It can also be done on a schoolwide basis, posting quotations in the hallways, cafeteria, gymnasium, and other highly visible places. To further illustrate this point, other quotations about values, morality, values education, and moral education are scattered throughout this book.

8

Praise, Appreciation

Calvinist tradition influenced many generations to believe it was best to withhold praise and appreciation from children lest it "go to their heads" and give them an overinflated opinion of themselves. More recently, we have come to understand the importance of self-esteem and to recognize that praise and appreciation can play an important part in helping young people feel lovable, capable, and worthwhile.[174]

Another benefit of praise and appreciation is its effectiveness as a direct method of inculcating values and morality. Children, teenagers, adults—*everyone* loves to be praised and appreciated. Because it feels so good to be praised and appreciated, we are likely to repeat doing what elicited the praise and appreciation before. This is basic behavior modification theory. If you "reinforce" or reward a behavior, it is more likely that behavior will be repeated. Praise and appreciation are powerful forms of reward.

Traditionally, we have corrected and criticized students for doing the wrong things. A new admonition has recently become popular among educators. "Catch them doing right." In other words, notice when their behavior reflects the values you want to instill, and comment positively on it. For example:

> *"John, that was a fine job you did on your report. Not only did you convey a good deal of information, but you included your own viewpoint on the subject as well. Very good!"*

> *"Yes, my daughter is fine, and I appreciate your asking about her. That was very considerate of you."*

> *"Nice work."*

> *"I have to tell you that I was really proud of you all at the assembly this morning. I thought the questions you asked the speaker were really thoughtful. And I particularly appreciated how, unlike some of the other students, you did not 'boo' when the speaker made that comment about the school. It showed me that you have really learned the meaning of 'respect'."*

Notice there are several different elements in these examples of praise and appreciation. There is positive evaluation—"fine job," "very good," "nice work." The behavior that is being praised is specifically described—working together, conveying lots of information, giving your own viewpoint, asking thoughtful questions, not 'booing' the speaker. The values behind the behavior are highlighted—cooperative, consideration, respect. Finally, the teacher expresses his own, positive feelings—"I appreciate," "I was really proud."

The more of these elements you include in your expressions of praise and appreciation, the more effective the inculcation will be. When a student knows specifically what you appreciate, the more likely he is to reproduce the behavior or attitude.

Because praise and appreciation are such important and universal tools for influencing values and self-esteem, two cautions are in order here. First, your praise and appreciation should be genuine. Don't force yourself to give a long, elaborate, "four-part" appreciation, and don't praise something that's not really there, hoping your appreciation will bring it into being. Students will sense that something is "fishy," and this insincerity will undermine other occasions when your praise and appreciation *are* sincere. Better to wait until you actually see something you like, even if it's a small example of the desired value, and take that occasion to comment. Better to say simply "Nice going!" if that's what you feel, than to deliver a more complex statement you don't genuinely feel.

Second, don't just praise and appreciate students when they exhibit traditional moral virtues like respect, responsibility, and self-discipline. That is necessary, but not sufficient. Find some *other* occasions to praise their creativity, their originality, and their individuality. There are two reasons for this. The first is that citizens in a democracy must learn to not just follow the crowd, but to think for themselves, to speak their minds, to act on their convictions, and, if necessary, to stand alone. It is important to reinforce qualities of individuality as well as conformity to expected group norms and values.

The second reason is that praising people only for what *you value* in their behavior and never for *what they value in themselves* erodes self-esteem. If we only praise students when they get good grades and behave properly, for example, they may develop the feeling that they are only worthwhile as long as they achieve success and conform to others' expectations. Since no one can always succeed and meet others' expectations, students may feel on some deeper level that they are not worthwhile and may feel a continual need for others' praise and reassurance. By sometimes praising them for "being themselves," for thinking their own thoughts, for having the courage to be different, and for the qualities and characteristics *they like about themselves*, we are conveying, "I appreciate you *for who you are* and not just for doing what I think is good." It's a subtle distinction, but one of the most important that teachers and parents can ever make.

9

Correction and Negative Feedback

Just as praise and appreciation are forms of positive feedback that let a student know you think he is on the right track, correction or negative feedback tells a student his behavior is not acceptable or desirable. While praise and appreciation are positive reinforcers that make it more likely a behavior will be repeated, correction and negative feedback are intended to encourage a student to alter his behavior in more constructive directions. Used as part of values education, praise, appreciation, correction, and negative feedback are all ways of inculcating values and moral behavior.

Correction and feedback, in this context, means *providing the student with information,* the sooner the better, *that what he is doing does not conform to the rules or expectations in this situation for appropriate, respectful, responsible, moral, or ethical behavior.* Sometimes the values or morals being inculcated are quite explicit; more often the moral implication is implied. The following examples illustrate both cases.

"He's not finished speaking." (*Moral implication:* "It's disrespectful to interrupt.")

"Hey, what did we say about put-downs in this class?" (*Moral implication:* "Hurting people is not an acceptable behavior.")

"That was wrong."

"I don't know if you realize it, but when you describe grown women as 'girls,' you are likely to offend quite a few people." (*Moral implication.* "Be considerate of other people's feelings; avoid using words that others find disrespectful.")

During a class discussion: "C'mon, she's being honest here, cut her some slack." (*Moral implication:* "We value honesty. You should be more sensitive to her feelings, more caring and considerate.")

"No, that would be stealing." (*Moral implication:* "Stealing is wrong.")

"There you go, putting yourself down again." (*Moral implication:* "You have worth; you should respect yourself more.")

"Hey, give me a break, will ya?" (*Moral implication:* "I would appreciate your acting more considerately.")

Students are calling out: "Remember to raise your hand." (*Moral implication:* "Be respectful of others.")

"I notice you only criticize people. How about saying something nice to someone once in a while? (*Moral implication:* "Try to be more caring and supportive.")

"That's not fair."

"It was wrong how you treated the substitute teacher yesterday."

It is one thing to state and explain to students our rules, values, and moral expectations. Correction and negative feedback, like praise and appreciation, are the daily reminders, year after year, of how and how not to put those rules, values, and moral expectations into practice. Correction and feedback are also the daily reminders of the importance we attribute to the rules, values, and moral expectations.

10

Rewards and Awards, Grades, Contests, and Prizes

Rewards and Awards

Beyond giving praise and appreciation, another way to inculcate values is by giving more concrete rewards and awards to students who demonstrate the target values. Not only does this reinforce the desired values in the students who receive the reward or award, it calls attention to and models the desirable values for everyone who knows of the award.

Rewards and "privileges" are often given for following the rules, completing one's assignments, and doing a good job—all indicators of desirable character traits, such as responsibility, perseverance, and pride in work. Such rewards include:

- Stickers
- Being first in line
- Early or longer recess
- Buttons
- Helping the teacher
- Snacks or treats
- Choice of assignments
- Relief from an assignment
- Right to leave school during lunch or free periods
- Right to use the student lounge
- A reserved parking space (!)

Obviously, some of these rewards or "privileges" are appropriate for different age levels, and others (like helping the teacher) might or might not seem like a reward to some students. Still, rewards are omnipresent in schools and can be used to acknowledge and encourage desirable behavior. For generations, schools have also given more prominent awards for academic excellence and for achievement in sports. Honor Roll, Dean's List, membership in Arista or other honor societies, a coveted school letter, college scholarships—these have long served as awards for good scholarship and athletic accomplishment.

More recently, elementary and secondary schools have gone further and begun to give awards for behavior that represents a broader array of values that the school wants to instill in its students. Awards can be given for:

- Good citizenship
- Helping another person
- Creativity
- Community service
- Demonstrating the Value-of-the-Month (#16)
- Giving one's best effort
- Academic achievement
- Sportsmanship
- Youth advocacy
- Patriotism
- Conflict resolution (the "School Peace Prize")
- Exemplifying the school's values

Awards like these can be given to students in individual classrooms, as a school award, or on a district-wide basis. The teacher alone, the principal, students, or others can be involved in selecting the award winners. Awards can be given casually or with great fanfare at school assemblies.

In some instances, only one student can win the award or honor, as in "Youth Citizen of the Year" or valedictorian. For the purpose of values education and moral education, *it is better if many or all students can potentially win an award.* Monthly awards can go to nine or ten students over the course of the year. Other awards can go to an unlimited number. For example, one school has a "Wall of Fame," with room for an unlimited number of names and photographs of students who demonstrate the desired values. A principal in another school uses her bulletin board in the hallway to acknowledge all award winners. In Penfield, New York, Burger King will give a free meal to any and all students who have received the school award for helping another person. At Malcolm X Elementary School in Washington, DC, students frequently receive parchment certificates, glittering trophies, medals, and pins, amidst much fanfare—tangible and immediate reinforcement for their self-discipline and good citizenship.

Grades

Grades or marks are another form of reward that almost all schools employ. In addition to recognizing different levels of accomplishment, grades are a potential means of inculcating values. The most common use of grades is in rewarding and reinforcing the values of hard work, diligence, perseverance, and excellence. Critics of traditional grading point out problems in the reliability and validity of grades; argue that grading can turn students off as well as motivate them, and suggest that there are better alternatives for evaluating and reporting pupil progress.[107]

These criticisms notwithstanding, it is hard to dispute that grades help inculcate values. The question is *which* values? When students ask, "Does this count?" they mean, "Will it be on the test? Will we be graded on this?" Inadvertently, they are raising a question of values. "Does this count?" is another way of asking, "Is this important? Does it have value?" Grades are one means the school has to communicate what it values. Grades typically are given for academic diligence, memorization, following the rules, and sometimes for conceptual understanding. They might also be given for critical thinking, independence, creativity, service, honor, and good citizenship. If the latter are among our target values, our grading and evaluation systems can reflect and reinforce them. Many schools are starting to do just that—communicating to students and their parents, in numerical grades or in written evaluations, the values they feel are central to academic and moral learning.

Contests

Compared to an *award*, where people are hopefully engaged in the activity anyway and some happen to be declared winners, a *contest* is a competition that people enter specifically for the purpose of competing for the award. Contests are another means of inculcating values. Having a contest for the best "whatever-it-is" suggests that "whatever-it-is" is important. A contest that highlights a particular value or moral precept emphasizes the importance of that value and engages students in thinking about and internalizing it.

The same values award categories listed above such as citizenship, creativity, peace, and patriotism can be used for "values contests." Again, the contest can be on a class, school, or district level.

The concept of an "essay contest" is fairly familiar. But there are many more forms of expression that lend themselves to contests, for example:

- Essay
- Speech
- Poem
- Play
- Story
- Artwork
- Music
- Dance

Let's say you wanted to focus on the value of compassion or caring for others. In your class or school or district, you would announce the contest. An award or prize will be given to the student who creates the best essay, story, or work of art that illustrates the value of caring. There are many permutations on this. You can have one overall award or one award in each category, for example, award both the best essay on caring and the best poem on caring. You could have first place, second place, third place, and honorable mention awards. You could limit the subject to one particular value, like caring, or expand it to several values you have been focusing on. If the whole district becomes involved, there could be contest winners from each class, a winner from each school, and a district winner.

Prizes

There are many different prizes or tangible awards that can be given to award or contest winners. These include:

- Certificates
- Individual plaques and trophies
- Medals, pins, and buttons
- The winners' names on a wall plaque
- Membership in a club, such as a good citizens' club or a community service club
- School mugs, sweatshirts, and letters
- A wide variety of gifts—basketball, dictionary, calculator
- Multiple awards, such as one elementary school's "star performer" award program in which winners receive a school pencil, a certificate from the principal, and their picture on a bulletin board
- Complimentary meals from local restaurants
- A special trip or event for the winners

Community organizations and businesses regularly offer scholarships and monetary awards to students who demonstrate good citizenship and good character, as well as good grades. For example, MacDonald's sponsors the Ray A. Kroc Youth Achievement Award to junior and senior high school students who have demonstrated all-around excellence in the areas of citizenship, leadership, scholarship, and extracurricular activities.

Awards, grades, and prizes can be overdone, resulting in: an emphasis on students' working for extrinsic rewards rather than intrinsic motivation; making students feel worthwhile only if they continually win awards; increasing students' anxiety about winning, and eroding the self-esteem of those who do not win or achieve high grades.[111] But when used as one part of a more comprehensive approach to values education, tangible and symbolic rewards can help emphasize the values we wish to instill and help students develop the good habits that lead to achieving the award.

11

Rules

Everyone knows that schools establish rules to maintain order and to control the movements of large numbers of students so that education can proceed in an organized fashion. We recognize less often that students, as well as teachers, appreciate rules and order, which reflects a universal, psychological need. When we know what the rules are, then we understand the limits of our freedom, and conversely, we can "feel free" to operate within those limits. For example, if a parent says, "You may play anywhere on this block, but do not cross the street," the child now knows the parameters within which he can feel free and in control. If we also know that others are required to observe the same rules, then we have a sense of moral correctness, of fairness in our world.

Psychologically speaking, then, an orderly world in which sensible rules and laws are fairly applied is a desirable world to live in. In contrast, a world in which we are confused about our prerogatives, where the rules keep changing, where they are applied unfairly, or where they make no sense, is a world of chaos, anarchy, and even tyranny. Such a world inevitably brings out the worst in individual selfishness, competition, and aggression. So, in schools, from both the adults' and students' viewpoint, appropriate rules help create a safer, more orderly, and more comfortable learning environment.

Rules are also an important aspect of values education and moral education. The first reason for this is that rules are a very clear way to indicate what the rule-makers value. Some rules emphasize obedience and order, such as "Walk single file in the halls" or "Don't talk back to a teacher." Some emphasize respecting other people, for example, "Let the other person finish before you speak" or "Racial slurs will not be tolerated." Some rules emphasize hard work, independence, loyalty, or respect for authority. Schools must choose which rules to emphasize. The list of rules chosen is an important way of saying to the students, "These are the things we value and we want you to value them as well."

Second, in a developmental sense, rules are an important step on the path to moral maturity. If you tell a youngster, "You should take responsibility for your own actions" or "You should not take advantage of other people," the child may not know what you mean. If you say, "The rule is: you may not copy anyone else's work; that's called 'cheating' and it's not allowed," then they begin to understand one example of the general moral principle. After several years of living according to various rules that stem from the same basic principles, eventually children begin to understand the more general principles—fairness, respect, reciprocity—and apply those principles in situations where no rules are given or where the given rules don't apply.

In other words, moral rules encourage moral behavior or moral habit formation. To those who would argue that rule-inspired behavior and habits are a far cry from internalized values and morality, Richard Sparks, Jr. writes:

Our basic assumption is that there is a reciprocal relationship between thought and deed. That is, individuals act in accordance with their perceptions, values, and beliefs, and, in turn . . . , an educational environment in which virtuous conduct is consistently nurtured, valued, and reinforced is presumed also to have an impact on the formation of one's values and moral reasoning. As individuals interact in a school environment where desirable behaviors are clearly communicated, systematically nurtured, and consistently reinforced, the values underlying those behaviors will become internalized and, ultimately, characteristic of the individual.[180]

So, at all levels of the educational enterprise, schools and teachers will and should have rules. There may be rules about promptness and tardiness, vulgarity, fighting, cheating, overt acts of affection, dress, respect and disrespect, or any area and behavior which the teachers and schools feel are important. The question then is: how do we make rules that actually contribute to the goals of values education, rather than making rules simply for the sake of having rules and controlling large numbers of people? Some hints for doing this are given below.

1. *State the rule in positive terms, if possible.* There are two important reasons for trying to state rules in positive terms. First, it is better to have students focused on visualizing the desired behavior than the negative behavior. Thus, "Raise your hand before speaking" is preferable to "Don't call out." Second, positively stated rules often do a better job of elucidating a moral principle, while negatively stated rules tend only to proscribe individual behaviors. For example, a negative rule might say "No hitting is allowed," while in positive terms this might translate to "Treat others with respect." Some teachers use a combination of positively stated and negatively stated rules.

2. *The rules should be clear.* Students have a right to understand the rule. Teachers need to communicate or explain the rule clearly to students, which includes examples of what the rule means. If there is a rule about doing one's own work, for example, students should understand the difference between legitimate collaboration and unfair copying. That can only be done by giving specific examples of each. Some teachers give students a list of specific "do's" and "don'ts" that follow from each rule. Teachers often find it helpful to write the rules down and, depending on grade level, distribute them to students, post them in the classroom or school hallway, or include them in a student handbook. One school emphasizing the value of respect posts different "Respect Rules" (get the triple pun?), with a somewhat different list in the classroom ("Share materials fairly"), in the cafeteria ("Keep your area clean"), in the hall ("Walk on the right"), on the school busses ("Be courteous to the driver"), and so on throughout the school.

3. *The reason for the rule should be explained.* This is the point where values education and moral education take place explicitly. "The reason that put-downs, ridicule, and teasing are not allowed in this classroom is that each of us is entitled to be respected. No one deserves to be hurt by another, but put-downs can really hurt. I think we will all enjoy participating in this class more if we feel safe from teasing and sarcasm."

This is one way we help young people develop a "conscience." When they reflexively make a sarcastic comment to someone, if they experience a half-conscious, nagging wonder as to whether they just broke the rule and hurt that person's feelings and, perhaps, remember the notion that no one deserves to be hurt, then they have begun to internalize a moral principle. Establishing and explaining the rule about no put-downs played a small but significant part in that student's moral education.

Explaining classroom or school rules also provides an excellent opportunity for helping students understand the rules and laws of the larger society.[125] It is useful to ask students if they know of any laws in the wider world that are similar to the rules of their classroom. It will help them understand that so many of society's rules and laws are based on the value of respecting the rights of others.

4. *Limit the number of rules.* If we tried, we could easily make a list of 100 rules for students to follow. Don't run in the halls. Raise your hand before speaking. Only one trip to the bathroom per person per period. No spitting on the floor. Don't stick your gum on the bottom of the desk. Don't write on the walls. You must wear shoes to class. To spell out all the rules that govern behavior in school settings would be absurd and would also establish a repressive atmosphere.

A better approach is to select a few (three, five, certainly no more than ten) key rules and emphasize these. Some rules can be more general, all-encompassing one's like "Show everyone respect" or "Respect other people's property." Those two rules alone encompass dozens of more specific applications. Remember, the Old Testament included over 500 laws, but only 10 commandments. So emphasize the rules that are most important. You can still apply others as needed, but some of the most effective values education and moral education will take place around those limited number of rules you choose to explain clearly and emphasize consistently.

5. *Remind students of the rules.* You need to do more than state the rules clearly initially. They need to be reinforced over time. In one elementary school, the principal and teachers frequently ask, "What's the rule?" and the students answer collectively, "No hitting, kicking, fighting, or other types of negative, violent behavior." That's the school's main rule and every student knows it.

Rules that are posted and visible provide a daily reminder. You can also refer to the rule from time to time. Teachers often remind students of a rule when it is broken. An even better way is to find an occasion to *compliment the students on how well they are doing in following the rule.* For example, after your class has had a good discussion, you might say, "I really want to appreciate you all on how well you respected one another during that discussion. You listened well to each other, and no one broke the 'put-down rule.' That's just great. I wish more classes could demonstrate such mutual respect."

6. *Establish appropriate consequences for breaking the rules.* This is such an important part of values education and moral education that it is discussed in its own separate section (#13).

7. *Apply the rules consistently and fairly.* Because young people, as adults, have an intuitive fairness meter operating at all times, they quickly recognize and resent any inconsistencies in the way rules are applied. It may be impossible for teachers to be totally consistent, because we are human and because seemingly similar situations are not always the same. Nevertheless, the more consistently rules are applied, the greater the likelihood students will accept, respect, and follow them.

This is sometimes easier said than done, because not all teachers agree on all rules. On some issues agreement is not a major problem. Many good high schools have operated for years with some teachers allowing gum-chewing in class while others forbid it. Part of the students' education can be to recognize that different teachers have different values and students need to learn to work with and work under teachers, employers, and others with different values. However, there are other rules that are too important to allow diversity among the staff. For example, if a school is experiencing problems of violence or interracial tensions and establishes certain rules as a first step in dealing with the problem (such as carrying weapons or making racial slurs will result in immediate suspension), then the school staff must be united, consistent, and fair in carrying out these rules in order to restore order and communicate that this school does not value but condemns violence and intolerance.

8. *Involve students in rule making and enforcement.* This is another useful approach to values education and moral education, which is dealt with in its own section under "Facilitating Values and Morality" (#75).

Well, that's enough rules . . . about making rules.

Coach Lou Holtz's Three Rules

1. Do what's right (what's honest and fair).
2. Do the best you can.
3. Treat others as you'd like to be treated.[84]

12

Requirements

A "requirement" refers here to the work a student must do to fulfill an assignment, pass a course, earn a particular mark, move to the next grade or, ultimately, graduate. As with rules, the requirements a school sets for its students demonstrate the values it wishes to inculcate.

Here are some new ways (and a few old ones) that schools have recently begun to alter their requirements to achieve not only more academic learning, but to further values education.

1. *Hard Work.* Some schools who have identified "the work ethic" as one of their target values are now requiring their students to work harder. Students are reading more, writing more, and doing more math and science.

2. *Excellence in Education.* Schools and teachers who have said they value excellence in education are now changing their expectations and requirements to reflect this value. Some schools, elementary and secondary, will no longer pass students on to the next grade or allow them to graduate, unless they have demonstrated the required competency levels. Individual teachers can inculcate this value by requiring students to do quality work (which they need to define) and handing back any student's work which does not meet the standards. This process continues until the student achieves the required level of quality, at which point he receives credit for that assignment.

3. *Community Service.* Many elementary and secondary schools who want to teach the value of caring, compassion, and concern for the common good are now requiring students to engage in community service—as short assignments, longer projects, or even courses (#21).

4. *Independent Projects.* Teachers and schools who value self-discipline, independence, and creativity are requiring students to do independent projects. As with community service, these can be short class assignments, longer projects, independent study courses or modules, or graduation requirements such as a "Senior Project."

5. *Physical Education Standards.* We have no problem stating expectations and requirements about student reading levels. Many schools have recently set standards for students' physical development. To receive credit for physical education classes, students must demonstrate various physical abilities and accomplishments. As the author's seventh-grade daughter put it, without much enthusiasm, "Now we have to run a mile."

6. *Life Skills.* More schools are now requiring students to learn important life skills and values in special courses designed to teach those attitudes, skills, and values. Whether the courses are called Life Skills, Human Relations, Health Education, Human Sexuality, Values, Current Issues, Career and Life Skills, Citizenship, or something else, one of the major goals is to enhance the values and moral development of the students.

7. *Family Involvement.* Some schools are now requiring a parent or guardian to become involved in their child's education—whether by reading to the child (adult literacy courses are also offered), enabling the student to complete an assignment ("interview your parent about . . ."), helping the child with homework, or coming to school activities. The goal is to enhance family values as well as help the child learn.

8. *Cooperative Learning.* Many teachers and schools who want to teach students the value of cooperation are now requiring cooperation in their courses. As the section on cooperative learning illustrates (#92), students work on academic tasks in small groups in which they must work cooperatively in order to complete the assignment.

Many more examples could be given. They all illustrate the main idea—that a school's requirements reflect and reinforce the values it wishes to teach the students. What values is a school teaching if all it does is require the students to show up, memorize information, feed it back on tests, and follow orders? As an individual teacher, as a school, or as a district, reconsidering one's requirements is a potent way of refining and improving a values education program.

13

Consequences and Punishment

What happens when students do not observe the rules or fulfill the requirements? There must be consequences; otherwise the rules and requirements will cease to have any meaning.

Initially, students often will observe rules not so much because they appreciate the value of the rules, but rather to avoid the negative consequences of not following the rules. That's alright, initially. In following the rules to avoid punishment, students *do* learn the rules. They come to understand the expectations that the school and society have regarding their behavior. We also want them to internalize the moral reasoning behind many of society's rules, and we have many other methods to help accomplish that; but it is important initially for them to learn the patterns of behavior that society expects of them. When they develop the habit of following rules and meeting requirements, they will have established a foundation for success in society and for making life's more difficult judgment calls about when to stretch or even break a rule.

The consequences and punishments teachers and schools have at their disposal, when students do not follow the rules or meet requirements, are very familiar and include:

- Negative feedback ("constructive criticism")
- Warning
- Detention
- Loss of privileges
- Not being allowed to participate
- Not receiving an award or honor
- A lower grade

- Parent notification
- Suspension or expulsion
- Retention—not being promoted

Several guidelines familiar to most educators for administering consequences and punishments are briefly:

1. *Let the punishment fit the crime.* This has come to have two meanings. The first is to avoid unduly harsh punishments for minor infractions—the educational equivalent of no "cruel and unusual punishment"—and, conversely, to avoid unduly light reproofs for serious infractions. Neither approach breeds understanding of or respect for the system of rules and requirements. The second meaning is to employ "natural and logical consequences" whenever possible.[46] For example, if several students deface school property, a more natural and logical punishment, and better moral education, would be to require them to clean up the school property rather than suspend them for three days. If a student insults another student, breaking a rule about respect, a logical consequence is to have the student apologize to the person he offended.

2. *Avoid mass punishment for individual infractions.* When an entire classroom is punished for the actions of one or two students, or an entire grade or school is punished for the actions of a few students, it creates resentment in the majority of students who feel unfairly punished. It is sometimes tempting to employ mass punishment, especially when you can't identify the individual culprit; but this strategy almost always backfires. Rather than fostering respect for rules and laws, mass punishment creates generalized resentment toward authority.

3. *Be consistent, yet flexible.* Now there's a contradiction; but it's one we have to live with. Unless a rule is applied consistently, students will become confused as to how important the rule is and will become resentful over its inconsistent application. "How come he got away with it and I got punished?" or "Why was my daughter punished when other students get away with this all the time?" are familiar refrains to experienced school teachers and administrators. So consistency is important. But it can be self-defeating to be 100 percent consistent. Sometimes there are good reasons to make exceptions. True, it takes a great deal of wisdom to decide which situations those are, and it takes a great deal of political savvy to figure out how to make an exception discreetly so it doesn't come back to haunt you. In spite of these difficulties, there are times when the cause of values eduction and child welfare is better served by setting the rule aside, "just this once." Good luck.

4. *Never use ridicule and self-esteem-eroding methods for negative feedback and punishment.* We not only want students to know that they did wrong, we want them *to believe they have the ability to do better.* By ridiculing or giving them negative labels to apply to themselves, we only reinforce the idea that they are incompetent or bad. If that's how they feel about themselves, that is how they will act. Instead, when using criticism or punishment, always try to convey the idea that it was their particular *behavior* or *choice* which was inappropriate in the particular instance, and, therefore, they must face the consequence for what they did; but you are sure they know better and are capable of making a better choice next time.

14

Codes, Pledges, and Guidelines

> *"I pledjaleegins . . ."*

A centuries-old method for gaining adherence to a group's value system is to ask or require members of that group to affirm their loyalty in the form of a ritual pledge or oath. The "Pledge of Allegiance," which begins almost every American school student's day, and the Boy Scout "Oath" are two of the most familiar such pledges.

> *"I pledge allegiance to the flag of the United States of America and to the republic for which it stands - one nation under God, indivisible, with liberty and justice for all."*
>
> *"On my honor, I will do my best to do my duty to God and my country and to obey the Scout Law; to help other people at all times; to keep myself physically strong, mentally awake, and morally straight."*

Many religions have statements that affirm their particular faith, and many clubs, lodges, and organizations have oaths of loyalty to the group and its values. These affirmations can be a powerful way of making explicit and emphasizing the group's most cherished values. They also are a way of gaining—at least on a superficial level and sometimes much more profoundly, a commitment from members to adhere to the values of the group.

School "honor codes" are a popular method for inculcating the values of honesty and responsibility. The code sets forth a high standard for personal honesty and integrity. Many honor codes include the requirement that students report others who violate these standards. An honor code is not optional. Whether or not the students are asked to actually sign the code, it is understood that everyone is expected to follow it. An honor code is no guarantee of student honesty, but it can make a significant difference. In a national survey of 126,000 teenagers, 29 percent said they would cheat on a test; but only 13 percent said they would cheat if they had signed a school pledge not to.[6]

Some schools have programs that encourage students to sign a pledge to "Just Say No" to drugs. The National Youth Sports Coaches Association sponsors an All-American Drug-Free Teams program, in which almost 10,000 young people across the country have signed pledges to refrain from using alcohol, tobacco, and other drugs, and from associating with peers who use drugs. (Coaches sign pledges not to use alcohol or tobacco at youth sports activities.) Many schools and communities have developed joint teenager-parent pledge forms in which the teenager commits to call his parents to request a ride home if he or his friends have been drinking, and the parents agree to give that ride, no questions asked, with the option to discuss the incident at a later time.

Other schools use "guidelines" as a somewhat less formal version of a code. For example, one middle school has a set of "Ethical Guidelines" that are posted, distributed, explained, and discussed regularly. They include such concepts as: "A Jefferson School student always . . . respects the rights of others . . . gives his or her best effort . . . keeps his or her commitments . . . cares. . . ." The guidelines are a way to communicate and emphasize the moral expectations to the whole school community.

Ft. Washington Elementary School in Clovis, California has a "Code of Participation." The code states the conditions for student participation in school activities and emphasizes personal commitment and responsibility. The code makes it explicit that with the privilege of participation comes the responsibility for maintaining a satisfactory level of academic progress, good citizenship and behavior, and a positive contribution to the group's effort. Each of these conditions is defined specifically, and the school stands behind its code. If a student's average falls below "C," for example, he may no longer participate in the activity. There is also a "no-quit" provision in the code, meaning that if a student commits himself to participate in the activity, he sticks with it for the duration.

15

Ceremonies, Rituals, and Traditions

Ceremonies, rituals and traditions are among the most important ways by which any culture instills and passes on values to the next generation. Schools can use these same vehicles for enhancing values and morality.

Some classroom teachers establish their own traditions and rituals, including:

1. *Comfort and Caring.* Teachers on both the elementary and secondary levels may call it by different names, but "comfort and caring" time is a few minutes at the beginning of the day or the beginning of each class to check in with the students. The question is: "Does anyone need anything that will allow you to be more comfortable or does anyone need any caring right now?" The idea here is that if students need to know something or are cold or distracted or hurting emotionally, then they are not going to be able to concentrate on their work. By taking a few moments or minutes to see if anyone needs this sort of help, it both helps accomplish the learning goals, but also teaches the value of caring. Many teachers report that "comfort and caring" time has helped the classroom be a much more pleasant, supportive, positive place to be.

2. *Appreciation Time.* Some teachers make a ritual, on a daily or weekly basis, of having a time for sharing appreciations. An "I appreciate . . ." sentence stem sometimes helps students begin. This is a time for students to appreciate one another, for the teacher to appreciate the students, and for the students to appreciate the teacher for things they have done or said or how they have acted since the last appreciation time.

3. *Opinion Time.* Some teachers set aside a particular time each week for the ritual of students speaking out on current topics. One teacher makes a greater ceremony of it by setting up a lectern. During opinion time, any students may come up to the lectern and deliver an opinion or editorial (there are no length requirements) on any topic they choose. Other teachers confine the topic to a particular subject area. This ritual inculcates the values of independent thought and respect for others' views.

4. *Song.* On the elementary level, some teachers have a tradition of the class singing a song at the beginning or end or at a regular time during the school day. Many of the songs have to do with values and morality—caring, friendship, family, working together, and making the world better. They also contribute to caring and cohesiveness within the group.

5. *Applause.* Some teachers develop the tradition of student applause or other verbal or nonverbal expression of appreciation whenever a student gives a presentation, volunteers, performs a service for the group, accomplishes a difficult task, or takes a risk. Students in these classes know that when they stretch their limits, their classmates will be appreciative.

There are many other traditions and rituals that classroom teachers create to fit with their own teaching goals and subject areas. These were only a few of the more frequently used examples. On a school-wide basis, there are many other opportunities for traditions, rituals, or ceremonies with a values and moral content. They include:

- Awards ceremonies
- Awareness days or awareness weeks
- Service days
- Dress-up days
- Appreciation days—for teachers, support staff, students
  principal, etc.
- Assemblies
- Parties and dances
- Flag salute
- Talent show
- Homecoming
- Ceremonies honoring graduates/alumni

Some of these ideas might sound like fairly traditional school rituals or traditions, like dress-up days or dances. However, they can easily be adapted for the purposes of values education. For example, one elementary school has a dress-up day as part of an annual drug awareness week (a tradition within a tradition). On that day, the students all make crazy-looking hats on which they put a serious message about drugs. Students look forward to this tradition and learn from it each year. Dances can be given a values theme as well—an annual dance to raise money for a local charity, a costume party where you dress up as an historical figure you admire, or a dance or party where the students bring their families.

The power of tradition, ritual, and ceremony is in the repetition. The repetition says, "This is important." The ceremonial or dramatic aspects highlight and intensify the meaning. If it is an enjoyable tradition, then students look forward to it and cannot help but absorb some of the values associated with the event.

16

Theme-of-the-Month

Teachers have many, many items to "cover" in the course of a year's curriculum and instruction. Adding on a long list of desirable values to instill in their students may seem overwhelming to some. Many teachers and schools have attempted to solve this problem by using a "Theme-of-the-Month" approach to organizing their values education program. Each month the teacher, and often the whole school, focuses on one of the target values. (A high school in Oregon uses a "Theme-of-the-Year" approach, focusing on a different value each year from ninth through twelfth grade; however, the monthly approach is more typical.)

In one elementary school, for example, October may be the month to focus on "Friendship," November on "Honesty," December on "Caring," and so on throughout the year. During October, then, the teachers' reading and writing assignments have to do with the value of friendship. Each class awards a "Friend-of-the-Month" award to the student in that class who most demonstrates the value of friendship. A school assembly is devoted to students' performing songs, stories, and dances on the theme of friendship. Posters on friendship fill the halls. And, in many other ways, the life of the school revolves around the theme of friendship that month. The next month, the focus shifts to "Honesty," with the same variety of methods for highlighting and inculcating the new value.

Secondary schools also use the Theme-of-the-Month approach to values education, adapting it to fit the departmentalized classes. Each subject area teacher tries to find connections between his or her subject matter and the Value-of-the-Month. Meanwhile the school as a whole utilizes morning announcements, assemblies, awards, and other means to emphasize that month's value. Fearing that the monthly theme approach might seem arbitrary or "phoney" to older students, some high schools have employed a variation on the theme approach which has been effective. Instead of taking the monthly theme from a predetermined list of target values, the school spends a week or a month focusing on *a theme that is particularly relevant to the students and the school.*

For example, in one school there were a few racial incidents, which caused many of the faculty and students some real concern. So they decided to designate the next month as a period to focus on the value of "Respect." For that month, the teachers, administrators, student government, coaches, and extracurricular advisors all tried to highlight, explore, and emphasize the value of respect for others. In another high school, a star athlete died from an overdose of crack cocaine. Naturally, many students were upset and felt the incident only illustrated a more general problem of drug abuse among teenagers. Student government leaders and the school counselors got together and planned a month of activities around the theme of "Taking Care of Ourselves and One Another." For the next month, many of the subject area classes, extracurricular activities, assemblies, parent meetings, hallway bulletin boards, half-time activities at sporting events, and other aspects of school life emphasized the value of taking care of ourselves and reaching out to others who are in trouble.

Obviously, other important values are not ignored during the period when a class or school is focusing on the Theme-of-the-Month, but special emphasis *is* given to the highlighted value. Similarly, focusing on the values theme does not mean the school suspends normal functions during this period. The subject area classes continue learning their subject matter; teams and clubs continue to function as usual. However, in all these activities, there is an overlay of the values theme and, whenever possible, the teachers, coaches, advisors, student leaders, and school personnel try to integrate the special theme into their normal activities. School continues as usual, but not really; because something very *un*usual is happening here. A whole school is learning values.

17

Library Selections and Highlights

The school library (and public library) plays an important role in enhancing values and morality among students. The library shelves are filled with books, magazines, and videos with values and morality among the central themes. Stories and novels—from *Dr. Seuss* to *War and Peace*—explore every values issue and moral dilemma known to humankind.[119,141] Biographies are filled with examples of admirable values and moral courage. And there are examples of moral weakness, villainy, and immorality as well, because good literature often explores the tension between right and wrong and good and evil.

When individual teachers, whole schools, or entire districts have identified particular target values for their values education programs, librarians have been particularly helpful in working with the teachers and students. Just ask the librarian, "I'm looking for some stories or biographies that demonstrate the value of_____. Can you help me?" Most librarians are delighted to be asked and come up with some excellent resources you can use. Similarly, when classes or schools have taken the values Theme-of-the-Month approach (#16), librarians are happy to set aside a section or bookcase or table to display books, magazines, and tapes on that month's values theme.

Because the library is a repository of the community's values and moral traditions, it is not surprising that controversies sometimes arise over library selections. Objections to particular titles can and do come from all parts of the political and religious spectrum. Those libraries and districts that have been most successful in handling controversies have usually employed the following guidelines:

1. There is a clear policy in place regarding how library materials are selected, how they are reviewed, and how objections are handled. The American Library Association, the National Council of Teachers of English, and others have developed some excellent examples of such policies, which take into account the legitimate rights of teachers, parents, and students.[104,134]
2. This policy is understood by librarians, teachers, and school administrators, and it is followed scrupulously if and when objections are raised.
3. Decisions about removing objectionable materials are made by the professional staff, after consultation and discussion with a broad cross-section of parent and community interests. Such decisions are not based on the input of a few individuals or a single-interest group.
4. Individual parents may request that their children not have access to particular library books; but they may not prevent other children from reading these books.
5. Library and curriculum materials should be judged on their merits in their entirety. For example, some books may be good literature and contain important value lessons, but also include several offensive words. Rather than throw out the baby (the otherwise good book) with the bath water (the offensive passage), it might be better to discuss the entire book with the students in a way that allows them to benefit from its good qualities and learn positive lessons from its shortcomings.

Note on Ideas #18–#22

The following four ideas all revolve around the values of taking responsibility and performing service to others. The ideas overlap and have many similarities. Some of them could easily have been grouped together as different examples of the same idea. In practice, many schools *do* combine these activities, for example, by having a "service requirement" that students can fulfill by performing responsibility tasks, school service projects, cross-age tutoring, or community service. The focus is on service, no matter how, when, or where it takes place.

However, many other schools employ only one or two of the following four service ideas. For example, some schools have classrooms take responsibility for school maintenance tasks, but do not require other school service, tutoring, or community service projects. Other schools employ school service projects, but not community service. Therefore, the ideas, although very closely allied, are presented separately. They may be used separately or together, as the teacher, school, or district sees fit.

18

Responsibility Tasks

In families, we are familiar with the concept of giving the children tasks and responsibilities in which they contribute to the operation of the household. This concept applies perfectly to school settings also. School responsibility tasks might include:

1. *Custodial tasks*—cleaning chalkboards, painting, washing walls, raking leaves, and cleaning up the cafeteria.
2. *Teacher assistance tasks*—grading papers, library research, activity planning, and assisting coaches.
3. *School operation tasks*—safety patrol, morning announcements, student court, hallway monitors, helping police operate the metal detectors to keep guns and knives out of the school, and watching for drug dealers loitering outside.

Some of these tasks are typically allotted to school "clubs," like the safety patrol or morning announcement squad, which is good for the students who participate in those clubs. The suggestion here, though, is that *everyone* would benefit by having some responsibility for the school's operation. This can be done by assigning different responsibility tasks to different classes or grades. For example, Mrs. Brown's class helps with cafeteria clean-up every Friday, while Mr. Jones's class handles morning announcements for the month. In other schools, the tasks are individually allotted. In another example, a junior high school made a list of two hundred different responsibility tasks. Some tasks require only one student, others need a dozen or more. Students indicate their first, second, and third choices, and tasks are assigned accordingly; but everyone is required to help.

One learns to be responsible by being given responsibility. Responsibility tasks are jobs or chores which students do on a regular basis. The idea is for students to feel that these jobs are *their responsibility*. We want them to feel pleased and proud when they fulfill their responsibility, when they step back and see what they have accomplished, when they realize that they have played a meaningful part in the operation of their school, when they are acknowledged and appreciated for meeting their responsibilities. And we want them to feel unhappy with themselves when they do not fulfill their responsibility, when they recognize that they have let their classmates or teachers down, when they see that the school is less attractive, less safe, or less organized because they did not do their part.

You should try, as much as possible, to match tasks with students and classes so they can all feel successful at the task, and the jobs assigned are not extremely difficult or unduly tedious. However, such tasks need not always be fun and may very well be boring at times; this is part of the learning experience also. Fulfilling one's responsibilities is not always fun and it is often hard work. Being responsible means getting the job done anyway. Valuable learning can occur as students discuss their feelings about their tasks (positive and negative), work through any resistance, figure out ways to make the work go more smoothly, and eventually, hopefully, celebrate the results.

19

School Service Projects

There is a subtle difference between *responsibility* and *service*, as embodied here and in the previous idea (#18). The responsibility task implies having a job to do and doing it. The service project implies helping others beyond one's basic or minimum responsibilities. Later in life, they will be responsible for many tasks, but no one will require them to be of service to others. In assigning responsibility tasks, we hope that students will learn the value of responsibility, of doing one's part and doing it conscientiously. In assigning service projects, we hope that young people will come to appreciate the value of serving others and, coming full circle, to believe that service to others is their responsibility.

As with responsibility tasks, school service can be organized on an individual or classroom level. On an individual basis, each student is required to engage in a school service project to fulfill the course requirements. This can be a one-time, short project, comparable to a homework assignment; a larger service project, comparable to a major project or paper; or an on-going assignment throughout the semester. On the classroom level, the entire class can engage in a service project together. Again, this can be your own requirement, or if the whole school is doing service projects, you might say, "Every class is required to engage in a school service project. Let's discuss and choose what service project *our class* will undertake for the school."

The fourteen examples of custodial tasks, teacher assistance tasks, and school operation tasks listed in the previous section (#18) as responsibility tasks can also be used as school service projects. Other school service projects include:

- Litter pickup
- Painting a mural
- Collecting soup or grocery store labels to obtain audio-visual equipment for the school
- School beautification projects
- Working on the school newspaper
- Cross-age tutoring (#20)
- Fundraising drive for a school-wide purpose
- Helping school secretaries
- Leading safety programs for other classes or a school assembly
- Joining student service groups, like SADD (Students Against Drunk Driving)
- Teacher aides
- Operating the school store
- Crossing guards
- Student government

School service projects should be integrated into the curriculum, rather than added on as an isolated, additional requirement. Elementary teachers, secondary subject area teachers, or school counselors—whoever is working with the students in the area of school service—should:

1. Help the students understand the rationale for the program and *motivate* them to participate.
2. *Orient* and, if necessary, *train* them to perform the service.
3. Oversee the *logistics* of the program.
4. Lead the appropriate *follow-up activities* to help students maximize their learning from the experience.
5. Give whatever *supervision, feedback,* or *evaluation* is appropriate.

20

Cross-Age Tutoring and Helping

Cross-age tutoring is one of the most frequently employed school service projects. The concept is elegantly simple: older students help younger students in their academic learning. Both groups of students benefit academically, and both benefit in terms of values education. The older students experience the value and satisfaction of helping others, while the younger students have a role model who appears to take education seriously.

"Tutoring" can mean anything from formal instruction in an academic task to reading aloud to younger children. The concept can be extended to include other forms of helping, such as coaching the younger children in sports, refereeing their games, or serving as Big Brothers and Big Sisters. Cross-age tutoring can be done with almost any age spread. Elementary students who have just learned to read can read simple stories to kindergartners. Junior high students can help fourth-grade students with their math homework. Advanced placement (AP) chemistry students can help introductory chemistry students with their laboratory experiments.

Cross-age tutoring typically is either organized on a one-to-one or a class-to-class basis. In the individual approach, older students are paired with younger students, and each pair gets together on their own time—after school at the school, after school at one of their homes, during the school day if schedules and locations allow, or on weekends. In the other arrangement, an entire class (for example, a fifth-grade class) gets together with a younger group (for example, a first-grade class) and, during their time together, the students are paired-off or grouped within the class. The logistics of class-by-class pairing are obviously simpler when both are self-contained classes within the same building; however, there have been successful examples of secondary subject-area classes walking or being bussed to a nearby elementary school for the tutoring period. In still another arrangement, when all students are responsible for participating in a school service project and cross-age tutoring is one of the options, the students themselves or the school-service coordinator makes the arrangements on an individual basis.

As with any learning activity, good preparation, supervision, and follow-up will increase the likelihood of success with cross-age tutoring. Preparation includes thoughtful selection and pairing of individual students and classes, attention to scheduling and other logistics, and adequate orientation and training for all participants. Supervision includes observation and coaching by the teachers or coordinators. And follow-up includes time to reflect on the experience in writing or discussion, problem solving, and feedback and suggestions to and among the tutors.

21

Community Service

A logical extension of the *school* service concept is *community* service. Students make a contribution to the well-being of their community, as they learn the values of caring, compassion, and responsibility.[72]

This idea has begun to catch on so much that many school districts and even some state legislatures have begun to require some form of community service for school students. In Maryland, for example, state law requires that high school students contribute at least seventy-five hours of community service over four years. In New York State, the Rye School District and Rochester City School

District's School Without Walls also have a community service requirement for high school graduation.

There are many different settings and types of service in which students can help their community. Some examples of the settings and types of community service that both elementary and secondary classes have engaged in include:

- Nursing homes
- Soup kitchens
- Litter pickup or Adopt-a-Highway programs
- Senior citizen centers
- Assisting public officials
- Working with handicapped children
- Reading to the elderly
- Writing letters for blind or for non-English speakers
- Fundraising for local charities and causes
- Visiting children or adults in the hospital
- Cleaning up a vacant lot
- Conducting home energy audits
- Creating a community garden
- Painting an outdoor mural
- Working on a clothing drive
- Collecting food for the needy

The previous sections on school service projects (#19) and cross-age tutoring (#20) contain suggestions for how the logistics of community service projects might be organized and the sort of preparation, supervision, and follow-up needed to maximize the effectiveness of the service component in education.

> *Many persons have a wrong idea of what constitutes true happiness. It is not attained through self-gratification but through fidelity to a worthy purpose.*
> HELEN KELLER

22

Values-Based Improvement Projects

- Correct an injustice.
- Reach out to someone who is lonely.
- Apologize to someone you hurt.
- Contribute something to a charity or non-profit organization.
- Tell someone you appreciate what they did.

- Do something to make the school more attractive.
- Do something nice for your parent(s).
- Right a wrong.
- Stop doing something you shouldn't be doing.
- Do something to improve race relations.

All these assignments have two things in common. First, they are all based on one or more values or morals we wish to instill in young people, and second, they all ask students to improve their world—to leave it a little better than they found it.

Assignments like this can be readily incorporated into your own classroom. Are you looking for a good writing assignment? Assign one of the values-based improvement projects listed; then have the students write an essay describing what they did and what they learned from the experience. Has the class just heard or read or learned about a historical or fictitious figure who made the world a better place? Help them understand the concept of improving the world by engaging in such an attempt themselves. Has a problem just emerged in the school? Assign your students to do something to fix it.

A good deal of learning occurs as the students undertake the assignment. Just as much learning takes place afterwards, as they reflect on it themselves and then discuss it with the class. Sometimes the students have a discouraging experience as they try, in some small way, to make the world a better place. It is valuable and very important to discuss these feelings and learn from them. More often, though, the students are surprised and moved to discover their own ability to make a positive difference. They feel personally empowered. They internalize moral values as they improve their world.

My role, I know, is not to transform the world, nor man: for that I have not virtues enough, nor clearsightedness. But it consists, perhaps, in serving, where I can, those few values without which a world, even transformed, is not worth living in, without which a man, even new, would not be worthy of respect.

ALBERT CAMUS

23

American History and Democracy

One of the most important things we can do to instill moral values in young people is to do a good job of teaching American history and democracy.

At the core of all morality is the idea of respect for others. To respect others is to believe that every person has worth and dignity, that every person is entitled to be treated decently and humanely—as some might say, that every person is a child of God. All morality flows from this basic attitude of respect and the belief in its importance. It is also, precisely, this concept of respect on which the American system of government is founded, the belief "that all [persons] are created equal, that they are endowed by their Creator with certain inalienable rights, that among these are life, liberty, and the pursuit of happiness."

True, initially it was believed that only white, land-owning males were fully entitled to respect. But now most Americans (and citizens of many other nations) recognize and believe that *every person* is entitled to respect. True, not everyone actually *gets* that respect, but with two steps forward and one step backward, we make slow and steady progress. It is not always apparent, but over decades and generations, real progress is made.

What a story to tell! American history is the story of extending the moral principle of respect to more and more people, and the American system of government is essentially a moral system that codifies the principle of respect in a body of law and government. When operating properly, the system protects individuals and their liberties—their freedom of conscience, speech, assembly, religion, and other basic rights. It prevents the majority or the minority from imposing its will on others, when they would deny others *their* liberties. To teach American history and democracy—to help students understand and value that democratic heritage—is to teach them to be more respectful, more tolerant, more considerate of their neighbors—in a word, more moral persons. To teach all seven of the American *civic values* listed in Chapter 2—the public good, individual rights, justice, equality, diversity, truth, and patriotism—is to teach public morality. Civic education and moral education go hand in hand.

Therefore, from a values education and moral education standpoint, the most effective way to teach American history and democracy would be to emphasize those aspects of American history and government that pertain to:

1. respecting other people, appreciating their differences, and valuing our national diversity.
2. respecting the rights of others, understanding and valuing the Bill of Rights and how it applies today.[178]
3. understanding the responsibilities of citizenship and developing the attitudes, skills, and commitment to be an effective citizen.

This is an exciting history and civics to teach. It includes, but is not limited to:

- The American Revolution
- The important, inspiring documents of American history—the Declaration of Independence, the U.S. Constitution, Abraham Lincoln's second inaugural address, Martin Luther King's "Letter from a Birmingham Jail"
- The Bill of Rights, especially the First Amendment
- Emigration and the contributions of different ethnic groups to American history

- The long and difficult struggles throughout history to extend respect and equal rights to all citizens—the abolitionist movement, women's suffrage, the civil rights movement[87]
- The contributions of religion to American history and society
- Current problems and dilemmas in society and how different groups are working to solve them
- How the political system actually works
- The law
- The rights and responsibilities of citizens

Separating the trivial and ephemeral from the important and lasting is the dilemma for teachers in every discipline. In teaching American history and democracy, when in doubt, go for the big ideas. If there is not time for both, better have them understand the Bill of Rights than the War of 1812. Hopefully there *will* be time for both; but American history is a living history. Its importance is not so much in the past, as in the present and future. In teaching the American system and tradition, perhaps the most important goal is to have the students embrace the moral value of respect which is at the heart of it all.

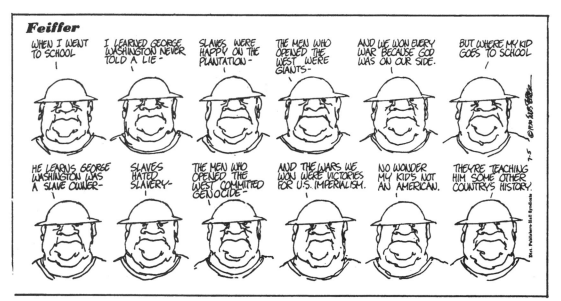

© 1970 Jules Feiffer.

24

Symbols

Organizations, teams, clubs, nations, and schools have symbols which stand for the characteristics or values of that group of people. The American eagle, for example, symbolizes the country's vision (the eagle's sight), strength (the arrows) and desire for peace (the olive branch). The Canadian maple leaf can symbolize national unity and pride in the country's rich natural resources. The cross, the star of David, and the crescent are powerful symbols of three of the world's great religions—Christianity, Judaism, and Islam.

Schools, too, have symbols, often reminiscent of national football teams— lions, tigers, and bears (oh, my), warriors, and an occasional bird. The symbols typically appear on school sports uniforms, sweatshirts, book covers, and the like, but for the most part are taken for granted. They are more often meant to be a logo for easy identification, than a conscious statement of the institution's values.

Yet symbols and emblems can have great emotional importance. Witness the reaction of war veterans when a protester burns an American flag, or the controversy over changing the Georgia state flag with its Confederate emblem. Another example was the hubbub in several communities when fundamentalist religious groups protested the school's "Red Devil" or "Blue Devil" symbols and mascots for their sports teams. The groups objected to the students' cheering for a symbol of Satan on the school's banner. The school district maintained it was a harmless symbol; the religious groups said no, it wasn't harmless, and it strongly offended their values.

It is interesting to consider. What *do* most school symbols symbolize? Most typically they stand for strength, power, and cunning. Those *are* values, and many people devote much of their lives to pursuing them. Yet few school districts, if any, have listed these among the target values they wish to inculcate.

What about those values the district says it wants to instill? You'll have to look a long time before you see a school's masthead or banner with the symbol of a book, a dove, a black hand shaking a white hand, a pine tree, or two silhouetted figures with their arms linked in a sign of cooperation.

A discussion of the district's symbol with respect to its values often generates some fruitful ideas and insights about values education in the district. In some instances, it may actually lead to a change of symbols. In most cases, however, school districts are reluctant to change their long-standing symbols, logos, icons, or mascots. So here are some other options to consider.

1. A class working with values and moral issues could adopt *a class symbol*.
2. One grade level in an elementary school, or each grade level, could adopt its own symbol.
3. An individual department in a secondary school, or each department, could adopt its own symbol.

4. School clubs and organizations could adopt different symbols and emblems which illustrate each group's values.
5. An individual school, or each school, could adopt its own symbol in addition to the district-wide sports symbol.
6. A school district could have *two* symbols, the current one and a new one.
7. The district *could* change its symbol to one that better represents its most important values.

25

Slogans

Malcolm X Elementary School is in the heart of one of Washington D.C.'s roughest neighborhoods. Every morning, as the children enter the building, they pass under two slogans, spray-painted on the wall graffiti-fashion, in foot-high black letters:

"WE FIGHT DRUGS THROUGH EDUCATION"

"EDUCATION—OUR KEY TO A BRIGHTER FUTURE"

A slogan is a short, cogent, memorable phrase or sentence that typically expresses a feeling, belief, value, or moral position. Here are some examples, both familiar and unfamiliar:

Just say no!
Friends don't let friends drive drunk.
Give a hoot, don't pollute.
I can do anything.
Don't put off for tomorrow what you can do today.
There is no "I" in TEAM.
Only YOU can prevent forest fires.

Slogans can be an effective means of inculcating values. A sex education curriculum that emphasizes abstinence (SEX RESPECT, Box 349, Badley, IL 60915) uses these slogans to drive home the point:

Score on the field, not on your date.
Don't be a louse, wait for your spouse.
Pet your dog, not your date.

Classes and schools sometimes use slogans—or mottos—to describe themselves. "East High School—Where Excellence Matters." "Valley School—We Care!" "The Class With Class." Mrs. Goodman's First Grade: "Where Every Student Counts" (get it?). One principal turned a failing school around, using slogans as an important part of his strategy. The main slogan was "We Can Do," and it appeared *everywhere*—over the school entrance, in the halls, on every classroom wall, on the school book covers and sweatshirts, on banners at sporting events, on every letter sent home to parents, etc. At Malcolm X Elementary School, the principal asks the students each morning, "What kind of school is this?" and they all reply in unison, "A school of love!" It may seem contrived, but it was one of a number of strategies that helped change a failing, violent, inner city school into, well, a school of love.

Some teachers have students write their own slogans about a particular value theme or slogans expressing their own values in general. One inner city class wrote thirty different slogans having to do with believing in yourself, including:

"I am somebody special."
"I can and I will."
"I am somebody, 'cause God don't make no junk."
"Believe in yourself!"
"Be patient with me. God isn't finished with me yet."
"The sky is the limit!"

The slogans were posted around the classroom, and each day a different one was displayed in the hall, outside the classroom door.

Like advertising jingles you can't shake, slogans penetrate the conscious and unconscious mind. They sometimes have a greater impact on beliefs and values than more sophisticated moralizing or intellectual arguments.

26

Posters

The poster is another effective means available for inculcating values. It is visually graphic and interesting; its message is short, simple, and clear; and it is visible on a regular, daily basis. It is no wonder that advertisers, political campaigns, and propagandists the world over employ the wall poster or billboard as a major tool for influencing public opinion and behavior.

Posters can be created to dramatize and reinforce any values or moral principles you wish to instill. Some are available in packaged programs and curricula. For example, as a part of their traffic safety program, the American Automobile Association (AAA) publishes a set of ten traffic safety education posters for elementary schools.[4] Each year students across the country enter their traffic safety posters in the national contest, with AAA selecting the winning posters and making them available through AAA's local clubs. In this way, thousands of students are engaged in becoming values educators themselves, as they try to express the importance of traffic safety artistically.

As this example suggests, having students create posters is an excellent teaching strategy. If your class is working on intergroup relations, your students can create posters for the school that promulgate respect for others, tolerance, and appreciation of diversity. If your school is working on an anti-drug abuse campaign, the students can make up posters conveying the anti-drug message in their own terms. Student councils can undertake poster campaigns as well. Slogans (#25) often translate well to a poster format. Slogans and posters can also be adapted as bumper stickers—an excellent way to drive your values message home (literally). As the examples in Figure 5-1 illustrate, posters can be used in an individual classroom, a whole school, or throughout the community, to deliver impactful, on-going messages about values and morality.

FIGURE 5-1 Sample Values Posters.[4]

(a)

Reprinted with permission of the American Automobile Association.

FIGURE 5-1   Sample Values Posters.[189] (*continued*)

(b)

Caheim Drake, Fourth Grade, *Kids Say Don't Smoke.*

27

Morning Announcements

"I want to thank whoever it was that turned my necklace in to the lost and found. It was a gift from my brother and it meant a lot to me. Thank you, whoever you are."

Morning announcements present an excellent opportunity to inculcate values. It can be a time for:

- Acknowledging individuals who have demonstrated honesty, courage, respect, and responsibility
- Thanking classes, clubs, and teams for contributions they have made to the school
- Appreciating the entire school for respectful behavior at a school assembly, cooperation on the fire drill, or participation in a community event
- Sharing disappointment with a number of classes or the school for misbehavior or failure to live up to the school's values or ideals
- Delivering a "values quote of the day," or "values thought of the day"—a daily quotation or thought containing a value-laden or moral message
- Reciting the Pledge of Allegiance
- A moment of silent reflection (or, in some private schools, a moment of prayer)
- Encouraging or exhorting students to behave respectfully, lawfully, and/or appropriately at an upcoming event
- Delivering a short lecture or moralizing message on some value or moral theme—perhaps using the occasion of a holiday (Thanksgiving, Martin Luther King Day, or Veterans Day) for the theme of the message

Morning announcements are an excellent opportunity for the school principal to become directly involved in values education and moral education on a regular basis. However, the goals of values education will be served best if this is also a role that is shared. Students and other teachers can and should participate in morning announcements that contain values or moral content. The wider participation conveys the notion of a whole community that supports these values, not just a particular authority figure. For example, at Public School 298 in Brooklyn, New York, the students recite poetry and read essays about the value of the month (#16) during morning announcements. A Friday morning announcement from SADD (Students Against Drunk Driving) encouraging fellow students to be careful that weekend and to always have a "designated driver" is a more effective message when it is delivered by a peer.

Most schools make morning announcements over a public address system. In some schools, announcements are made separately in each classroom. Most of the announcements listed above will still work in individual classrooms, or they can be adapted to fit that setting.

Some schools begin with a short assembly each morning, where attendance is taken and morning announcements are delivered. At the Emma Willard School, a private, girl's high school in Troy, New York, the students make most of the announcements themselves. It is a school tradition to applaud, encourage, or cheer any girl who makes an announcement. Even if she just reminds people to turn in their money for the yearbook, the student gets applauded and supported as she comes up to make the announcement and when she is finished. In the process, the students are learning the value of caring for and supporting one another, which conveys the notion that everyone has something worthwhile to say and reinforces the value of individual dignity and respect. It's not explicit, but values education is taking place.

28

Clarifying Moral Questions

Morally clarifying questions are designed to encourage students to think beyond their own self-interest, to consider the implications of their ideas and actions on others, and to apply standards of fairness and justice when thinking about values issues.

Some examples of morally clarifying questions are:

1. How will your actions help, hurt, or affect others than yourself?
2. What would be the consequences on society if others followed your example?
3. Would the world be a better place if everyone shared your viewpoint or acted as you do?
4. What's the right thing to do?
5. Is that fair?
6. If you did not have a financial interest in the situation, how would you feel?
7. If you did not know the particular individual(s) involved, would you feel any differently?
8. If you were an objective, independent judge trying to reach the fairest solution, how would you decide?
9. How would you feel if you were on the other side?
10. How would you like it if someone did that to you or treated you that way?
11. Is this simply a matter of personal choice, or are there questions of right and wrong involved also?
12. What would your parents, or the law, or your religion say is right?
13. What does your conscience tell you?

If you continually ask a young person, "What's in it for you?" and "What are you going to get out of it?" he will develop the idea that it is very important to look out for his own interest. Similarly, if you ask clarifying moral-dimension questions, like these, often enough, students begin to get the idea that such questions are worth considering; that it is important to think about how their actions will affect other people; that it is important to look beyond their own self-interest, and to consider what is right and fair. Asking clarifying moral questions helps young people develop the habit of asking these questions themselves. As they begin to internalize such questions and as they begin to ask themselves these questions when value dilemmas occur, they are developing a moral conscience.

Morally clarifying questions are typically asked in dialogue or in group discussion settings, although they can also be used on students' written work. For example, if an elementary student says, "Joey hit Janie first; it's all his fault," the teacher might say, "If you weren't Joey's friend, but instead you were Janie's friend, how do you think Janie would explain how the fight started?" Or if a high school student says, "It was a creative solution for the owner to burn his building down and collect the insurance money," the teacher might ask, "What would happen if everyone who was in financial difficulty burned down their building to collect the insurance?"

The effectiveness of these questions in getting students to really think about the moral implications of their views and actions is influenced by the tone and intent of the questioner. If you don't appear to have a particular correct answer in mind, and you seem genuinely interested in their thoughts on the question, they are more likely to give your question some serious thought and perhaps gain some real moral insight. They might say, for example: "Oh, yeah, now that you mention it, I don't think I'd want to live in a world where everyone did that," or "Now that I think about it, I see that my viewpoint was based mostly on supporting my friend's position, not necessarily on what was fair."

On the other hand, if your tone suggests that what they said or did was wrong, and your "question" is telling them how they should think about the situation, then they will feel like they are receiving a moralizing lecture in the form of a question. This description probably applies to 90 percent of the times when the classic, clarifying moral question—"How would you like it if somebody did that to you?"—is used. The student knows he is being reprimanded; he is not thinking about the rights of others. While phrased as a morally clarifying question, it is really a statement of admonition or moralizing in disguise (#6). The value of the question is in its moralizing, not its clarifying effect. It is better to keep moralizing separate from clarifying, for example, "I'm sure you wouldn't like it if somebody did that to you. I know *I* wouldn't." Then, when you *really* ask a clarifying moral question, students will not get defensive but will actually think about the moral dimensions of the issue.

29

Hypothetical Moral Choices: What Should You Do?

Many of life's values dilemmas and moral dilemmas come to us unexpectedly. We must make a choice, sometimes under the pressure of the moment, and live with the consequences, good or bad. Sometimes in the actual situation, especially when peer pressure may be operating, we forget to examine the moral dimensions of a problem and make a choice purely on immediate self-interest. Presenting students with hypothetical choices gives them an opportunity to think about difficult situations and explore possible solutions when it doesn't really "count." With input from you and their classmates, it is a time for them to learn and reaffirm values and moral principles and get in the habit of applying moral criteria to life's value dilemmas.

A hypothetical moral choice is essentially a hypothetical situation, with some important values or moral issue at stake, followed by the question, "What should you do?" Notice the focus is personal. These are not abstract dilemmas to determine how someone else should resolve the problem. The questions cause the students to imagine *themselves* in the situation and consider what *they* should do to solve it. Here are some hypothetical moral choices, appropriate to different age levels:

- A nice looking man you never saw before shows you this beautiful teddy bear and tells you, if you get into his car, he will give it to you. What should you do?
- You find a wallet with money and ID in it on the street. What should you do?
- Someone cuts in front of you in the movie line. You think you are stronger than that person. What should you do?
- What should you do if someone asks to copy your homework?
- What should you do if you see someone cheating on a test?
- You are at a party. A guy you really have been wanting to get to know seems to be interested in you and asks you to dance. You spend the next half hour together dancing and talking. You are really hitting it off together. You're really excited about it. Then he takes out a marijuana cigarette and asks you to join him. You tell him no thanks, and he tells you there are other girls who would like to have a good time with him and, if you're not interested, he'll go ask one of them. What should you do?
- Your brother has been getting in trouble a lot lately. He's hanging out with some pretty tough guys. One day he comes to you and says he needs help. He gives you a gun and asks you to hide it in your room for him until he asks for it. He tells you how much he appreciates your help and he wouldn't have asked you if it wasn't *really* important to him. What should you do?

The structure of these questions implies that there are right and wrong answers, from either a moral or strategic perspective. The child above *should not* get into the car with that stranger under any circumstances. The wallet *should* be returned to its owner, although there may be a number of ways to do that. In many instances, there is no *one* correct answer. There may be a number of ways to solve the dilemma that reflect moral principles. The goal of the hypothetical moral choice activity is to be sure that each student understands what the correct answer is from a moral, legal, safety, or other standpoint; or if there is no single, correct answer, to understand the moral principles that should apply to any solution.

To do the activity, first present the hypothetical situation or dilemma to the class. Ask the students to consider, individually, what they *should* do in that situation. Then, in small groups, ask them to try to reach an agreement about what a person in that situation should do. Finally, engage the whole class in a discussion, and see if the class can come to a consensus on the right way to solve the dilemma. They may very well recognize the right thing to do themselves and affirm this collectively without any intervention on your part. On the other hand, your explanation (#6) or clarifying moral questions (#28) may be helpful or necessary for them to understand the moral dimensions of the problem.

A variation on "What *should* you do?" is the question "What *would* you do?" which is a valuable and legitimate question also. It encourages students to move from moral understanding to right action—to committing themselves beforehand to do the right thing in such a situation. The "What *would* you do?" approach to exploring values and moral dilemmas is presented as the "hypothetical values choice" (#72) in the chapter on Facilitating Values and Morality. "What should you do?" and "What would you do?" questions work very well together, in either order.

30

Teach Empathy

Almost all moral and religious systems and school district lists of target values include compassion, caring, and consideration among their highest values. A correlate of compassion is *empathy*. Carl Rogers described empathy as the "sensitive understanding of another person's internal frame of reference" or, in schools, the "awareness of the way the process of education and learning seems to the student."[106] In more informal terms, empathy is the ability to "stand in someone else's shoes," to "walk a mile in his moccasins."

Empathy comes easier to some people than to others, but everyone can learn to be more empathic. The following ways are most often used by teachers to teach students to be more empathic and, therefore, inevitably, more compassionate human beings.

1. *Listening skills.* This is probably the most obvious and effective way to teach people to be more empathic. A separate section on listening skills (#89) is included in Chapter 8 on Skills for Value Development and Moral Literacy.

2. *Sensitivity modules.* A sensitivity module is a learning assignment, out in the community, in which students get to experience the world from a different perspective.[102] Such experiences might include: spending the night in the inner-city (or the suburbs or country), standing in line at a food pantry, shadowing someone at her work for a whole day, spending Saturday working in a day care center or agency, making rounds with a visiting nurse, reading two issues cover to cover of a magazine with a focus that is totally foreign to you, or canvassing for a political candidate.

3. *Role-playing.* This is a dramatic means of getting students to take another person's role—they literally are assigned the role in a little play with no script. It could be a role-play on a particular moral issue, for example, stealing. The teacher assigns roles to different students—the victim, the victim's family members, the thief or thieves, and the police officer. Then the teacher sets the scene. "The court case is over. The robber has been found guilty. You are all waiting outside in the hall for the sentence, and you begin talking to one another. Victim and victim's family, you want the thief to understand how this robbery has affected you and to make restitution to the victim. Thief, you want the family to understand and forgive you. Police officer, you want them to realize how crime is ruining the city and to sympathize with how hard your job is. Alright, begin!"

A role-play also can be on a subject not directly related to values education. This is often done when teachers have their students assume the roles of different characters from their reading or roles of historical figures and then give these characters a discussion topic or situation to resolve. Whether the issue to be resolved is moral, political, intellectual, or a values dilemma, the students must still place themselves in another person's shoes to play their role.[171]

4. *Simulation exercises.* Simulations are more elaborate role-plays. They generally are structured more extensively, last longer, and involve more students than a role-playing situation. For example, a high school social studies teacher assigned each of her students the role of different community members—government officials, business people, religious leaders, union members, ethnic group representatives, parents, children, health care workers, social workers, etc.—everyone had a role. Over the course of several weeks, she had them study community problems, talk to people whose roles they were playing, and then, once a week in the classroom, have "community meetings" and discussions among the various parties for the purpose of improving their simulated community. The goal was to truly understand the legitimate needs and concerns of each of the interest groups and to work out solutions that would maximize everyone's well-being. Over the weeks, the students really began to understand and empathize with people from all these different backgrounds and interests, as well as learn a great deal about civics and government.

In another example, an elementary teacher wanted her class to appreciate how difficult the Pilgrim's voyage across the Atlantic Ocean was. She drew an outline of the Mayflower's deck in chalk on the gym floor and got several third grade classes to all stand "on the deck" so they could feel and appreciate what it was like to be on such a crowded ship.

5. *Disability simulations.* Many teachers have asked students to go blindfolded or sit in a wheelchair or in some other way experience something of what the world is like to a person with a disability. Students typically develop greater empathy in two ways—they both appreciate the problems that the disability causes *and* they realize how disabled people are people just like them.

6. *Role-reversal.* There are a number of ways to ask people very quickly to assume another perspective. One way is to ask a simple, clarifying moral question (#28), such as "How do you think you would feel if you were on the other side?" Another way is used in a classroom discussion, when two people are disagreeing. Stop the action and say "Reverse roles!" The students must then switch perspectives, each doing his best to argue the other's viewpoint. When this has gone on long enough for them to appreciate the other's outlook, you say "Reverse roles" again. Role-reversal can also be employed in a dramatic role-playing situation, where the students literally change positions and assume the other's role.

In all these examples of "role-taking" and "empathy training" experiences, time should be allotted to thoroughly discuss what happened during the activity and to explore what the students learned or could learn from the experience.

7. *Literature.* One of the best ways to help young people develop empathy is to have them savor the experience of others through reading. For elementary students, Jane Yolen's *Encounter* tells of the arrival of Columbus from the perspective of a young Taino, native American boy. For junior high and high school students, Conrad Richter's *A Light in the Forest* follows two teenagers—a native American and a white settler—as they come to understand and appreciate each other's cultures. John Howard Griffin's *Black Like Me* tells the true story of a white man who dyed his skin black and travelled through the South in the early years of the Civil Rights movement. Talk about walking in someone else's shoes! The reader vicariously experiences the African-American experience, as Griffin vividly describes how differently he was treated when his skin color was black. (Aside from teaching empathy, reading literature has many other benefits for values education, as discussed in Idea #2.)

> *Real education should educate us out of self into something finer; into a selflessness which links us with all humanity.*
>
> LADY NANCY ASTOR

31

Teach Ethics

If morality is the subset of values that pertains to right and wrong, then ethics is the subset of morality that pertains to fair and unfair, just and unjust. Something may be wrong because it violates the moral values of respect and compassion. But if it violates the principles of fairness and justice, then it is not only wrong, it is also unethical.

For millennia, philosophers, theologians, scholars, and educators have attempted to understand and define fairness and justice. It is a large field of study. In the broadest sense, teaching ethics might include:

1. *Ethical concepts.* What do the terms *ethical, fairness* and *justice* mean? What is the difference between something being *legal* and being *ethical*? What are the major rules, principles, or guidelines for determining fairness or justice?

2. *History of ethics.* What contributions did Plato, Emmanuel Kant, John Rawls and others make to our understanding of ethics? From Socrates (in *Crito*) to Watergate, what are some of the famous historical examples of ethical and unethical behavior?

3. *Current applications.* What ethical problems and issues exist today in the fields of business, government, criminal justice, education, medicine, personal behavior, and other areas?

4. *Exercises and activities.* What learning activities can the students engage in to better understand, internalize, and value ethical thinking and behavior? Literature, which is usually filled with moral and ethical issues, is an excellent way of raising ethical questions for thought, discussion, writing, and further reading.[165] One major way to inculcate ethical thinking is to give the students ethical dilemmas and problem situations and ask them to use the ethical concepts and guidelines they have learned to find the most ethical, fairest, most just answer to the problem. Situations and dilemmas can be hypothetical ones, like the "leaf raking" example that follows in Figure 5-4. They can also involve actual, contemporary situations, such as asking students to study and evaluate how fair the current national health care system is and to make recommendations for a fairer system.

Just how far you might want to go in this area will depend on the age level of your students, your curriculum area and overall objectives, and your understanding and interest in the subject of ethics. But make no mistake: *all students are capable of understanding ethical concepts on some level.* There is hardly a first-grade student to be found who does not say "That's not fair!" when he perceives his rights have been violated. The statement "That's not fair!" is an excellent starting point for a study of ethics: What does it mean when we say something is not fair?

Cartoon by Bradford Veley.

The goal of teaching ethics is to get each student to internalize a set of ethical filters that will immediately be used to evaluate ethical issues that arise. Among other ethical principles or filters they might use, they will ask themselves:

1. Would I want the same solution applied to me if roles were reversed? (The principal of *reciprocity* or *reversibility*.)
2. Would I want everyone in the world to employ this solution or follow this example? (The principal of *universality*.)
3. Is this rule being applied similarly to other individuals or groups? (The principal of *equity*.)

4. How would I view the situation if I did not have a personal interest in it? (The principle of *neutrality*.)
5. What solution would be best for the greatest number? (The principal of *utility*.)

The principal of reciprocity is embodied in the Golden Rule: "Do unto others as you would have them do unto you." If teaching ethics accomplished nothing but instilling that one principle in students' lives, the world would be a much better place.

FIGURE 5-2   What Would You Do?

PROBLEM 6

> Suppose a neighbor asks you to rake some leaves in her yard. She suggests you ask a friend to help you. You and your friend, working side-by-side, finish the job in a little over an hour. The neighbor gives each of you five dollars. The following week you run into the neighbor and she gives you three more dollars, telling you, "I really appreciated the fine job you did removing the leaves from my yard."

1. a. Would you split the money with your friend?
   b. Would you keep the money and not share it with your friend?
   c. Would you tell your friend what happened but explain to him/her why you feel you do not have to share it?
   d. Would you share a portion of the money with your friend but keep most of it yourself?
   e. Would you do something else? What would you do?

2. What if your neighbor told you the three dollars is just for you?
   a. Would you keep the money and not say anything to your friend?
   b. Would you keep the money and explain to your friend why you are keeping the money?
   c. Would you split the money with your friend anyway?
   d. Would you do something else? What would you do?

3. Would it matter if you feel that you worked much harder than your friend? Why would this affect or not affect what you would do?

4. Would it matter if your friend receives money from his parents every month and your parents never give you money? Why would this be important or not be important to your decision?

Source: © 1989 Critical Thinking Press & Software, P.O. Box 448, Pacific Grove, CA, 93950. 1-(800)-458-4849.[11]

32

The Sports Program

Participation in sports has long been considered an excellent way to develop character. Such participation teaches the value of hard work and perseverance, of sticking with a task until excellence or mastery is achieved. Participation in sports teaches the values of cooperation and teamwork. Sports give young people who might be having difficulty in other areas of school and life an opportunity for success, which enhances their self-esteem and increases the likelihood they will be positive members of society. Sports teach the values of fairness and of playing by the rules. Sports provide another opportunity for teachers and coaches to be positive role models for students and to inculcate sound health practices concerning nutrition, smoking, alcohol, and drugs. Finally, and sadly, in our society, sports is one of the few areas where different ethnic groups share a common sense of purpose, where the value of respect and the appreciation of diversity are nurtured.

There are many reasons, then, for considering school sports to be an integral part of the values education and moral education program. Several recommendations follow from this recognition:

1. *The right values should be emphasized within a sports program.* Too often we justify school sports as promoting the values of perseverance, hard work, cooperation, self-esteem, fairness, playing by the rules, and tolerance; and then proceed to glorify *competition* and *winning* as most important aspects of the program. Unfortunately, when competition and winning become too important, the other values are eroded. When football coach Vince Lombardi's famous dictum that "Winning isn't the most important thing; it's the *only* thing" reigns, then fairness, playing by the rules, self-esteem from playing one's hardest, cooperation, maximum participation, and mutual respect fall by the wayside. Clarifying the *real* values of one's sports program will often lead to:

- Holding athletes and spectators to the highest standards of sportsmanship, courtesy, and decorum, on the field and in the stands.
- Denying awards or participation to those who fail to meet these standards.
- Putting sports awards and sports assemblies on a par with other extracurricular participation awards, honors, and assemblies.
- Applying the rules for participation of star athletes just as rigorously as they would be applied for average athletes.
- Making the dictum that "Winning isn't the most important thing; *giving your best effort is the most important thing*" the guiding principle that is stated, modeled, and taught by coaches, principals, and teachers at every opportunity.

2. *The benefits of participation in sports should be extended to a wider number of students.* If sports are such an important part of values education, why not extend this opportunity to more students? Physical education classes do this to some extent, but a three-week unit on soccer or basketball is a far cry from a season-long commitment to participating in a competitive sport.

Some schools have a policy that any student who wants to can participate in the sports program. They create as many teams as are required based on the number of students who show up. At the elementary level, this constitutes the intramural sports program. At the secondary level, the best athletes make up the varsity and junior varsity teams that compete with other schools, and the remaining teams compete among themselves in an intramural program (unless they can find another school with a similar philosophy, in which case the third and fourth teams can compete with their counterparts from the other school). Whatever the mechanics, the goal is to give more young people the chance to become involved in an on-going sports program.

If a school sports program is fulfilling its potential as a prime vehicle for values education and moral education, then it will not be considered a frill that can be easily dispensed with or cut back in difficult financial times. Rather, it can be defended as an integral part of the district's educational program.

33

Extracurricular Participation

The debating team, the chess team, the science club, the French club, the school band, the cheerleading squad, the ski club, the Students Against Drunk Driving chapter, the computer club, the math club, theater groups, and myriad of other teams, clubs, and activities available in most secondary schools and in some elementary schools all provide countless opportunities for values education. Most of the benefits of a school sports program, previously discussed (#32), apply equally well to these other forms of extracurricular participation.

They teach the values of hard work and perseverance.

They teach cooperation and teamwork.

The provide expanded opportunities for success and enhancing students' self-esteem.

They teach fairness and following the rules.

They give students the chance to be exposed to other positive role models, in a setting less formal than the classroom, where they can better observe and appreciate their coaches or club sponsors as whole persons.

They give students the opportunity to work with and get to know a wider diversity of students than they might find in their academic or vocational classes.

Many extracurricular activities also provide opportunities for students to learn leadership skills, to develop career or life-long interests, and to be of service to the school or the community.[58] Other activities reinforce particular values or positive behaviors, such as the 15,000 or so "Just Say No" clubs around the country, whose approximately half million young members support one another in refraining from using alcohol, tobacco, and illegal drugs.

The Ft. Washington Elementary School in Clovis, California believes so strongly in the value of extracurricular activities that it calls them "co-curricular" activities and requires that all their fourth-, fifth- and sixth-grade students participate in them. Co-curricular activities include sports teams, student government, instrumental and choral music, oral interpretation and drama, journalism, spelling team, and the arts festival.

Short of requiring students to participate in extracurricular activities, other schools encourage participation by:

Extending a wider variety and number of awards for extracurricular participation

Having more assemblies that focus on the activities and performance of extracurricular clubs and teams

Having exhibits of the activities and products, if any, of the various clubs and teams—on the hallway walls, in the lunch room, or in other prominent places

Scheduling some activities before school, during school, on the weekends, or at other times that might be more convenient for students who have after-school jobs

Developing a section of the report card or finding another method of communicating to parents the value that the school attaches to extracurricular participation.

34

Maintain and Enhance Self-Esteem

The connection between self-esteem and morality was explored in Chapter 2. People who feel good about themselves are more likely to behave in ways that are caring and compassionate to others than people who feel badly about themselves. People who are hurting inside, who feel angry and inadequate within themselves, are more likely to behave in ways that are selfish, aggressive, and noncooperative. The correlation is certainly not absolute. Almost everyone has some self-esteem issues to work out, yet most behave in socially constructive ways. Nevertheless, there is a relationship between self-esteem and behavior. Having low self-esteem increases the likelihood of realizing fewer personal goals and values in life and of having less energy and attention for the needs of others.

Therefore, teachers who wish to enhance values and morality are conscious of maintaining and enhancing students' self-esteem. "Maintaining" involves avoiding words and actions that will erode self-esteem. "Enhancing" involves employing words and actions that will build up self-esteem. Many books and programs have been developed to do just this.[31,32,194] What follows are some of the most frequent suggestions for accomplishing this goal.

1. *Have high expectations.* Conveying the notion that "I believe you can do well and I expect that you will" is one of the most important ways to enhance self-esteem. Your believing in your students helps them to believe in themselves.

2. *Structure for success.* Nothing enhances self-esteem as much as success. Try to structure classroom tasks and assignments and provide the support so that students can and do succeed. This is one of the trickiest but most important tasks teachers at all levels face: how to challenge the students and help them stretch the limits of their capabilities, while still helping them succeed.

3. *Validate the positive.* "Validate" means to affirm what is real. All students, even those who are angry and destructive, have good qualities, perform constructive deeds, or do quality work—at least sometimes. Noticing and commenting on those positive qualities and actions affirms and reinforces them. It is usually easier to notice students' good work—a good test score, an assignment well done—than students' good character. But, if anything, good character is more important to validate, because good character leads to good work.

4. *Avoid put-downs, ridicule, and invidious comparisons.* "Negative feedback," which gives students' specific information on what they did wrong, what the consequences were, and how it made you or others feel can be a helpful learning experience (#9). Negative feedback is different from put-downs, ridicule, or criticism that labels students in a negative light or embarrasses them before their peers. It is also different from making statements or using grading or class rank in such a way that "rubs in" how much worse a student is at something than his fellow classmates.[175]

5. *Self-concept/self-esteem activities.* There are two kinds of activities designed to maintain and enhance students' self-esteem. The first is those activities in which *other people* say and do positive things to affect one's self-esteem. Some examples of this are:

- "I Appreciate _____ Statements," in which students share things they appreciate about one another.
- "Strength Bombardment," in which each student hears from a small group or the whole class what they perceive his strengths to be.
- "Validation Envelopes," in which each student has an envelope on the wall in which other students can drop positive messages.

- "Positive Telegrams," in which teachers and principals use preprinted school telegrams to communicate short appreciations and validations to students and have a stack of telegram forms available in every classroom to encourage students to send positive messages to each other.
- "Secret Buddies," in which each student draws a classmate's name for whom he or she does thoughtful, caring, or self-esteem-enhancing acts (anonymous notes, gifts, etc.) and only later reveals his or her identity.

The second type of self-esteem activity teaches students to *manage their own self-esteem*. These approaches teach them to:

- Make self-affirmations.
- Understand and appreciate their own strengths and good qualities.
- Accept themselves, with strengths and weaknesses combined.
- Accept weakness or failure without feeling like a failure; reframe failure as a step on the road to success.
- Engage in "positive self-talk."
- Become effective goal-setters.

Recently, it has become fashionable to criticize self-esteem curricula as fostering narcissism, selfishness, and unrealistic self-images and future expectations.[99] As Muhammad Ali put it, "When you're as great as I am, it's hard to be humble." Certainly any good idea can be carried to the extreme. Whether that usually happens with self-esteem programs in schools is a debatable question, and some critics set up straw men by taking an example out of context and exaggerating its importance. Obviously, overdoing self-esteem activities is not what is being recommended here. By including self-esteem maintenance and enhancement as *one part* of a comprehensive values education, we insure a balance between personal values realization and moral and ethical behavior.

(Note: This section could also be placed in Chapter 7 on "Facilitating Values and Morality" or, along with #35 and #99, in a separate chapter on "Preconditions for Values Education." However, since the goal of most of these suggestions is to instill or inculcate the feeling of positive self-worth in all students, in that sense it seemed appropriate to include this activity among the methods for inculcating values.)

Chapter 6

Modeling Values
and Morality

35

The Emotional Bond

A third-grade student came home from school one day and asked her mother to buy bananas the next time she went shopping. As her daughter had always claimed she hated bananas, the mother was more than a little curious. On further questioning, the mother discovered that the daughter's teacher had told the class that bananas were good for them and that she, the teacher, often had a banana with her lunch. The daughter really liked her teacher and was looking forward to bringing a banana to school the next day with her lunch, to show the teacher that she, too, liked bananas.

This was more than a case of modeling, in which the girl wanted to eat bananas to *be like* her teacher. It was important to her that the teacher *know* that she ate bananas, too. Why? Because then the teacher would like her more. The teacher would recognize that they shared something in common; they were both banana-eaters. It would strengthen the bond between them. At least the girl imagined it would.

Social learning theorists describe the emotional connection between child and parent as the most potent factor in socializing children into the ways of society. In the infant and child's world, the most fearful and terrible prospect is to lose the love and support of the parent. The child will literally do anything to maintain that love and support. Sometimes that vulnerability is taken advantage of, but in healthy homes throughout the world, it is also the most powerful tool for inculcating values and moral standards. Children and teenagers will go to great lengths in adopting their parents' values in order to maintain their love, affection, and support and, conversely, to avoid disappointing or angering them.

This is true with teachers as well. To put it bluntly, if your students like you and respect you, they will listen to you. They will listen more carefully to whatever you may say about values and morality. And they will avoid behaving in negative ways that might lessen your liking or respect for them. On the other hand, *if your students don't like you, you have lost much of your moral authority*. When a child or a student reaches the point of thinking or saying, "I don't care what so-and-so thinks of me," the opportunity to be a values model or moral force in their lives is greatly diminished.

From this rationale, one is tempted to conclude that, if you want to be the most effective values educator you can be, make sure your students like you, as well as respect you. If they don't like you, at least make sure they respect you (respect being different from *fear*); but to maximize your effectiveness, they should experience an emotional bond with you that they do not want to jeopardize and they want to enhance.

Well, that's easy to say, but there is also a problem. Teachers cannot violate personal standards or integrity to get their students to like them. That would be a sure formula for disaster, equivalent to a teenager being willing to do anything his peers advocate to get *them* to like *him*. Students need to see adults as role models who stand up for their values without pandering for popularity.

Still, it would be glaringly incomplete to consider the many ways to enhance values and morality in schools without acknowledging a basic truth that underlies the entire values education and moral education enterprise. And that truth is that how students feel about you is going to strongly influence the outcome of almost every suggestion in this book. It's a paradox, but one we have to live with. Perhaps, in the end, all we can do is to be aware of this phenomenon, of how the emotional bond between student and teacher, as between child and parent, can be one of the most helpful aids for inculcating and modeling values and morality. Many of the more specific ideas below for modeling values and morality will have the indirect effect of strengthening this emotional bond.

36

Share Your Beliefs and Reasons

First, let's make a distinction between your beliefs on controversial issues and your beliefs regarding honesty, respect, responsibility, tolerance, and other target values that your school and district have agreed are important for all students to learn.

In many cases, it is *not* appropriate for elementary and secondary school teachers to discuss their beliefs on controversial issues that are polarizing or might polarize the community. In other instances, teachers can and do share their views on controversial issues, especially when the issue is an appropriate part of the school curriculum and the teacher's viewpoint is one among others that are fairly presented.

Stating your beliefs about the school's target values and conventional morality is quite another matter. Such sharing is almost always appropriate. You are an important person in the lives of your students. They are interested in your beliefs. You have a great opportunity, therefore, to influence their values and moral attitudes.

For example, a fourth-grade teacher, at an apt moment, tells her students, "I believe that people are people. There are many white people and black people who are good and decent and law-abiding, and others of both races who are mean and selfish. When I meet someone who is different from me, I don't assume they are one way or the other until I get to know them. I believe that is the American way and that there is no place for prejudice in our society."

A high school health education teacher tells her students, "I believe that, if you really love someone, you will want to do what is best for that person. I don't understand how some people can say they love someone and then put that person at risk of getting pregnant or getting AIDS or a venereal disease. If anyone ever says to you, 'I love you, and you shouldn't worry about getting pregnant or getting a disease,' then I would seriously question whether that person really loved or cared about you."

These examples may sound a little like inculcating values by moralizing (#6), but there is an important difference. Instead of or in addition to saying, "*Society* believes that prejudice is wrong," the teacher is saying, "*I believe* that prejudice is wrong." This changes an abstract principle into a living belief that someone they know holds. When the health education teacher says, "I believe . . . I don't understand . . . I would seriously question . . . ," it gets the students' attention in a personal and powerful way.

It is not always easy to distinguish between those controversial issues about which it would be inappropriate or unwise to share your beliefs versus those matters of values or morality on which there is enough of a consensus or little controversy that you can freely communicate your own viewpoint. Despite this dilemma, more and more teachers are finding ways to share their beliefs about good and bad and right and wrong with their students. Short of using the classroom as a soapbox for personal causes, there are many appropriate occasions for teachers to state their own values.

If we want our students to become adults who are willing to stand up and "be counted" for their beliefs, they will need to see adults as role models who do the same. You are one of those adults who can show them the way.

37

Share Your Feelings

"Boys and girls, I'm disappointed in you. Just yesterday we talked about the importance of respecting one another and how, if you have a problem with something someone does, you should talk it over with them and, if you can't work it out, you should come to me. So what happened today on the playground? I had to break up two fights and . . . ."

Why are Mr. Silverman's fourth-grade students hanging their heads and unable to look him in the eye? Possibly because they know they were wrong, but certainly because he is disappointed in them. Mr. Silverman shared *his feelings* with his students, and that is something quite different and usually even more impactful than sharing one's beliefs.

"It really upsets me when . . . "

"I'm very proud of how you all . . . "

"I'm worried for you when I hear you talk like that, because I care about you and I fear that . . . "

"This is something that's really important to me."

Teachers are people too. They have feelings. Very often those feelings are attached to their values. When a teacher expresses the feeling of being upset after he sees some children picking on another child, he is communicating the importance he attributes to the values of kindness and respect. When a teacher talks of how proud he is of how his biology students did at the science fair, he is underscoring the values of hard work, quality work, and self-discipline. When a teacher expresses his anger and disappointment about an incident of cheating, he is showing his students how important honesty, integrity, and responsibility are to him. When the principal tells an assembly about to hear a program on drug abuse, "This is something that's really important to me, because I can remember students sitting right where you are sitting a few years ago who are no longer alive today," he is telling them how he values human life, how he values *their lives*.

Some teachers find it easier to share their positive feelings with students but would not dream of sharing sadness, hurt, frustration, or disappointment. Others have no difficulty communicating negative feelings but never communicate positive ones. It can be risky to share our positive or negative feelings with students, because to be human is to be vulnerable. Yet teachers who are willing to share their feelings. who are willing to communicate what they are feeling inside, will find a whole new realm through which they can help their students develop values and morality.

38

Share Your Experiences

John Dewey believed that education was the re-evaluation of experience.[43] Our experiences profoundly shape our attitudes, beliefs, and values. Just as *we* have learned much from our experiences, we want our children and our students to benefit from our experience—both our personal experience and the collective experience of our culture. While we realize they must live their own lives, we still hope that, by sharing whatever wisdom our experiences have given us, we can save them from making serious mistakes and help them learn how to more efficiently achieve their goals. It follows, then, that if we wish to influence our students' values, we will find occasions to share with them experiences that influenced our own values.

Some of *your* experiences that you might share with your students include:

- Stories from your childhood
- An important learning experience you had
- How you got or lost a job and what you learned from it about the value of responsibility or education or honesty
- A relationship that went sour and what you learned about respect and communication from that experience
- An experience in political activity and what you learned from it about the value of freedom and democracy
- How you handle various value and moral dilemmas in your own life

Our own stories can be communicated in two ways. If they are told in a classic, repetitive tone such as "When I was your age, I milked the cows, stoked the furnace, and then walked six miles through the snow to get to school each morning," then students will hear only the moralizing, and they will probably not pay much attention to your experience. But if you can talk about your experience with enough detail and reality that, to some extent, *they experience* your experience, then they cannot help but learn from it, as you did.

For example, a high school social studies teacher participated in the Civil Rights Movement in the 1960s. Every year, he finds an appropriate time to tell his students his story of being thrown in jail and beaten simply for helping other Americans gain the right to vote. He speaks of the black family he lived with and how, poor as they were, they risked everything they had for the right to vote. He shows them pictures from this period of history. He tells the stories of the people he knew and their quiet heroism. He talks of how, to this day, he cannot miss voting in an election, because he remembers how people he knew died to gain the right to vote. Each year students tell him that that time, when he told of his experiences, was one of their strongest memories of his class.

You may think, "Well, that's fine, but I was never a part of history," but if you think about it, you were. You have lived through many changes and important periods or events in American history. What was it like back then? Beyond national history, your own history affected your values even more directly. Thus, the science teacher describes the excitement she felt working on a science experiment in college.** The health education teacher talks of her experience with dieting and weight loss. The English teacher talks of her attempts to get her stories published. The home economics teacher discusses how she and her husband work out the household chores and roles in their house. The school principal, at a school assembly on drug abuse talks about the students she knew who died in the last two years because of drugs. These are real experiences that can make real impacts on your students' aspirations, choices, and values.

Many of your students are searching, some of them desperately, for adult models they can respect, admire, and emulate. Sharing your experiences can help move you one step closer to being one of those models.

Here's a little experiment. *Think of the five experiences in your life that have been most influential on your values today.* Then find a way to share *one* of those experiences with one of your classes. You may be amazed with what a *valu*-able lesson it turns out to be—for your students and yourself.

39

Share Your Skills

Students often have the image of teachers as uni-dimensional creatures who do what they do in front of the classroom and don't do anything else. They are often amazed to discover that their teachers have many other skills in life.

What are *your* skills? What do you know how to do besides teach? Can you . . . ?

- Play a musical instrument
- Sew
- Write poetry, fiction, or nonfiction
- Play a sport
- Build or repair things
- Cook
- Use a chainsaw
- Juggle

**The male pronoun was used throughout the first half of the book. The female pronoun will now be used throughout the second half.

- Dance
- Sing
- Act
- Do a craft

Even if it's only wiggling your ears, it's a skill that makes you a more real, more interesting person to your students. When you are more interesting to your students, then they become interested in other aspects of your life, including your attitudes, beliefs, and values. So, if you wish to be a role model in terms of values and morality, it is consistent with that goal to find or create occasions to demonstrate and share with your students one or more of your skills.

For example, a high school biology teacher sometimes has her students work on group projects and experiments during class. On occasion, when she does not need to circulate among the groups, she plays her cello for 10 or 15 minutes, while her students work. Naturally, they tease her about it; but in truth, they enjoy it, and when she discusses values or moral behavior, they listen a little more carefully, because she is a fuller, richer human being to them.

In another example, a third-grade teacher is pretty good at hitting a softball. At recess, she often joins the class and hits balls to the students in the field. Not only is she influencing the students' values by expanding their concept of women's capabilities, but again, she becomes a more intriguing person to the students, which rubs off on everything else she does with them.

There are also circumstances when you have a skill in the area you are actually teaching. Physical education and music teachers do this all the time—demonstrate the skills they are teaching to the students. So if you are teaching your students poetry or story writing, consider reading them poems or a story that *you* have written. If you are teaching them about citizenship, show them a letter to the editor or letter to a congressperson that you wrote and sent. If you are teaching foreign language, have the students watch you actually converse with someone else in that language.

Beyond the benefits already cited, by sharing your skills with your students, you are modeling an adult with skills. In other words, you are suggesting to them, "Hey, it's good to know how to do something well. That brings enjoyment and enrichment to your life. Skill or quality is its own reward."

40

Share Your Personal Lives and Interests

Like most teachers, you probably have had the experience of encountering one of your students in the grocery store or the mall and having the student act surprised and disconcerted at seeing you outside of school. It is as though students think that teachers are locked up in their classrooms at night and let out when school starts the next morning. It is difficult for students to model themselves after such a stereotype, especially as they get older.

Consequently, another useful way to be a more effective role model to your students is to let them know something of your personal life and interests. Of course, there is a lot you will want to and should keep private; but there are many things you could share with them if you feel comfortable doing so. You can:

- Tell family stories.
- Show photographs of the trip you took over the vacation.
- Bring examples of your hobby to class.
- Talk about the club you belong to.
- Introduce your family member or friend to the class (or to the student at the grocery store), if the occasion arises.
- Give examples from your own life to illustrate a point you are making.

Some occasions for doing this may be directly related to the subject you are teaching. For example, you might mention that a character in a story the class is reading is a lot like a family member of yours and describe the similarity. Not only are you helping them understand the story better, but you are becoming a more real person to them and, in this instance, possibly teaching them something about family values. In many instances, however, this sharing of your personal life and interests will probably be done in passing—a sentence here, a reference there, or a one-minute story of the "a funny thing happened to me on the way to school this morning" variety. In many instances, what you share may have an implicit or explicit message about values in it, or it may simply be another way to interest them in you as a person, which will pay off when you *do* have something to say about values and morality.

41

Your Personal Bulletin Board

This is an easy way to share your values with your students and to counteract the all-too-prevalent image of teachers that "Linus" expresses in the accompanying cartoon. Any teacher, principal, guidance counselor, school nurse, group leader, or other adult who works with children and youth can do it.

First, get a bulletin board of any size. Put your name and a good-size picture of yourself in the middle of it. Then fill it with photographs, quotations, news clippings, letters, excerpts, award certificates, the family picture that sits on the corner of your desk, membership cards, and things you've written or drawn—anything that conveys who you are and what you value. This is your "personal

PEANUTS reprinted by permission of UFS, Inc.

bulletin board"—a collage of images that convey who you are and what is important to you.

Then hang it in your classroom, or outside your office, or another appropriate place. If the rest of the faculty picks up on the idea, the personal bulletin
boards can be hung in one place in the hall, with a different faculty member
featured each week.

If you want to get your students involved in this activity, they can make personal bulletin boards themselves. It's another good idea for facilitating their values development. Your students' personal bulletin boards can then be hung in
the classroom or in the hall. Eventually, many will end up hanging in their rooms
at home. As yours might.

> *He that gives good advice builds with one hand; he that gives counsel and ex-*
> *ample builds with both.*
>
> FRANCIS BACON

42

Live Your Values Openly

The previous examples describe different ways to be a role model to students by sharing with them your beliefs, feelings, experiences, skills, and interests. The key word was *sharing*, that is, telling about, describing, or showing them in the classroom. Another form of modeling is to *live your values* in everyday life, in the community, in a visible way. For example:

- Participating in a theater group
- Working in the soup kitchen
- Singing in the church choir
- Supervising a youth group
- Carrying a picket sign in a demonstration
- Writing a letter-to-the-editor
- Being a "big brother" or "big sister"
- Displaying a bumper sticker with a values message
- Taking your family to a school event or to a picnic in the local park

The old saying about actions speaking louder than words applies here. What people see us doing often has greater impact than what they hear us saying about what we do.

This is not to suggest that teachers and youth leaders' lives must be a totally open book. You are entitled to your privacy, and certain beliefs, interests, and aspects of your personal life you may rightfully choose to keep private. The point is that, when you choose to live your values openly and visibly, your opportunities to serve as a role model increase significantly.

It is well to think well. It is divine to act well.

HORACE MANN
Thought and Action

43

Avoid Hypocrisy

Have you heard the one about the education professor who gave his students long lists of teaching rules to memorize, and Rule Number 42 was: "Don't give your students long lists of rules to memorize"?

Or, more to the point, have you heard the one about the social studies teacher who bragged to his class about how he was going to get out of jury duty? Or the health education teacher who smoked? Or the unduly overweight physical education teacher? Or the school principal who liked to give lectures on fair play, but seemed to favor one race or gender over another? Or the state superintendent of public instruction who was convicted of felony conflict of interest charges shortly after his article on the importance of teaching values in the schools appeared in a major ethics journal.[85]

These are true stories. But certainly these caricatures do not describe us! Unfortunately, contradictions are easier to see at a distance. Consider this psychology experiment. A number of graduate seminarians were assigned to prepare a sermon on the Good Samaritan, to be delivered to a gathering across the campus. As each student was being escorted separately to the lecture hall, slightly late, they encountered an apparent drug addict who asked the seminarian for help in getting to a nearby campus clinic. About one half of the young ministers passed the person in distress without stopping to help—a rather obvious case of not practicing what they were about to preach.[127]

Most of us probably are sometimes like those ministry students, and like those professionals described earlier—basically good, caring people, but human, with instances of blindness. Sometimes we do not see our own inconsistencies, contradictions, and even hypocrisy, when we are not at our best. The problem is that young people have incredibly fine-tuned antennae for contradiction and hypocrisy. And their judgments are merciless. Their pronouncements about what is hypocritical or inconsistent are not always accurate; but they make them anyway, with a good deal of self-righteousness.

What this means is that we don't have much leeway for error. To the extent we are perceived as not practicing what we preach, we lose our moral authority. In one study, middle school students identified as "poor models" those teachers who admonished the students to "respect others," but would then "choose favorites," "treat us like babies," "not listen," and "give us busy work." The "good models," from the students' point of view, included those teachers who:

- present clear, consistent, and sincere messages,
- do not pull rank—are never authoritarian,
- communicate high expectations,
- really listen,
- communicate their commitment through actions,
- are hard-working and really care about student learning, and
- deserve respect.[197]

Probably none of us lives up to such an ideal all the time. So here are a few filters for reducing or eliminating any inconsistency or hypocrisy that might interfere with your ability to be a positive role model of values and morality for your students.

1. *Be honest with yourself.* What do you tell them is important? What do you harp on? Now ask yourself: how would an unbiased person describe your behavior in that area? Is your behavior consistent with the values you teach?

JUMP START reprinted by permission of UFS, Inc.

2. *Take their feedback seriously.* If students seem to be saying to you, possibly in friendly teasing, that your deeds are not matching your words, think about it. They may be right, and it may be more important than you realize. Or they may be wrong, yet you are conveying that impression. That's a problem, too.

3. *Admit you are wrong.* If and when you don't live up to your own ideals, and the matter is relevant to the classroom (for example, you "lost your cool" and were overly harsh with a student), then be willing to acknowledge your error. They will learn much more about values and morality from someone who is honest enough to admit she was wrong than from someone who pretends to be perfect.

4. *Solicit feedback.* Whether it's once a year or once every five years, take a deep breath and ask one of your classes, or ask a few students in your class, if they have seen any contradictions in what you say about values and morality and how you behave. Do it privately and/or anonymously, so it will not be embarrassing to you. It is a valuable reality check.

44

What You Wear

Of all the ideas described in this book, this one may be the easiest to misunderstand. You may want to remember that this idea is being described by someone to whom clothes are not very important, someone who once had a tenth grade student ask him, "Mr. Kirschenbaum, why do you always wear such dull combinations?"

The fact remains: many students take more than a passing notice of what you wear. This is particularly true when students get older and more fashion-conscious themselves. If you dress attractively, stylishly, or "cool" by their terms, many students will find you, to a degree, a more interesting and attractive role model. Conversely, if you dress in a manner they regard as dull, dumpy, or old-fashioned, they may initially regard you as someone whose ideas and values have little relevance to them.

Are these initial impressions superficial? Of course they are. Should they be encouraged? Certainly not. Do we adults frequently make the same superficial judgments ourselves? Indeed we do. It is well known in personnel work that interviewers develop strong opinions about interviewees in the first few seconds of the interview. The question "Does he or she look like *our* sort of person?" is an important initial screen applied before the more important qualifications are even examined. In fact, teachers have long been accustomed to conforming to the dress expectations of the community and the profession. Not long ago, any male teacher who did not wear a jacket and tie or any female teacher who wore pants to school would be regarded as morally suspect, certainly not a proper role model for his or her students. Such dress codes, formal or informal, still exist in many schools today.

The point here is that young people, just like adults, have their own ideas about appearance. Just as some fourth grade boys will walk through fire for their teacher who can hit a baseball over the left field fence, some students who think their teachers dress attractively will be more likely to view them as role models in other areas also.

Would you, therefore, consider modifying your dress or hair style to fit your students' expectations? Before taking umbrage at such a notion, remember that you already probably modify your clothing, hair style, and similar choices because of the expectations of your administrator, colleagues, and the community. Other professionals often modify their attire to fit their *clients'* expectations as well. Is it so unreasonable for teachers to consider doing the same?

Of course, you may feel that society puts too much emphasis on superficial and material values to begin with. It may be your goal to have your students come to value qualities of character, intelligence, and morality in people rather than Hollywood images of glamor and unrealistic expectations for male and female identities. You have so much to offer your students beyond your appearance. Granted all this, the question remains: will they be more likely or less likely to attend to all you have to teach them if you appear to them attractive and contemporary or if you appear out-of-date and out-of-step with the world they live in?

There is also the matter of wearing buttons, religious symbols, red ribbons, arm-bands, or other symbolic expressions of one's values. The courts, over the years, have developed some fine lines between permissible and impermissible behavior with respect to such "symbolic speech" on the part of teachers and students. Depending on the particular symbol, the age of the students, the curriculum and instructional purpose, and how much certain symbols might distract students from learning, the courts have allowed or disallowed the practice. Without going into the fine points of the law, suffice it to say that, within certain limits, the wearing of buttons and symbolic adornments is another means of modeling values and morality.

45

Invite Students Along

Although there are many ways you can be an effective model of values and morality to your students within the confines of the school building, school is only a part of your life. School is a more or less formal setting, where the roles of teacher and student are somewhat proscribed by convention and school culture. Outside of school, you are more of a three-dimensional person. Your personal qualities and values have a greater chance to emerge. Students have an opportunity to learn from you in a greater variety of ways.

For some students, the opportunity to see and participate in your life outside of school will be further enrichment for their otherwise healthy, normal, personal, and family life. For other students, you and your family might provide a rare glimpse of sanity, order, and kindness in their otherwise disordered and dysfunctional lives. In either case, it would be a mistake to underestimate how much students can learn from seeing you "in your element," participating in your family, or accompanying you on your interests, even for a brief period.

Teachers have found many ways to invite students to participate in their lives. One teacher extends an open invitation to any of her students to join her when she jogs every Saturday morning. Another teacher invites her students to help her and her husband at the annual Christmas party their church puts on for a local senior citizens' home. Such events can involve small groups of two or three students to occasions where the whole class participates. Events and activities that you can invite students to include:

- A play, concert, or cultural event
- A party
- The circus
- A fundraising event
- Community service projects
- Visiting your parent(s)
- A picnic
- A sporting event
- The lake or beach
- Camping
- Fishing
- A sing-a-long
- Church or synagogue
- Babysitting and child care

You may look at this list of possibilities and feel faint at the thought of involving students in this much of your personal life. This is understandable. You work hard and are surrounded by students all week. The last thing you may want to do is to use your free time to extend your teaching role into the evening or the weekend, let alone without pay. This idea is not for everyone.

However, it need not be an all-or-nothing situation. *Once a year*, you might ask some or all of your students to join your family for a picnic or a ball game. Or once every month or two, you might extend such an invitation to a different one of your classes. So it need not take up a great deal of your free time.

Teachers who have involved students in their lives on a regular basis have reported that it is a meaningful time both for themselves and the students. Not only do the students get to know the teacher better and get a chance to see how her values pervade her life, but the teacher gets to know the students better. As it turns out, they, too, are much more complicated and interesting people than is revealed in the classroom. The mutual learning that takes place outside the classroom often pays rich dividends, enhancing the teachers' ability to be a more effective teacher with the students and motivating the students to do well in that class. Teachers with children of their own have also reported how the students have sometimes been a big help to them, serving as big brother/big sister and models to their own children, and vice versa.

Two other reasons some teachers are reluctant to consider this idea is the issue of liability exposure and the risk of students, parents, or peers misunderstanding their intentions. In these days of litigation and of concern over child abuse and sexual harassment, these are realistic considerations. However, there are ways to deal with these concerns, including:

- Carry personal liability insurance.
- Avoid being alone with individual students, particularly of the opposite sex. The chaperone idea worked well for generations of our Victorian ancestors. Use it when appropriate.
- Sometimes arrange to meet students at the event, or have them arrange their own transportation.
- Make it clear that this is not a school-sponsored activity (unless you want to go through the proper channels and turn it into one).
- Make appropriate contact with the students' parents. This will depend on the students' age, the nature of the activity, and the individual students and parents involved. Each situation is different and may require no parent contact, a courtesy phone call, a short permission note, or even a written emergency medical authorization form.

46

Highlight Other Models, Past and Present

The previous ten ideas all discussed ways that *you*—the teacher or group leader - can model values and morality. The following ideas suggest ways that you can enlist *other good role models* to assist in that effort.

Many people believe that exposing students to history's best examples of virtuous behavior is one of the most important and effective means of values education. According to former U.S. Secretary of Education William Bennett:

> If we want our children to know about honesty, we should teach them about Abe Lincoln walking three miles to return six cents. . . If we want them to know about courage, we should teach them about Joan of Arc, Horatius at the bridge, and Harriet Tubman and the Underground Railroad. If we want them to know about persistence in the face of adversity, they should know about the voyages of Columbus, and the character of Washington during the Revolution and Lincoln during the Civil War. . . If we want them to know about respect for the law, they should understand why Socrates told Crito: "No, I must submit to the decree of Athens." . . . From the Bible they should know about Ruth's loyalty to Naomi, Joseph's forgiveness of his brothers, Jonathan's friendship with David, the Good Samaritan's kindness toward a stranger, and David's cleverness and courage in facing Goliath.[18]

His point is important. Our civilization's history and literature are replete with examples of the highest values and morality we want to instill in our students. These models not only contribute to the students' "cultural literacy," they present vivid examples of the values and morality we hope young people will emulate.

This is nothing new. Cultures have always created heroes and stories about heroes to teach the youth and socialize them into the culture's values and norms. At least until recently, what American child did not hear the story of George Washington and the cherry tree? Young George's reply, "Father, I cannot tell a lie," became a conscious or unconscious standard of honesty that tens of millions of children carried with them into adulthood.

Not all models need be from the past, however. Contemporary life and times provide numerous models who can contribute to the moral development of youth. Many of these models are close at hand. They may be found among:

- Your students' parents
- Your own family and friends
- Other teachers in the building or district
- The principal or other administrators

- Community members—including political leaders, business people, people in the local news, religious figures, professional and tradespeople, police officers, and social activists

Beyond the immediate community, there are also models from the state, national, and international scenes. These include people in the news, sports figures, people from the entertainment world, Nobel Prize and other award winners, and other exemplars of particular values or moral virtues. In fact, any person whose life and behavior demonstrate one or more of the values you wish to inculcate can be held up as a model for the students to understand, appreciate, and hopefully emulate.

There are many ways to convey these past and present models to students:

They can read books, magazine articles, or newspaper articles about them.

You can read the books or articles to them, which is especially appropriate for younger children.

You can tell them about these models—as a story, as part of a lecture, or in the course of discussion.

They can view a video or film about these models.

Your students can also teach one another about these and other models. For example, you can assign your students to each learn about a different model (from a list you give them and/or ones they choose themselves) and then report back to the whole class, telling their classmates about the model they studied and what they admire about that person.

You can arrange *personal contact* between the students and good living role models, an idea discussed separately in the next two sections.

CALVIN AND HOBBES copyright 1986 Watterson. Distributed by UNIVERSAL PRESS SYNDICATE.

47

Older Students as Models

When we say younger children "look up" to older children, we obviously mean more than they tilt their heads back to see their taller counterparts. Children and teenagers associate being older with being stronger, more knowledgeable about the world, more confident, and more independent. They are fascinated with older children and teenagers, looking for clues and signs of how they will be in a few years and how they might act now to hasten the process. Older students, then, can be influential role models for younger ones. Unfortunately, the modeling is not always positive. That is why many teachers have found ways to expose their students to older students who *do* model positive attitudes and behaviors.

Modeling can take place between just about all age levels. High school seniors can serve as models for high school sophomores *and* for fourth-grade students. Fourth-grade students can serve as models for second-grade students. Here are some of the many ways that teachers have utilized positive, older student models in their classroom and school:

- Cross-age tutoring and helping (#20)
- Guest speakers—about drugs, getting along with others, doing well in junior high and other topics
- Teacher helpers—in the classroom, on the playground, and on class trips
- Assemblies—where older students speak
- By reference—using older students as examples when making a point
- Morning announcements (#27)
- Teaching—inviting older students in to teach something to the whole class
- Service projects—having older students lead and work with younger students on responsibility tasks and school and community service projects (#18,#19,#21)
- Ceremonies, traditions—with older students leading or participating in the ceremonies (#15)
- Student government and community meetings—with older students taking leadership roles (#78,#77)

Modeling can take place on several levels. When a fourth-grader reads a story to a first-grader, the first-grader gets the idea that it's "neat" to be able to read. If she learns to read, then she will be more like her fourth-grade idol. She also observes the model of an older student who acts in a helpful and caring manner and who appears to take her school work seriously. To a small degree, the values of caring, hard work, and learning are passed on from the older to the younger student.

In Rochester, New York a group of teenagers in the "Not Me, Not Now" program helped write and produce a series of TV commercials promoting sexual abstinence. Students in the program visit area high schools to share their message and provide positive role models for other teens. In other communities, when high school juniors and seniors from Students for a Drug Free Community or other local student drug abuse prevention organizations, visit the junior high health classes, they offer the model of young people who seem to be having a good life without resorting to drugs. It is an important lesson, which can shape the younger students' images of how they would like to be when they get older.

48

Resource Persons

In addition to older students as role models, there are many other "resource persons" who might visit your class or school and serve as models for the students. These include:

- Community leaders
- Civil servants
- Professionals
- Business people
- Tradespeople
- Religious leaders
- Parents
- Other teachers
- The principal
- People in the news
- Representatives of various organizations

You probably will not introduce these guests to the students by saying, "Here is someone I hope will be a role model to you." Rather they are invited to talk to the students about their area of knowledge, which is relevant to the academic subject you are studying or the values issue you are exploring in class. A black police officer, for example, may be invited to an inner-city classroom to talk about the laws and law enforcement. But, in the process, as she shares her experience about how she became a police officer, and as she answers the students' questions, they will be exposed to a positive role model of someone who is dedicated, works hard, and is succeeding in the world.

Similarly, when a chemistry teacher invites an actual chemist into the classroom to teach the students a particular laboratory process and to talk about her work, the students not only learn chemistry but meet another adult role model. Does this person like her work? How did she decide what career she wanted to pursue? Might I want to continue in chemistry or science? What else do I like or not like about this person? What other lessons in life can I draw from this person's example? Obviously, much of this is not a conscious process on the students' part; still it occurs. Young people do not typically get to meet new adults and hear them talk about their lives and work. When they do, it is natural for them to use the occasion to clarify who they themselves are and to think about the kind of lives they want to live.

There are many representatives of organizations—like Mothers Against Driving Drunk, Amnesty International, and Habitat for Humanity—who regularly go into schools to talk with students. Police officers around the country, as part of the DARE (Drug Abuse Resistance Education) Program developed by the Los Angeles Unified School District, visit schools to lead students through a multi-session program in drug abuse prevention.[49] Beyond these organizational representatives who regularly visit the schools as resource people, there are many other fine and talented people in the school community and the larger community who would be flattered and delighted to be invited to talk with your students. Most would be comfortable doing this on the classroom level, and some would be willing and able to address a larger school assembly. The latter setting may reach more students at once, but unless the speaker is very skillful or charismatic, a smaller audience in the classroom provides more opportunity for questions, interaction, and effective modeling. In either case, using resource people can make an excellent contribution to both academic learning and values education.

Another way to utilize resource persons is to have the students visit them at work or at home. If the students are old enough, they also can go as groups or as individuals to visit the resource people or shadow them at work. The Ms. Foundation initiated a "Take Our Daughters to Work Day," a program designed to plant the seeds of self-confidence and success, which has grown to include a million girls each year. The students visit their mothers, fathers, and other adults at their places of work and learn a great deal about work-related and other values.

49

Your Family and Friends

In the section on "Resource Persons" (#48) your own family and friends were not included in the list of possible resource persons who might serve as role models for your students. These people were saved for a separate section to emphasize their special potential for values education.

As mentioned before, your students are anywhere from mildly interested to fascinated with you as a person. This enhances your opportunity to be an important role model for them. Their interest in *you* carries over to your family and friends who are, after all, extensions and reflections of you and your values. To use the examples from the previous section to illustrate this point, you might invite a police officer or a chemist to serve as a resource person to your class. But if that police officer happens to be *your sister* or the chemist happens to be *your personal friend*, then your students will be doubly interested in what they have to say.

This enhances the strength and extent of the role modeling that takes place. On the one hand, the resource person becomes a more interesting, more real person to the students because of his or her association with you. It is likely that students will attend to and benefit from their knowledge, experiences, and example a bit more than if they had no relationship with you. At the same time, *you* become a more interesting, more real person to the students because of your association with the resource person. And, finally, your relationship with the resource person, which the students witness, becomes another source of modeling. The students get to see you with your sister or friend—or parent or child or college roommate. As they observe how you introduce your sister, what your friend says to or about you, or the banter and interaction between you, they see a positive example of family and friendship in action. It's another model for them.

So, when you are considering inviting resource persons to class, don't forget your family and friends. They may have knowledge and experience to contribute to your learning outcomes; but, in addition, they and you *together* have a greater opportunity to serve as role models and provide a positive example of the values of family, friendship, caring, and respect.

50

Symbolic Leadership

Symbolic leadership refers to those specific actions a leader takes that have meaning far beyond the actions themselves. They are actions that send a signal about the values the leader stands for, actions which symbolize the values the leader wants to instill in the organization. For example:

- The principal jogs with the elementary children who are struggling to run the mile. She says, "C'mon, *we* can do this!"
- The school superintendent joins the teachers and students in a community clean-up day.
- The principal announces that, next Friday, she is going to fast during the lunch hour and donate the money she would have spent on lunch to famine relief. She invites all students and teachers to join her on Friday.
- A teacher walks down the hall with his arm around an autistic student.
- The principal wears a red ribbon to symbolize drug awareness and saying "yes" to a healthy lifestyle.
- As a teacher is telling an ethnic or gender joke in the teacher's lunchroom, a department chairperson stands up, says, "I'm sorry, I don't find jokes like that funny," and leaves.

Acts of symbolic leadership are memorable. They are especially impactful when done by the leader of an organization. When a principal engages in a symbolic leadership act, students and teachers talk about it, they interpret the action, and they re-examine their own values and actions. Sometimes they are immediately inspired and sometimes they become defensive, but they are rarely unmoved or unaffected. Symbolic leadership behavior is a powerful statement of values that conveys far more than words alone. It is one of the most effective means for modeling values and morality.

51

Negative Models

All the previous ideas have described ways to use positive models—yourself and others—to enhance values and morality in young people. It is also possible to accomplish this goal by using *negative role models*. A negative model is someone who demonstrates the *un*desirable way to act, the *wrong* way to live, the *im*proper way to be.

The "boy who cried wolf" is one such negative example. See what happened to *him*? Let that be a lesson to *you*. You remember the hare, who because of pride and self-indulgence, lost the race to the tortoise, and the other animals in Aesop's fables who were too foolish or proud or thoughtless to escape the cunning fox's schemes and machinations. From Natasha and Boris Badonov (pronounced "bad-enough") of "Rocky and Bullwinkle" cartoon fame, to Benedict Arnold, to Judas Iscariot, there are myriad villains, anti-heroes, and no-goodniks who can serve as object lessons in the values of patriotism, loyalty, and courage—the very *opposite* of the values these negative models stood for and for which they have earned the opprobrium of posterity.

Not all negative role models are unattractive or unsympathetic figures, however. Sophocles and Shakespeare's tragic heroes were not without their virtues. Magic Johnson is one of the most beloved sports heroes of the 1980s and 1990s. After contracting AIDS, he became an important negative role model (as well as a positive model, taking responsibility for his problem and working to help others) to millions of young people as he toured the country telling them, "Don't make the same mistake I did." Former drug abusers, criminals, male chauvinists, sinners, Watergate conspirators, and con-artists have all served as useful negative role models, in schools and other settings, describing the errors of their ways and how they have changed their values.

Saint George slaying a dragon or George Washington saying "I cannot tell a lie" are both important positive role models; but especially as young people get older and life gets more complicated, these exalted models can sometimes appear other-worldly or unrealistic. That is where enlightened negative models, realistic people whom young people understand and identify with, can be important positive influences on their values and moral development. A teenage, single mother (without her baby) explaining how she became pregnant, describing the reality of raising a child by herself, getting by on welfare, and having to forgo her personal goals and dreams, teaches a lot more about responsibility and self-discipline than all the lectures you might deliver on that subject.

Negative models can be brought to the students' attention and integrated into classroom lessons and activities by the same methods used to expose students to positive role models (#46,#48).

52

Role Model Analysis

This activity enables students to better recognize and appreciate the value (and the values) of the positive role models in their lives. It also allows them to affirm the values of these role models as their own values.

Begin the activity by helping students understand the concept of a role model. In simple terms, a role model is someone they admire, someone they look up to, someone they would like to be like, or someone whose example influences them. They should understand that they need not admire or want to be like this person *in all ways*. A person can be a role model in some respects, but not in others. A role model can also be a positive influence or a negative one. In this activity they will be thinking about the role models in their lives who have influenced them to be better persons—to do and be their best.

Once they understand the meaning of the concept, ask them to suggest all the types of people who might be role models. Write their ideas on the board. You can add to the group's list. A list of possible role models might look something like this:

- Parent
- Brother, sister
- Other relative
- Elementary school teacher
- Junior high school teacher
- High school teacher
- Coach, or extracurricular leader
- Youth group leader
- Religious leader
- Friend
- Coworker
- Employer

- Author
- Political figure
- Sports or entertainment figure

Have the students divide a full page of paper into three columns, as shown in Figure 6-1. Have them write the word "Model" at the top of the first column. Then, referring to the list of possible models they just generated, ask them to try to think of *five* people they personally know who serve or who have served as models to them in positive ways and to write the names of those five models in the left column, skipping a few lines between each name. (For older elementary students, *three* models is enough. For younger elementary students, writing or thinking of *one* model is sufficient.) Some students may have trouble thinking of five models, and that's alright; but help them along by encouraging them to think of any people—relatives, neighbors, teachers, and others, living or dead—whose example they have appreciated, who have helped them to be better people, whom they would like to be like, or whom they admire in some ways.

After writing the names of their role models in the first column, students should then write the words "Personality or Character Traits" at the top of the middle column. In this column, next to each of their role models' names, they will write down one or two qualities of *personality or character* that they admire in that person. You may have to explain what you mean by personality or character. The phrase "personal qualities" may help. The point is to eliminate people whom they admire simply because they are rich or good-looking and to have them focus on more enduring and important qualities and values.

Have students head the third column "Influence." Here they should write a few words to indicate how each of their models influenced them personally and how they are a different or better person because of that model's example.

To further reflect on and learn from this "role model analysis," students can complete "I Learned Sentences" (#65). Finally, students should have the opportunity to share some of their reflections with others. A good way to do this is to divide students into groups of two, three, or four, and give all members a minute or two to talk about one of their role models and how that person influenced them. Then, in the whole group, ask for volunteers who will share one of their examples with the class.

At Harris Hill Elementary School in Penfield, New York, teachers do a much simpler version of this activity. Children identify positive role models and represent them and their good qualities on a poster, in a report, or on a medallion.

FIGURE 6-1   A Role Model Chart

Model	Personality or Character Traits	Influence
Dad	reliable, devoted	Being reliable is important to me.
Carl	good listener	Taught me to be a better listener
Marianne	friendly, happy	Reminds me people can be happy.

> *One must be extremely cautious in his speech so as not to utter anything disgraceful in front of his child . . . and even more so not to do anything disgraceful . . . since the child may learn from what he observes. If later, the father will ask the child "Why did you do such and such?" the child will reply "Did you not do thus yourself?" . . . If a father hears that someone performed a disgraceful act he should let his disgust and aversion be most emphatically known to the child so that he will distance himself from such behavior . . . And if the father learns of a meritorious act performed by others he should emphatically praise it in the presence of his child so that he should aspire to behave in a similar manner . . . When the father goes to perform a deed of kindness such as visiting the sick, providing assistance to a bride, or burying the dead, he should take his child with him so as to train him in deeds of loving kindness.*
>
> RABBI ISRAEL AL-NAKEWA
> 14TH CENTURY, SPAIN[169]

53

Thank You Letter to Models

In this activity, students write a letter to one of their role models. It can follow the role model analysis (#52), or it can be used independently.

First the students should think of a living person who has been a positive role model in their lives. (The previous activity gives several ideas for how to explain the concept of a positive role model and how to help students think of possible models in their experience.) Have the students select *one model* they have known whom they could thank for serving as a role model to them. Their assignment is to write a letter to that person, thanking him or her for being a good model for them. Let them know right away that *they will not be required to actually send this letter,* although they can if they choose to. In the letter, they should tell the person what it is they appreciate about that person's personality or character and explain why or how that person's example has been important or helpful to them. The letters can be written in class or as a homework assignment.

When students have completed their letters, give them the opportunity to share their letters with at least one other person. This can be done in pairs or small groups, in which they read one another's letters silently or read their own letters aloud to others. You can also ask for volunteers to read their letters to the class or you may collect them to read later on your own.

Now here's the icing on the cake. *Invite them to send their letters to their role models.* Some teachers actually make this a required assignment, letting the students know this before they write their letter. Whether or not you take it that far, at the very least, *suggest* that they mail or hand deliver their letters of appreciation. Some teachers actually bring envelopes, stamps, and a phone book for local addresses to facilitate the process. At first, students typically seem embarrassed at the thought of sending their letters and think it would be very strange for their role model to receive a letter like this. You can assure them that receiving the letter will make their day and probably make the *year* of any teacher, parent, uncle, aunt, or grandparent who got such a letter. Invite students who do send their letters to later report back to the class how it went and if they received a response from the recipient.

This activity serves several purposes. First it highlights the values of the positive role models that students select and allows the students to affirm those values themselves. Second, it guides students through the caring act of expressing their appreciation to another person and to experience the satisfaction in giving such a gift. And, finally, in many cases, when students actually send their letters, it helps establish positive communication between the students and their role model, further reinforcing those positive values the students recognized in the relationship in the first place.

54

Participate Yourself

One of the best ways to be a model to your students and to share your beliefs, feelings, experiences, and interests (#36-40) is to participate in many of the activities in this book yourself. Your participation will do more to make these activities work than anything else you can do.

For example, if the class has a responsibility task assignment for the school (#18), you work along with them. If you ask them to write a thank-you letter to a role model (#53), then write one yourself and read it to the class. If you ask them to vote on values and moral issues (#57), vote yourself. If you ask them to indicate their priorities and preferences among conflicting choices (#58), indicate your own priorities and preferences. If you give them the opportunity to be interviewed in front of the class (#60), then volunteer to be interviewed yourself. If you have them write a poem or story about one of their values (#69), write a poem or story yourself. As the students see you doing what you ask them to do, as they hear what you have to say about your feelings, beliefs, experiences, and values, you will become that much more real, interesting, and influential in their lives.

Here are five guidelines for making your participation most effective from a modeling standpoint, particularly when discussing values and moral issues:

1. *Listen to them.* If your students perceive you as truly interested in what they have to say, they will be much more interested in what you have to say. If they see you listening to them impatiently and perfunctorily, just waiting for your chance to tell them what *you* think, they will listen to you the same way. The best guarantee that they will respect your views is to respect theirs.

2. *Don't monopolize.* You have many other occasions to lecture and teach them about values, morals, and academics. When you are doing activities and discussions aimed at getting them to express themselves, then don't take too much of the air time. Participate, but don't monopolize. If you speak occasionally, your words will have that much more impact.

3. *Share, don't preach.* Preaching or moralizing (#6) is a valid method for inculcating values. However, it is usually not an effective strategy when modeling and facilitating values and moral development. Preaching gets in the way of students seeing you clearly as a person (a model) or of them thinking more deeply about what *they* believe. When you participate in discussion activities, students will hear what you have to say better if you are sharing your own deeply felt views with them, rather than telling them that this is what they should think. It's a fine, but important distinction. Save the moralizing for another time.

4. *Choose the best time to participate.* It is often best to let all those students who want to speak do so before you share your feelings, opinions and experiences. In that way, you make sure they are thinking for themselves and developing their own values and morals. On the other hand, sometimes it is best for you to re-spond first, to give students a better idea of what the question or activity calls for or to help get them started in a positive vein. And sometimes you might take a turn in the middle—to keep the discussion or activity moving forward and to demonstrate that you don't need the last word on every subject. It's tricky, but again, it's important. You want your participation to encourage them to think for themselves and to speak up, as well as to share your own views and values. By keeping these dual goals in mind, you will be able to judge the best times for you to participate.

5. *Use your right to pass.*   Remember, you are no more obliged to share your feelings, beliefs, and experiences on every values and moral issue than your stu-dents are. You, too, have a right to privacy. By occasionally exercising your right to pass, even if you do not feel the need to do so, you model self-respect, as well as remind students of their right to pass, while showing them how to do it.

55

Staff Hiring Policy

Most school districts would state that values development, moral development, good citizenship, and academic excellence are *all* top priority goals for their stu-dents. Yet, when it comes to hiring teachers, it is the candidates' academic prepa-ration, teaching experience, and how they handle themselves in an interview that determine who gets the job. Little or nothing is said or asked about their values, moral commitments, or citizenship traits.

A satirical journal article once suggested that, when schools interview teacher candidates, they should have a child stand on the corner crying pitifully, and see which candidates, as they drive away from the interview, stop to ask the child what's wrong. While such a means of measuring a prospective teacher's level of compassion may be a bit extreme, there is a valid point to be made. If we want teachers to be positive role models for our youth, why not spend a little time asking some interview questions that are relevant to this objective? For example:

- In what ways do you think you might be a positive role model for your students?
- What do you do in your life and work to keep on learning and growing?
- What does it mean to you to be a good citizen? In what ways do you demon-strate those good citizenship qualities?
- Are there any community activities you participate in that you think enrich your teaching or make you a more positive role model for your students?
- Who was one of your most important role models as a youth? Do you think

you model those same qualities, or will model those qualities for your students? How?

- Here are some of the values our school has identified as being values we want to teach our students. (List your school's target values.) In what ways do you demonstrate these values in your life?

Surely this line of inquiry can go too far. There was a time when single women had to give up their teaching positions after getting married, because, incredibly, married women were not regarded as decent role models for impressionable youth. What teachers do with their private lives is their own business (unless they choose to share it), and the last thing we want to do is to begin inappropriate inquiries about prospective teachers' politics, hobbies, or personal lives. There is a fine line between an inappropriate inquiry and an appropriate one. Nevertheless, if we are serious about wanting teachers to be positive, active role models, then we will take the risk of asking some different and perhaps difficult questions to find out more than the superficial information that can be gleaned from their dress (they look neat and clean), their speech (they don't use swear words), and the absence of any morals charges on their record.

If the idea of asking clarifying questions at the interview such as those listed above is uncomfortable, here is another approach that gets at the same objective. Every candidate to be interviewed receives the following message, hopefully at least a week before their interview:

> "It is important to us that our teachers be good role models for our students in terms of their values and moral development. Recognizing that none of us is perfect, we would like our teachers to be people who model caring relationships, compassion, commitment, service, integrity, involvement, tolerance, intellectual inquiry, perseverance, patriotism, and good citizenship. Please put together a portfolio, to bring to your interview, which will help us appreciate how you demonstrate many of these values in your life. Feel free to use letters, photographs, documents, or any other creative means you like to illustrate these values in your life and work. We appreciate your taking the time to do this. We would not ask this of you if it weren't important to us. Thank you."

However it is done, using staff hiring policy and procedures to identify those candidates with the most potential as values educators is one of the most effective methods available to enhance a values education or moral education program. If we want our teachers to share, live, demonstrate, and model the target values we have chosen, then we must find ways to get to know candidates better and to make their ability to be good role models an important criteria for selection.

Chapter 7

Facilitating Values and Morality

An Introduction to the Facilitation Activities

Facilitating values and moral development is a very different process from inculcating values and morality. The two go hand in hand, but it is important to understand the distinction and to determine when to do one or the other. These issues were discussed in Chapters 3 and 4, but before conducting many of the facilitation activities below, it will be helpful to consider the following, specific guidelines:

1. *Structure the choices to encourage thinking.* If you are asking students a series of voting questions (#57), the questions should not have obvious answers, with the result that everyone votes the same way. If you are giving them a number of choices to prioritize (#58), make the choices equally competitive. If you are presenting two ends of a continuum for students to place themselves upon (#59), don't make one end of the continuum an obviously "good" or attractive choice and the other end a "wrong" or unattractive choice. In other words, when giving the students choices to encourage them to think for themselves, don't make the choices too easy or obvious. Give them something to think about.

2. *Don't telegraph your own answers.* This is an extension of the previous point. You may want the students to think for themselves, but there are subtle ways you might unconsciously "stack the deck" in favor of your own beliefs and opinions. When giving students a series of choices, don't always make your own choice the first in the series, or the last, or the one on the left, or some other predictable placement. Try not to use "loaded words" that reveal your position. Watch your tone of voice, which can easily reveal your attitude about a choice you are presenting.

3. *Participate yourself.* Idea #54 presents a number of guidelines regarding your own participation when facilitating discussions on values and moral issues. These include the importance of being a good listener, not monopolizing the discussion, sharing your own viewpoint without preaching, choosing the best time to participate, and exercising your right to pass. It would helpful to reread that section before beginning the activities below.

4. *Treat all responses with equal respect.* Don't correct, reward, punish, or praise students' responses, lest they get the idea that the point of asking these questions is for them to give you the correct answer, rather than think for themselves. That might be alright if you were trying to inculcate values, but if your present goal is to facilitate *their* thinking and decision-making, then you don't want them shifting into a "right answer mentality" in which they are trying to guess *your* answer.

However, it is important for everyone to realize that your treating student responses with equal respect does not mean you agree with every viewpoint expressed. You might remind students, "Whenever we discuss a value issue in this class, freedom of thought gives you the right to form and express your own opinion. But remember, your right to your opinion doesn't mean your opinion is right."[122] As indicated above, you can also participate in the discussion yourself, which includes disagreeing with students if you think they are wrong; but if you want to *facilitate* their values development, your participation should be done in a sharing, not a moralizing mode, which encourages them to keep thinking for themselves.

5. *Shift to inculcation with awareness.* As Chapter 4 discussed in more detail, one of the greatest challenges in comprehensive values education is to shift back and forth skillfully between the inculcating, modeling, facilitating, and skill-building modes. There are points during a facilitative discussion of values and moral issues, when you may want to ask a clarifying moral question to encourage the students to think more deeply about the moral dimensions of an issue (#28), or when you may want to go beyond the personal sharing of your beliefs and employ moralizing (#6), praise (#8), correction (#9), or other forms of inculcation.

There is nothing wrong with doing this, per se, except you will be setting in motion two, potentially contradictory teaching modes—inculcating and facilitating. Students can handle a certain amount of ambiguity. They can understand that you *do* trust them to think for themselves and be responsible *and* that you have some things you wish to teach them about values and morality.

However, if you shift back and forth too often or abruptly between facilitating and inculcating, students get confused. They begin to feel, "Hey, wait a minute. She says she wants us to think for ourselves, and she asks us an interesting, thought-provoking question, and a few students give their response, and then she starts asking questions implying we're wrong and launches into a big lecture on the topic. I'm getting the feeling she doesn't really want us to think for ourselves after all; she doesn't really trust us to have a good discussion and learn from it. So why bother thinking about this stuff? I might as well just try to figure out what answer she wants to hear and make some brownie points by saying that answer; or else I might as well just sit back and wait for the inevitable sermon."

The point is that *it is difficult to inculcate and facilitate simultaneously.* It takes a combination of skill, artfulness, and intuition to move back and forth smoothly between the two modes, without doing a disservice to one or the other or both. For that reason, some teachers prefer to do one at a time. When they facilitate, they facilitate, sticking rigorously to the first four guidelines above. Then, at other times, they inculcate. Students understand their teacher has two goals—to help them be responsible, independent thinkers and actors and to teach them values, morals, and ethics.

There is some merit to having separate times for inculcation and facilitation. There are times when it's best to make a clear statement of moral values and leave it at that, so there is no ambiguity about it and no further discussion to dilute the message. There are other times when it's best to let the students have their say and discuss a topic at length without interruption or teacher input. They need and deserve to have some "space," that is, some time to think for themselves without further inculcation.

However, it is a shame not to capitalize on a teachable moment, to miss the opportunity for some good facilitation or inculcation just because you happen to be working primarily in the other mode. Chapter 4 suggests that, in spite of the pitfalls, teachers *can* learn to operate in several modes simultaneously or in quick succession. That is why the guideline here reads to do so *with awareness.* Be aware of your students' responses. If you are having a good, active, facilitative discussion, and you ask a few clarifying moral questions, and at first they appear to be responding thoughtfully, and then they start slumping down in their seats and losing attention, that's your cue. Change gears; ask an open-ended question, with no right answer implied; start facilitating again; draw them back in. It may feel a little awkward at first, but with experience, you will feel increasingly comfortable and skillful in moving back and forth among several modes of values education.

6. *Vary the discussion period.* Many of the following ideas contain thought-provoking questions and activities that the students respond to individually and then discuss with others. The class will be much more interesting and these activities will go a lot further if you vary the format of the discussion. Conduct some discussions with the whole class, allowing students to answer randomly. Other times, go around the room in order, giving each student a chance to respond or pass. On other occasions, divide students into groups of four for a freewheeling discussion, or into groups of three where each student gets exactly one minute to be the "focus person" and give her ideas on the topic. There are numerous combinations of different group formats, group sizes, time limits, and discussion methods. Use many of them.

7. *Go beyond the superficial.* Just as many of the inculcation ideas in Chapter 5 can be applied superficially, so can facilitation activities, if all they involve are brief, random exercises that are not built into a larger educational plan. The goals of values education are much more likely to be achieved when facilitative activities are done often, are followed by in-depth discussion, are combined with subject area study, involve reading and writing, and are combined with inculcation and skill-building activities.

8. *Respond to irresponsible statements appropriately.* There is an understandable fear that is often expressed that encouraging students to voice their own opinions opens the door to their saying things or advocating positions that reflect negative values or antisocial attitudes, and that such expressions might negatively influence other students. There are a number of reasons to be reassured about this legitimate concern:

- Other students will often contradict the negative statement themselves.
- You can voice a different opinion, then or later.
- The students have probably heard those viewpoints already—from the same student, in the hallway, on the playground, in television, or in the movies.
- If they haven't heard the stated viewpoint yet, they probably will soon. Either way, better that it come out in the classroom, where the teacher or other students can deal with it and offer a more enlightened response.
- Research indicates that moral reasoning, as measured by Kohlberg's stages (#70), does not go backward.[110] In a classroom with several levels of moral reasoning, interaction helps some students move to the next level, while others stay at the same one.
- You can always change the subject.
- Some students will make socially irresponsible comments whether you permit them to or not—even when you are inculcating values.
- Often they don't really mean it, and no one takes it seriously.
- Young people can be a lot more serious and responsible than we often give them credit for. Once they realize that you want them to be honest with themselves and one another, they will become increasingly thoughtful in their comments.

There is no formula response to negative or antisocial comments by students. You have to evaluate each specific case. As in other teaching situations, you will then determine whether to take it seriously, let it pass, ask the student clarifying values questions or clarifying moral questions, ask if any students have a different viewpoint, give your own different viewpoint, share your feelings about what was said, correct the student, or speak to the student privately after class.

9. *Consult other resources. Values and Teaching*[154] and *Values Clarification*[176] contain many more suggestions and hundreds more examples for implementing Ideas #56–66 and #71. *Educating for Character*[122] and *Moral, Character, and Civic Education in the Elementary School*[19] contain scores of good suggestions and examples for implementing Ideas #74–80, particularly those related to class rule making, class meetings, and community meetings.

56

What Are Your Purposes?

One of the most effective ways of helping people develop and actualize their own values is to ask them frequently, "What are your purposes, your aspirations, your goals?" This can be done in general, in terms of specific life decisions, or in terms of school classes and subject areas.

Some elementary school teachers take five minutes every morning to ask their students to identify, depending on their age, one, two, or three goals for the day. It helps students focus their energy, set priorities, and become better goal-setters. In secondary classes and subject areas, periodic consideration of purposes is an effective way of motivating students, as well as helping them define their goals. It is also fruitful to ask students one or more questions like the following at the beginning of a school year or semester:

- What are your goals for this school year?
- What are some things you would like to learn?
- What "new year's resolution" might you make for this math class this year? (Or social studies, science, etc.)
- What have you liked about your English class in previous years? What have you disliked?
- What is one thing you have always wanted to know or one thing you would like to know that you might be able to learn in this class?
- What is one thing as a student that you plan on doing the same as you did last semester? What is one thing you plan on doing differently?
- What is one thing you can do to achieve your goals for this class this year?

Questions like these work with students at all grade levels. Depending on their age and how you wish to handle it, students can tell you their responses individually, write their answers, discuss them in small groups, discuss them as a whole class, or a combination of these means. The process of exploring their own purposes helps students take responsibility for their experience in the class. It helps students discover and develop their *intrinsic* motivation for learning. The conversation between you and the students surrounding these questions also provides you, the teacher, with useful diagnostic information and helps give you ideas for how to work with a particular class and individual students so as to better meet their needs and achieve your goals.

In a more general way, asking students, "What do you want out of life? What do you hope to achieve in the future? What would it mean to you to have a successful life?" and similar questions about their purposes is a useful means to get them to shift from thinking about short-term desires to long-term goals and values. There are many occasions for raising such questions: in discussions of careers; when a well-known person dies and there is commentary on his or her

life; in discussing a book or story the class read involving a person's life decisions, mistakes, or accomplishments; upon learning of this year's Nobel Prize
winners in your subject area; as a general writing assignment for English or language arts; as a topic for students to give speeches on, and other occasions you
will recognize or create.

Finally, asking questions about purposes is good training in decision-making
skills. When making decisions, individuals and groups often loose sight of the
goal and focus on minute aspects of the dilemma. To teach students to always go
back to the big questions like What are we trying to achieve here? What are my
goals and purposes? and What values do I want to realize in making this decision? is a most valuable lesson in decision making and in life.

When people stop to consider their long-range purposes and values, they
generally make more personally satisfying and socially responsible decisions. It
is when we focus on immediate desires and short-term considerations that we
are more likely to make poor decisions for ourselves and ignore the rights and
needs of others around us. When we step back, take a deep breath, and ask
ourselves, What is *really* important to me here? What are *all* my purposes? we are
much more likely to remember our basic values and to think of others as well as
ourselves.

> *Perfection of means and confusion of goals*
> *seem—in my opinion—to characterize our age.*
> ALBERT EINSTEIN

57

Voting

Giving students the chance to vote can have the same educational benefits that
adult elections often provide. Especially when the choices are difficult, voting
provides the opportunity for clarifying one's own values, for sharing beliefs and
priorities with others, for listening more carefully than ever to varying viewpoints, and for taking a stand on one's beliefs.

There are many opportunities for students to vote—selection of class officers; where to go on a class trip; options the teacher offers regarding an upcoming
assignment; the best solution to a current problem; what project their small group
will work on, or perhaps which community service project the class will undertake. All these examples are situations where a real vote is required. These are
not simulated experiences in voting and self-government; they are the real thing.
Whether the issues are major or minor, the vote counts. The results will really

affect what happens next. A number of the strategies for facilitating values and moral development—for example, student choice in curriculum (#68), class meetings (#76), and meaningful student government (#78)—will utilizing voting, as well as methods for consensus building, which honors the goals of the minority as well as the majority.

There is still another form of voting that can readily be used to further the goals of values education. It is a simple classroom activity called "values voting," which asks students to get in touch with and express their feelings, beliefs, choices, and values in the form of a straw poll, simply by raising their hands. Values voting questions always begin with the words, "How many of you _____?" Here are some examples of values voting questions for different age levels; although many of these could easily work for multiple age levels.

Elementary: *How many of you . . .*

1. would return a wallet you found with the money left in it?
2. have ever picked on somebody else?
3. would watch television all the time if you could?
4. have a favorite candidate in the upcoming election?
5. like vegetables? think you'll like vegetables in the future?

Middle School: *How many of you . . .*

6. plan on never smoking cigarettes?
7. believe there is life somewhere in outer space?
8. enjoy reading on your own?
9. think kids are getting involved with sex too early in this community?
10. are certain you will complete high school?

High School and Adult: *How many of you . . .*

11. think a woman will be President of the United States in your lifetime?
12. believe we have too many environmental protection laws and regulations in this country?
13. can think of three ways to avoid or reduce your chances of getting AIDS?
14. think the United States is the best country in the world?
15. are too hard on yourself when you make a mistake?

Students respond to values voting questions by raising their hands to indicate a positive response, pointing their thumbs down to indicate a negative response, or folding their arms to indicate they are uncertain or wish to keep their answer to themselves. After all the questions have been asked, discussion follows, during which time students can explain their votes and hear one another's viewpoints.

Values voting questions can be asked: (a) on a variety of subjects, as above, (b) on a particular values or moral issue you are discussing, such as ten questions

"Just a simple 'yes' or 'no' if you please, sir."

Source: Masters Agency.

about drug use and abuse, six questions about honesty, or eight voting questions about the current election, or (c) on the subject you are studying in class (#67).

Whether voting on real choices or employing the values voting technique, the act of voting is an excellent way to get students to think for themselves, to take a stand, and to consider different viewpoints. It is also a very easy, brief, and effective way of involving *all* the students in the class, not just those who speak up the most frequently. You will be impressed at how such questions help increase participation in the class discussions that result.

58

Prioritizing

Any time we give students the opportunity to set priorities, we give them practice in developing values of their own.

The "rank order" is one of the easiest and most effective ways of encouraging students to choose their preference between competing alternatives. Based on the topic you are considering, you ask the students a question, typically give them three or four answers to choose from, and ask them to arrange all the choices in order—from their most preferred to least preferred response. Some examples of rank orders appropriate to elementary, middle, and high school levels follow shortly.

Remember, the point of the activity is not for them all to choose the same best answer, but to get them to think more deeply about the issue and to get to know themselves and their values better. The benefit is not so much in their arriving at a particular answer, for they may change their minds many times about this issue as they grow and mature. *The benefit is in the thinking and feeling they do in order to arrive at their answer* and the additional thinking they do when they hear other people's answers and reasoning on the same topic.

Elementary School:

1. If you see a bigger kid picking on a little kid on the playground, what would you do? (Possible follow up: What *should* you do?)

   _____ Ignore them
   _____ Try to get them to stop
   _____ Tell a teacher

2. What kind of work do you prefer the most (or mind the least)?

   _____ Outdoor work
   _____ Housework
   _____ School work

3. What do you like to do best with your family?

   _____ Eat together
   _____ Take a car trip together
   _____ Watch television together
   _____ Go shopping together

4. If you were spending a Saturday afternoon with friends, what would you like to do the most?

   _____ Play a sport
   _____ Go to the mall

_____ Play around the house
_____ Hang out around town

5. What do you really believe about an allowance?

_____ Every child should get an allowance, without having to do any work around the house
_____ Every child should get an allowance, as long as they do some work around the house
_____ Kids shouldn't get an allowance and shouldn't have to work around the house.

Middle School:

6. If you had a friend who you found out was smoking marijuana, what would you do? (Possible follow-up: What *should* you do?)

_____ Urge him/her to quit.
_____ Ignore it.
_____ Talk to his/her parent or teacher.
_____ Join him/her.
_____ Report him/her to the police.

7. What is the most important thing you could do for your physical health?

_____ Quit or don't start smoking.
_____ Quit or don't start drinking alcohol.
_____ Get plenty of exercise.
_____ Eat healthy foods.

8. Which is most important to you?

_____ To be popular
_____ To be healthy
_____ To be intelligent

9. (For a religious school setting) Which of the following Bible stories do you like the best? (Or: Which has the most meaning to you?)

_____ Noah and the Flood
_____ The Exodus from Egypt
_____ Jesus's Sermon on the Mount

10. If you were going to give $5 to a worthy cause, to which would you prefer to give it?

_____ To feed hungry people
_____ To clean up the environment
_____ To improve the way the government works

High School and Adult:

11. Which of these careers would most suit you?

_____ Working in a large office or factory, with many people around
_____ Working in a small office or shop with a few people
_____ Working independently, mostly by yourself

12. What do you think is the best solution to the national budget deficit?

_____ Raise taxes.
_____ Lower spending.
_____ Raise taxes and lower spending.
_____ Do neither.

13. What do you think is the best way to avoid getting AIDS?

_____ Choosing your partner carefully
_____ Abstinence
_____ Using a condom

14. When is the wisest time for people to get married?

_____ Whenever they fall in love, no matter what the age
_____ After high school
_____ After age 20
_____ After age 25
_____ When they can support themselves adequately

15. Which comes closest to your feelings about people who don't vote in elections?

_____ I sympathize with them.
_____ I disagree with them.
_____ I don't understand them.

Be sure to have the students rank *all* the choices given, not just their first choice, as it requires much more thinking to select among all the alternatives than to select only their top choice. In many instances, students may have another answer they prefer over any of the choices you have given them. That's fine. Your goal in the rank order is not to list all the possible responses to the question, but to start the thought process rolling. Tell them to hold their additional answers until the discussion period and, meanwhile, prioritize all the given choices.

The "rank order" is only one way to encourage students to set priorities. It is a structured way to get all the students to grapple with the issues involved. But any clarifying question or activity that asks them to seek the *best* or *most* or *favorite* or *worst* or *least* desirable has the same effect. It causes them to get in touch with some of their priorities and values. For example, you could simply ask a group of students, "What are the most important factors you will consider when choosing your career?" You don't always need to structure the question as a rank order; it can be open-ended and still elicit values and priorities.

Having said that, however, the rank order is such a useful tool, that someone experienced in using it would find it hard to resist the temptation to record all the students' answers about important career factors on the board and then have everyone rank order the group's responses. Or you could ask them, using the list of career attributes the whole class just generated, to select the three career factors that are most important and the three factors that are least important to each of them. This is another form of prioritizing. "Circle your favorite. Cross out your least favorite. Put a 1, 2, and 3 next to the three best choices." There are many ways to ask students to make choices based on their priorities and values.

> *To laugh often and much; to win the respect of intelligent people and the affection of children; to earn the appreciation of honest critics and endure the betrayal of false friends; to appreciate beauty; to find the best in others; to leave the world a bit better, whether by a healthy child, a garden patch or a redeemed social condition; to know even one life has breathed easier because you have lived. This is to have succeeded.*
>
> RALPH WALDO EMERSON

59

Spread of Opinion Exercises

On many issues of values and morality, the array of possible positions can be spread along a continuum. It is a good critical thinking exercise (#86) to have students recognize the distinctions among the various positions on a continuum. A good way to facilitate values development is asking students to determine what *their position* is along the continuum.

Once a topic is identified, by either the teacher or students, you draw a line on the board and identify the extreme positions on either end of the line. Several examples are given below. In some cases, the choices speak for themselves. In other instances, you will have to say a bit more to help the students understand the issues involved. For example, in the second, middle school example below, you might explain that "Loose Louie" is someone who doesn't care what people think; he just acts however he feels. On the other hand, "Cool Carl" always does the "in thing"; his behavior always appears appropriately sophisticated.

Elementary Level:

1. How neat a person are you? (Or how neat would you like to be?)

   Fastidious Frannie . . . . Cyclone Cicilia

2. How much do you respect bigger or stronger kids who pick on smaller or weaker kids?

   Don't respect or admire them at all. . . . . Respect and admire them a lot

Middle School Level:

3. How important is it for your future for you to do well in school?

   Not at all important . . . . Extremely important

4. How spontaneous a person would you like to be?

   Loose Louie or Laura . . . . Cool Carl or Carla

Secondary and Adult Level:

5. How concerned are you about fat and cholesterol in your diet?

   Not at all . . . . Extremely

6. If you could make the law, under what circumstances would you permit abortions?

   Under no circumstances . . . . On demand for anyone

Ask each student, individually, to choose her own position on the continuum. You might have them draw a line in their notebook and put their initials on the place on the line that represents their position. Then ask for volunteers or students you call on to place their names on the continuum on the board. If you call on people, remind them of their right to pass (#66). If students are all grouping themselves together at one end, ask if there are other students with a different position, to legitimize diversity. *Then* ask students to explain their various positions. At the end of the discussion, you might ask if any students have changed their positions based on the reasoning they just heard.

If students continually group themselves together, it is a sign that the choices are "stacked" or obvious. The best continuums—those which produce the most thinking and discussion—generally have students placing themselves on both sides of the middle.

Two variations are: (1) Give students a topic on which there are many positions and have them identify four, five, or six positions along the continuum. Then have small groups each take a different position, research it, and explain its pros and cons to the class. After they have thoroughly understood the issues in this way, they then indicate their own positions within the spread of opinion. (2) Place the two ends of the continuum at either end of the room, and have everyone in the class physically move to the place between the two ends that represents their position. After everyone has physically moved to a place along the imaginary line, have them pair off with someone standing near them and explain why they chose to position themselves where they did.

60

Interviews

An interview can be a beneficial learning experience for both the interviewer, the interviewee, and the observers. The interviewer and observers get to hear the feelings, opinions, and experiences of the interviewee. The interviewee gets to think about interesting and important questions, express her beliefs and values publicly, and clarify how she wants to be perceived by others. After the interview is over, interviewees invariably "replay" and re-think parts of the interview and learn more from their experience.

Two types of interviews readily lend themselves to values education in the classroom. In a "public interview," the teacher calls on a student volunteer and asks that student a series of questions. In a "group interview," all the students get to ask questions of the volunteer interviewee. The group interview is like a press conference, with the class taking the role of the reporters. Group interviews can also be done in small groups—for example, groups of five, in which each member gets several minutes to be interviewed by the other four.

The questions asked can be on a particular topic the class is studying or about a "smorgasbord" of topics, such as school, work, friends, family, money, health, politics, likes, dislikes, television, sports, etc. Posting a list of such topics on the board often helps you or the student interviewers think of questions to ask. Public and group interviews generally last from five to ten minutes, depending on the age of the group, who is conducting the interview, and your overall objectives. Interviewees have the right to pass on any questions they would prefer not to answer.

Here are some generic examples of interview questions. Insert a dozen different topics into the blank spaces, and you have hundreds of potential questions that can be asked in public and group interviews. Once you and your students get the hang of it, there is no end to the thought-provoking questions you will think of.

1. What is one thing you like about _____?
2. What is one thing you dislike about _____?
3. How do you feel about _____?
4. What is your opinion about _____?
5. What do you do about _____?
6. What is your favorite _____?
7. How do you think you would react in the following situation?
8. Who would you vote for in the election?
9. When we were discussing _____ earlier, what was your position?
10. What would you say to the person who _____?
11. Would it be right to _____?
12. How do you handle the dilemma of _____?
13. Do you prefer _____ or _____? Why?

14. Have you had any experience with _____ and what did you learn from your experience?
15. What do you think about _____?
16. Do you like _____?
17. Do you like to _____?
18. What is your stand on _____?
19. What do you typically do about _____?
20. In such and such a situation, which of these would you choose?
21. What would be the fairest solution to _____?
22. What do you think you will do about _____?
23. What is one thing you would like to learn about _____?
24. Have you ever _____?
25. How did you get interested in _____?
26. Rank the following _____ in order of your preference.
27. What would your parents say about the answer you just gave?
28. Where would you place yourself on the continuum between _____ and _____?
29. Which _____ do you like least?
30. Are you proud of _____
31. What is one thing you would change about _____?
32. Would you ever _____?
33. Can you understand how someone would _____?
34. Are you planning to _____?
35. How often do you _____? Why?

Notice there are few "information questions" here such as How old are you? and How many children are there in your family? The idea is to ask questions that require a person to discover, clarify, and express her thoughts, feelings, beliefs, daily choices, goals, and values, and to allow other students to hear and think about the interviewee's answers. Everyone learns and grows in the process.

Some teachers employ the interview activity occasionally. Some use it once a week, eventually giving each student the opportunity to be interviewed. Some teachers use interviews in connection with the subject matter being taught. For example, interviewing a student about her feelings, thoughts, and experiences on the subject under discussion, or having a student take the role of a historical figure or literary character and answer interview questions as that character would.

Many teachers who have used the interview method have found that it helps to volunteer themselves to be interviewed by the class. This demonstrates a fairness and reciprocity that the students appreciate. It is an opportunity to model a thoughtful, honest, caring approach to the issues that are raised. It is also an occasion to communicate many of your own values in a format where the students are, by definition, interested; since they are asking the questions. Of course, you have the same "right to pass" (#66) as the students do on any questions asked and to say as much or as little as you wish to on any topic. In fact, it is sometimes a good idea to pass on one question just to demonstrate the viability of the pass option, thereby giving the students the confidence to do the same.

61

Inventories

Inventories help students to assess their lives and values more closely. They provide the opportunity to step back, observe patterns, and then analyze the patterns from a variety of perspectives.

First, choose an inventory topic on a subject you wish to explore. Then ask students, working individually, to make a list which fits that topic. For example, make a list of:

1. Ten adults you respect
2. Every TV program you watched in the last week
3. Everything you spent money on in the last week
4. Twenty things you love to do
5. Fifteen things you think are wrong to do
6. Everything you ate in the last 48 hours
7. All your friends
8. Your five favorite books
9. Ten games or sports you like to play
10. Ten Bible stories you remember (in an appropriate setting)

Ideally you will find topics that are relevant both to the values and moral issues you wish to discuss and to the subjects you are studying. For example, you could move from their inventories of ten adults they respect, to which characters they respect in the book they just read, to which personal characteristics or values are most deserving of respect. You could use their inventories of everything they ate in the past 48 hours in your unit on nutrition. You could use their list of five favorite books as a way of getting them to share their excitement about reading with one another.

Sometimes making the list itself produces self-awareness, insight, and motivation to consider the issue further. However, a follow-up step of *coding the list* usually produces even more self-knowledge.

For example, the list of TV programs could be coded as follows: "Put an 'Ent' next to those programs that were *entertaining*. Put an 'L' next to those you *learned* something from. Cross out the program you could most easily live without. Circle the last one you would give up. If you had one hour a day to watch TV, put a check mark next to those programs you would choose to watch." For another example, the inventory of "15 things you think are wrong" could be coded this way: "Where did you learn these things were wrong? Put a 'P' if you learned it from your *parents*, an 'R' if you learned it from your *religion*, an 'Sc' if you learned it at *school*, and an 'Se' if you decided it was wrong your*self*, from your own experience. You may use more than one letter, if you learned it in more than one place. Next, put a 'Me' next to any item on your list that you think is wrong for you, but not necessarily wrong for everyone, and put an 'Ev' next to those things you think are wrong for *everyone*. Finally, put a plus sign (+) next to the three things on your list you think are most wrong and a minus sign (–) next to the three you think are least wrong."

Any inventory can be analyzed more deeply by coding it in the fashion described. Following the coding, students should be given the opportunity to discuss what they learned about themselves and the subject from doing the inventory. "I Learned Statements" (#65) are a good way to follow-up an inventory.

62

Values Journal

When a class is regularly discussing, reading, and writing about values and moral issues, a "values journal" can be a powerful way of deepening the students' thinking.

Ideally, a values journal is a separate notebook devoted solely to this purpose. That gives the students a sense of its being special, something different from their other activities. However, the journal can also be a separate section in a loose-leaf notebook, or a file folder in which individual papers are collected.

The values journal is the place where students write freely on different values topics. The topics may be assigned by the teacher or chosen by the student or both. Here are a few examples of how different teachers use the journal.

1. An upper elementary school teacher has her class write in their values journals every Monday and Friday. She usually gives them a topic, for example: "Your Favorite Relative," "Three Things You Would Like to Learn," "Honesty," or "How Important is Money?" Other days she lets them write about any subject they choose. They have five minutes to write about the subject. She calls on a few volunteers to read their entries aloud to the class. Then she collects them all, reads them, and puts them back in her drawer until the next Monday or Friday.

2. A junior high school teacher has her students keep their journals at home, where they are responsible for writing one entry in it each week. They may write about either the topic she gives them or one they choose themselves. She collects them on Tuesday, reads them, and returns them on Wednesday.

3. A high school health education teacher requires her students to write three entries per week in their values journals about any topic relating to health—topics they are discussing in class, topics they read about or see on TV, or things they observe or think about themselves. Each entry must be at least 100 words in length. On Thursdays, students bring their journals to class, and everyone chooses one of their three selections to read aloud. Each week, the teacher collects one-third of the journals to take home and read.

4. Secondary English, social studies, home economics, art, physical education, and other subject area teachers have also used values journals, in a way comparable to the health education example above. Foreign language teachers have used them, too, having their students write short entries on value-laden topics *in the foreign language.*

5. A high school "school-within-a-school" has its students write in their journals daily. They do this on their own time, writing their thoughts or feelings on any subjects that interest them. There is no length requirement. Once a month, the students turn in their journals to their advisors, a few days before their scheduled monthly meeting with their advisors.

The values journal serves several purposes. Regular writing of this sort helps young people become more reflective, sensitive, and observant persons. It helps them to think more about the topics the teacher believes are important to think about or the student believes are important to think about. It provides an occasion for students to work out problems or confusions they are experiencing. It helps them to clarify and discover their own values. It provides a vehicle for enhancing communication between teacher and student. When journal entries are read aloud in class, it helps students learn from one another and realize that others share their concerns.

Values journals are not corrected for spelling and punctuation, as this might thwart the primary goal of having students explore their thoughts and feelings freely. (Ironically, writing experts believe that regular, freestyle writing, which is not corrected, helps students become more comfortable with the writing process. Combining this approach with other occasions where their writing *is* corrected for form and style helps maximize writing improvement.) However, many teachers *do* make comments and write clarifying questions (#28,#71) in students' values journals. The private dialogue that results is an excellent occasion to inculcate, to model, and primarily, to facilitate values and moral development.

63

Proud Questions

Pride has long been considered to be one of the "seven deadly sins." *Hubris*, or pride, was the character flaw that brought many heroes of Greek and Shakespearean drama to their tragic fate. Braggadocio, boasting, *machismo*, and arrogance are hardly the character traits we want to instill in our youth.

There is another kind of pride, however—the kind associated with prizing and cherishing someone or something. Feeling pride in one's family or country, feeling proud of one's effort and accomplishments, not feeling shame or embarrassment but feeling satisfaction in how one handled a difficult situation—these are examples of the sort of pride we would hope all young people develop.

There are many ways to help students recognize and develop areas in their lives where they can feel pride. One way is to ask the clarifying question, Are you proud of that? whenever the opportunity arises: Are you proud of this piece of work you just turned in? Are you proud of how you behaved while running for class office? Are you proud of your effort thus far in this sports season? Are you proud of your team's effort? To ask someone if they are proud is to ask them to consult their conscience and their highest ideals. The implicit message in asking such a question is: *Go for the gold. Don't settle for less than your best effort and your highest values.*

Another very useful way to encourage this positive kind of pride is the *proud whip* or *proud circle* exercise. Some teachers do it once a week, perhaps on a Monday or Friday. Simply ask, What is something you were proud of this week? or What is something you are proud of having done this week? Start with any student, then whip around the room, giving every student a chance to respond or pass. When it is their turn, they begin with the words "I'm proud _____" and complete the sentence with something they are proud of in their lives.

"I'm proud of how I did on the book report."
"I'm proud of my sister. She was just accepted at a college this week."
"I'm proud of how I didn't quit in the mile run, even though I felt like it."

Do this activity regularly and you will see how students begin to recognize and choose more things to be proud of in their lives.

You can also use the proud whip in relation to a particular topic or activity. For example, What is something you are proud of concerning:

- your family?
- your health?
- school?
- how you are doing in school this year?
- your religion?
- your role in this election?
- a belief of yours?
- alcohol and drug use?
- sports?
- reading ?

64

Sentence Stems

Your elementary school class is studying fire safety. You could get the whole class involved in the subject matter by asking them to complete one or more of these sentence stems. If they are not old enough to write their responses, they can say their answers aloud.

- Fire is _____.
- Firefighters are _____.
- If I woke up at night and smelled smoke, I would _____.
- A good way to prevent fires is _____.
- To report a fire, I would _____.

Your high school class is discussing the topic of citizenship. You might give them some unfinished sentences like these to complete:

- If there is no candidate on the ballot you like, you should _____.
- The most important thing a citizen can do is _____.
- One issue I would write a letter to the editor about is _____.
- I think _____ is a very good citizen, because _____.
- I think it is bad citizenship to _____.
- The news media should _____.

Not only are incomplete sentences an excellent way to involve students in the subject you are studying, incomplete sentences foster individual thinking. To complete the sentences, students must consult their feelings, their thoughts, their beliefs, and their values. In sharing and discussing their responses, students learn from one another and deepen their individual thinking about the issues.

65

I Learned Statements

This is one of the simplest, most widely applicable, and most powerful tools for helping learners reflect and grow. When students have completed an experience — a reading, story, exercise, experiment, activity, trip, etc.—in which values or moral issues were implicit or explicit or in which they were asked to do something new, give them this sentence stem to complete. If possible, write it on the board.

"I learned that I_____."

For third- or fourth-grade students to adults, ask students to individually write out a completed sentence, beginning with the same four words, completing it with anything they learned about themselves as a result of that activity. (Primary age children can do the activity without the writing step.) Then ask for several volunteers who would be willing to share their answers aloud. You will often be quite impressed with the quality of the students' responses and how hearing from one another this way deepens the learning experience for everyone.

Some teachers like to add other, comparable sentence stems to the basic one. You might make a chart of these, keep it handy, and use it frequently at appropriate times. For example:

- I learned that I _____.
- I re-learned that I _____.
- I was surprised that I _____.
- I was pleased that I _____.
- I was unhappy that I _____.
- I need to _____.
- I felt _____.
- I thought _____.

There is nothing wrong with asking students to complete the shorter sentence stem, "I learned _____." This typically produces responses that focus on the subject matter, like "I learned that Canada has ten provinces and two territories." "I learned there is more saturated fat in cashews than in peanuts." This can be a very useful method to highlight and reinforce student learnings about the subjects they study. However, by extending the sentence stem to say, "I learned *that I* _____," you invite the students to reflect more personally on their learnings and to connect the subject matter to their own feelings, beliefs, and values.

66

Respect the Right to Pass

Students should always be given "the right to pass" when doing activities that require sharing their feelings, beliefs, choices, experiences, and values with others. In so doing, you convey the implicit and explicit message to the students that, "You are entitled to your privacy. You should feel free to share as much or as little as you wish to. You do not need to participate in this activity if it makes you feel too uncomfortable or vulnerable in any way."

You should remind them of their right to pass each time you do an activity that elicits their thoughts and feelings about personal values and morals. "Remember, you can pass if you want to." Then all they have to do is not volunteer to speak, or if you are calling on people, to say "I pass" when their turn comes. You answer "Fine," "Thank you," or just smile and go on to the next person; no questions asked.

On one level, this is simply a hint or technique for maximizing the effectiveness of these exercises. Experience shows that when students feel compelled to participate, they seem to be less willing and eager to do so. On the other hand, when they are invited to participate, when they are encouraged but not required, and when the activities are inherently interesting, they are more willing and even more enthusiastic about joining in. Ironically, you get more participation by not requiring it.

But there is a more important reason for respecting the students' right to *not* participate in these facilitating activities. Giving them the right to pass shows a deep respect for them as separate, autonomous, responsible persons. It suggests to them that they are old enough to make intelligent and responsible decisions about their participation. It suggests that they are capable of behaving maturely as they consider these issues of values and morality. It suggests, therefore, that they are old enough *to have intelligent opinions and positions* on values and moral issues.

A corollary benefit is that when they participate and share their ideas, they are *choosing* to do so. They are not participating because they have to, but because they want to. They are expressing their real feelings and thoughts on the topic under discussion. Knowing this, it adds to the drama and impact of the activity, because it is not typical in school settings for students to be sharing their honest thoughts and feelings on a variety of important issues. The net effect is that students' interest, attention, and participation is maximized and a great deal more value is derived from it.

One should not overstate the case. Everyone still participates to the extent that they are present, observe, and listen to what is going on. To some degree, every student probably is also thinking about the subject. They simply are not required to state their views aloud if they do not wish to.

At the same time, if you sense a student is willing and able to participate but is feeling a little shy, you should feel free to give her gentle encouragement. You would do this in many other situations—encouraging students to answer a subject matter question or participate in a discussion or go out for a team or try some new learning experience. Your sensitivity toward and knowledge of your students is a good guide. You will know when some encouragement to participate is in order and when a student is saying she would really rather not take a turn.

67

Three-Level Approach to Subject Matter

One view of teaching suggests that every school subject can be taught on three levels—*facts, concepts, and values.*[78] The facts level includes learning separate pieces of information and isolated skills. The concepts level includes seeing the connections between separate facts, understanding principles, and mastering the complex skills of the discipline. The values level involves exploring the relationship of the subject matter to one's personal life and values.

For example, an elementary school teacher teaching the Pilgrim Story on the facts level would teach the students the basic facts of the story—what happened in England, in Holland, the Mayflower, Plymouth Rock, 1620, the hard winter, the friendly natives, and the First Thanksgiving. On the concepts levels, she would explore with the students the more complex ideas behind the story—prejudice, cultural assimilation, emigration, suffering, helping, and rituals. She would use other historical examples of prejudice, emigration, and rituals to help these concepts come alive. Finally, on the values level, the teacher would relate the story and its concepts to the students' own feelings, beliefs, experiences, and values. Have *you* ever experienced prejudice? What is something *you* are proud of in *your* cultural, ethnic, or religious background? Make an inventory of all the rituals *you* participate in over the whole year. What do these rituals mean to *you*? What is something *you* are thankful for?

Similarly, a high school biology teacher doing a unit on digestion and nutrition, on the facts level, might teach the parts of the digestive system, the different food groups, and the meaning of words like carbohydrate, fat, and cholesterol. On the concepts level, she might help students understand how digestion is its own "system," the meaning of "balanced diet," how to understand and interpret food labeling, and how experiments on measuring calories in food are conducted. On the values level, she might have them inventory all the foods they ate that week, evaluate if their food intake fits the definition of a balanced diet (which would be concepts level again), and ask them how they feel about their own eating habits. She might give one student a public interview (#60) on her food choices—how she learned them, what choices are conscious and unconscious, what she might like to change now or later, what else she would like to know about digestion and nutrition.

These two examples convey the important idea that values education need not be a separate endeavor from teaching traditional school subjects. Indeed, there is such pressure to increase reading, writing, math, and science skills that many teachers feel they have precious little time to do anything else. "Three-level teaching" is a way to combine the goals of both academic and values education. These are *motivating* activities; they help the students become much more interested in the subject matter, while simultaneously facilitating values and moral development.

Three-level teaching can be done in just about every subject area (Reference #78 provides numerous examples). Begin by asking yourself: "What does this book or lesson or unit or skill or subject I am teaching have to do with my students' lives, now or in the future?" Then consider asking them variations on the following questions:

- What would you like to know about this subject?
- How do you feel about this book, character, subject, or skill?
- What do you think about the facts or concepts I just taught you?
- What do you think about the viewpoint of this literary or historical figure or the speaker on the film you just saw?

- What examples from your own life can be used to help understand this subject? Have you had any experiences that relate to what we are studying?
- Do you agree or disagree with this viewpoint?
- How can you use this in your own life?
- What have you learned from this?
- What did you like or not like about what we just studied or did in class?
- What else would you like to know about it?

These are generic questions that will help you and the students relate the subject matter to their own feelings, beliefs, choices, experiences, and values. Such questions can be asked as open-ended discussion questions. They can also be asked in the form of the various facilitation activities described in this chapter. For example:

- Voting questions: "How many of you would have made the same choice that Lincoln did? How many would have waited? How many would have done it earlier?"
- Prioritizing question: "Rank the following three desserts in the order you believe is healthiest."
- Spread of opinion: "Where do you stand between these two extremes?:
      The worst story I've ever read . . . . The best story I've ever read?"
- Sentence Stems: "On this Thanksgiving, I'm thankful for ____ ."
      "Lincoln should have ____." "The healthiest food I like to eat is ____."

What avail is it to win prescribed amounts of information about geography and history, to win ability to read and write, if in the process the individual loses his own soul; loses his appreciation of things worthwhile, of the values to which these are relative; if he loses desire to apply what he has learned, and, above all, loses the ability to extract meaning from his future experiences as they occur?
JOHN DEWEY [43]

68

Student Choice in Curriculum

We teach basic skills like reading, writing, and mathematics by having students actually participate in those activities. The skills and values of democracy also require active learning. There is no better way to learn to be a responsible decision-maker than to be given the responsibility to make decisions, initially in a structured environment like the family and the classroom.

Students' taking on increasing responsibility for their choices and decisions as a means of fostering values and good citizenship can be advanced in many ways—for example, voting (#57), self-evaluation (#73), class rule making (#75), class meetings (#76), and meaningful student government (#78), to name a few. Another way to help young people learn to be better decision makers and to develop their own values is to give them some choices in the curriculum.

Alfie Kohn has summarized a significant amount of research that demonstrates that giving students and others choices in their learning and living situations enhances academic learning and mental and physical health.[112] Within reasonable limits that honor the teacher's learning objectives and protect students' safety, students can be given greater choice and control in both what they learn and how they learn it. For example:

1. *Reading.* While there are probably books, stories, or articles you want every student to read, you can also give the students a choice on other reading selections. This can be done in many different ways: having a classroom library from which students can select readings; giving them a list of acceptable titles from which they choose; letting them find their own readings as long as they meet certain criteria (such as length or subject area); or giving the option of reading the recommended book or another of their choice with your approval. This can be done once, occasionally, regularly, or all the time, depending on your goals and your beliefs about reading instruction.

2. *Writing.* Again, there are times when you will give all your students the same writing assignment. Other times, however, you can give them a choice. That can mean giving a particular assignment where you choose the style parameters and they choose the topic ("Write a 300 word essay in which you try to persuade the reader to your point of view on a topic or controversial issue of your choice"), giving them the topic and they choose the style ("You may write an essay, a short story, or an epic poem"), or giving them a number of topics to choose from.

3. *Courses.* On the secondary level, there are many possible choices students might make among various courses. The concept of elective courses is certainly familiar. So is the choice among different foreign languages and between academic and vocational courses. However, many schools have been successful in giving students choices among English, social studies, and other departmental courses. For example, one school allows its tenth-grade students to choose either Classics, Contemporary American Fiction, Science Fiction, or Creative Writing as their English course. All four classes do enough reading and writing to achieve common language arts objectives, but they emphasize the different themes as well.

Giving students choices such as these provides an opportunity for them to develop their own interests in greater depth, to discover their calling, and to develop their own values. It also helps motivate them with respect to the subject matter. If they have had a part in choosing their subject or assignment, they are more likely to become involved in it. And, very importantly, it gives them practice in making choices. Especially when accompanied by some guidance, discussion, and follow-up, they can learn from their good and bad choices and be wiser the next time.

4. *Other choices.* On the same grounds, any reasonable opportunity to give students choices is an opportunity for values education. Beyond the examples above, you can give choices to whole classes—for example, a choice of units, choice of learning mode (working individually or in groups), choice of assignments, choice of due dates, or choice of how to decorate the classroom. Individual students can be given choices, too—where to sit, when to go to the bathroom, or how to spend a block of free time. Sometimes even trivial choices—asking kindergartners to rank in order their preference for vanilla, chocolate, or strawberry ice cream, for example—can be a learning experience, especially when part of the learning is that not everyone has to make the same choice, that people are different and these differences can be respected, and we can work out our differences in a cooperative, problem-solving manner.

Just as some rulers of nations fear that giving citizens greater freedom of choice will lead to chaos and anarchy, so do teachers often fear the consequences of allowing students greater choice and control in the classroom and the school. Yet *these structured situations are the best places to learn to exercise responsible freedom.* As a part of a comprehensive values education that also teaches respect, responsibility, and democracy directly and indirectly—through inculcation, modeling, and skill development—facilitating students' own decision-making plays an essential part in their developing personal and civic values.

69

Values Story or Values Poem

Choose a particular value or character virtue—for example, honesty, family, tolerance, health, courage. Or give students a list of these and have them each choose one to work with. Their assignment is:

Write a poem or a story about this value.

Their poem or story should illustrate their particular viewpoint or concept or feeling about this value. As an alternative they might write a *fable*. It helps to read them one or two fables first, so they can learn the format—a story followed by a "moral," that is, a moral principle.

This seems like a simple enough assignment at first, but to do it, the students have to ask themselves, "What do I really think about this value?" To some extent, simply asking the students to focus on the value is a way of inculcating it. But it is also a way of facilitating their values development, because in order to do the assignment, the students must discover *their own* feelings about the value.

In the process, they will, to some degree, internalize that value. It will become more their own.

If students are then given the opportunity to read their poems, stories, or fables to the class, or edit them further for a class publication, they will derive additional benefits both in terms of reading, writing, and speaking skills *and* values and moral development.

For primary age students who are too young to actually write out a story, you can ask them to make up a story and tell it aloud, or tell it to an older child or parent who can write it down for them.

70

Moral Dilemma Discussions

This technique was pioneered by Lawrence Kohlberg and his associates who studied the process of moral reasoning.[108,109,110,146] They documented how children and young adults move through successive stages of moral development, believing that what is "right" is: what they can get away with without being punished (Stage 1); anything that serves their own immediate self-interest (Stage 2); that which gains them social approval (Stage 3); what the laws and rules say is right (Stage 4); what is reciprocally agreed upon as fair (Stage 5); and that which is consistent with universal principles of justice and ethics (Stage 6). The researchers demonstrated that when young people were exposed to moral reasoning levels one stage higher than their own, they typically moved to the next stage of moral reasoning; while conversely, the person at the higher moral reasoning level did not regress to a lower stage.

In a typical classroom, since students represent two or three different levels of moral reasoning, having them discuss moral dilemmas creates the situation where students are exposed to higher levels of moral reasoning. One type of moral dilemma is the *hypothetical dilemma*, such as Kohlberg and his colleagues used in most of their research. For example:

> A sick child desperately needs a particular medicine. The poor, single father cannot afford the high price the druggist is charging. The father cannot earn the money needed in time, and the druggist won't give him credit. Should the father steal the drug to save his child's life?

In conducting the discussion, the teacher is not concerned with the students' answers as to whether or not it is morally permissible for the father to steal under these circumstances. Rather the teacher wants to get students to verbalize *the reasoning by which they arrived at their answer*. The teacher wants the students to hear arguments one stage higher than their own. For example, if a third-grade student says, "It's not nice to steal. People won't like you if you steal from them" (a Stage 3 argument), another student might say, "I think the reason he shouldn't steal is because it's against the law and it's wrong to break the law" (a Stage 4 argument). The teacher, too, can present higher levels of moral reasoning. For example, when a tenth-grade student says, "He should have let his child die, because it's wrong to break the law" (Stage 4), the teacher might ask, "What if the father took the drug to save his son's life and then later earned the money and paid the druggist back for what he took? Would it be alright then?" This would expose the students to Stage 5 thinking. Whether or not one likes the particular solution offered, the point is to expose students to the level of moral reasoning that approaches life's dilemmas with the attitude: "Is there a way we can solve this dilemma that meets everyone's legitimate rights and needs?"

Moral dilemma discussion topics need not be hypothetical cases. As you read this paragraph, parents in Africa or Eastern Europe may be stealing food from United Nations relief convoys to feed their starving children. Is that morally justifiable? History offers many moral dilemmas for discussion as well. Was it right for the North to pursue the Civil War in which millions of lives were lost in order to preserve the Union and free the slaves? Was it right for the United States to drop the atomic bomb on Hiroshima and Nagasaki?

Literature presents endless moral dilemmas. Was it right for the fox to trick the hare? Did the King come up with the fairest solution? Were the senators justified in killing Caesar? Is it ever right for subjects to kill their monarch? Was it right for Anna Karenina to leave her husband? Science and health has its share of moral dilemmas as well—allocation of health care resources, euthanasia, biomedical research, experimentation on animals, and legalization of marijuana, not to mention abortion.

The most fruitful subjects for moral dilemma discussions are those for which there are no easy answers. Such dilemmas are more likely to elicit a wide range of moral arguments at different reasoning levels. The important thing in leading such discussions is to realize that it is moral *reasoning* that is the major focus. It takes some practice, but after a while you will begin to distinguish the student's moral reasoning from her opinions and intellectual arguments. It is her *reasoning* you want to highlight in the discussion. "So you think it's always wrong to break the law, Jane. Why is it always wrong?" "Jim, are you saying you will do *anything* to be well liked? Would you do something you thought was wrong?" "If they knew how many lives would be lost in the Civil War ahead of time, would you still say it was right for them to have fought the war?" Questions like these cause the students to consider and to verbalize the moral foundations of their viewpoints. As students hear one another do this, their own moral reasoning gradually moves to higher levels of development.

One caution here. It is important not to overuse the moral dilemma discussion method, lest you convey the impression that all of life's moral choices are complex dilemmas. That is not so. In most instances in real life, the right thing to do should be apparent immediately. *Perhaps* there are some cases where stealing can be justified, but in almost all cases it is wrong—clearly wrong. *Perhaps* there are some cases where not telling the truth is excusable, but honesty *is* the best policy. Young people's first experiences with hypothetical moral dilemmas should present clear cases, so they can readily recognize or be helped to recognize the right and moral course of action. And even when they begin to contemplate moral dilemmas with less obvious answers, they should occasionally be given simpler dilemmas to consider, to reinforce the basic principles of right and wrong. The "What *should* you do?" approach of the hypothetical moral choice strategy (#29) is a good counterpoint to the complex moral dilemma discussion. Moral dilemma discussions are most effective in enhancing higher moral thinking when they are used as part of a comprehensive approach to moral education.

71

Clarifying Values Questions

Louis Raths and his colleagues developed the concept of the "clarifying question" as a means of helping people develop and implement values in their lives.[154] They believed that a fully-developed value meets seven criteria. These are the seven criteria, along with examples of clarifying questions that help a person move toward meeting those criteria:

CHOOSING

1. Values are chosen after *considering alternatives*. Clarifying questions help people consider alternatives viewpoints and courses of action.

   a. Have you considered any alternatives?
   b. How would you answer people who have a different opinion and say
   _____ ?
   c. If you couldn't do that, what would the next best choice be?

2. Values are chosen after *considering the consequences*. Clarifying questions help people consider the consequences of their ideas, decisions, and actions.

   a. What are the pros and cons of that approach?
   b. Do you think you'll feel the same way a year from now?
   c. How will doing that affect the other people in your life?

3. Values are freely chosen, which means they are chosen without undue authority pressure or peer pressure. Clarifying questions help people consider the sources of their choices and take responsibility for their choices.

   a. Is that what *you* want to do?
   b. How did you develop this belief?
   c. Do *you* believe this is the best choice?

PRIZING

4. We *prize and cherish* our values. Clarifying questions help people better understand what they prize and cherish.

a. How important is this to you?
b. What do you *really* want to happen?
c. Are you proud of how you are handling this?

5. We are willing and likely to *publicly affirm* our values in appropriate circumstances. Clarifying questions help people consider if they do and when they would affirm their values publicly.

a. Have you told anyone about this?
b. Would you be willing to let others know your viewpoint?
c. Would you write a letter-to-the-editor about it?

ACTING

6. People *act* on their values. Values show up in people's behavior. Clarifying questions help people consider what they are doing or might do about their beliefs, goals, and values.

a. Are you doing anything about it?
b. What might you do to achieve your goal?
c. What would the first step be?

7. People *act repeatedly* and with *consistent patterns* on their values. Clarifying questions help people examine their patterns of action and consider new ones.

a. How do you typically handle this issue in your life?
b. Would you like to do more of it?
c. Are you consistent in this?

Questions like these can be asked in classroom discussions, in private conversations, in brief exchanges at the classroom door or in the hallway, or in comments on student papers. However, these twenty-one examples only begin to suggest the hundreds of different ways a teacher or group leader can ask young people to think more deeply about their feelings, beliefs, goals, and values. It should also be noted that many of the activities in this chapter—for example, prioritizing or interview questions—are structured ways of asking clarifying questions.

The clarifying *values* question and the clarifying *moral* question (#28), when used together, make a powerful combination for enhancing values and morality in young people.

72

Hypothetical Values Choices: What Would You Do?

Politicians hate hypothetical choice questions. "What will you do if your income projections turn out to be too low?" "If you have to cut programs, which programs will you cut?" The voters would like to hear honest answers to those questions for the same reasons the politicians want to avoid them—because considering hypothetical choices reveals a great deal about a person's values and how they think about values and moral issues.

Anytime you ask students, "What would you do if ____?", you are creating a fruitful occasion for facilitating values and moral development.

- What would you do if a nice looking man you never saw before showed you this beautiful teddy bear and told you, if you got into his car, he would give it to you?
- What would you do if you found a wallet with money and identification in it on the street?
- What would you do if your friend failed to meet you at the mall as you had arranged?
- What would you do if someone directed a nasty racial or religious slur at you?

There are packaged curricula containing hypothetical choice situations,[23] but most teachers construct their own. For example, a ninth-grade health teacher gave her class this hypothetical situation to confront:

You like this boy. It's your fifth date. You were kissing pretty passionately on your last two dates. Now he says he wants to go further with you. You don't want to. He says there are other girls who would be glad to have sex with him and that, if you're not interested, he's going to stop dating you. He's been a great guy and you've had a lot of fun together. You enjoyed the kissing, but you really don't want to go any further right now. The thought of losing him makes you feel awful. What would you do?

Hypothetical choice questions typically generate a great deal of animated class discussions. The hypothetical can quickly become "real," as the students project themselves into the situation and evaluate it from all sides. Fortunately, the situation is not real, at least not now. In real situations, people often feel pressured or confused and forget to think carefully, or to think about the future, or to think about their moral and ethical beliefs. In real situations, people make mistakes, sometimes serious ones, and later wish they had a chance to relive the experience and make a wiser and better choice. Hypothetical choice questions give students the opportunity to think and learn in a safe setting, to develop criteria for wise and moral decision making which can then carry over into "real life" when the value choices and moral dilemmas come fast and unexpectedly.

An alternative to "What *would* you do?" is "What *should* you do?" This is a valuable and legitimate question as well. Called the "hypothetical *moral* choice," this strategy (#29) is discussed in Chapter 5 on Inculcating Values and Morality. The main goal of a hypothetical moral choice question is to be sure that each student *understands* what the correct answer is from a moral or safety standpoint. For example, the child above *should not* get in the car with that stranger under any circumstances. The wallet *should* be returned to its owner. The hypothetical moral choice strategy advances moral understanding, an important first step. The hypothetical values choice strategy moves to the level of moral commitment and challenges students to confront the many values and moral issues that go into their personal choices.

Hypothetical values choices and hypothetical moral choices need not be entirely hypothetical. Students can help you identify good value dilemmas and moral dilemmas in their own lives. You can pass out 3 x 5 index cards and ask them to write down, anonymously, one of their own value or moral dilemmas—perhaps a difficult decision they have faced or a situation where their personal values and their friends' values are in conflict. This will produce many realistic choice situations to serve as the content for discussion, role-playing, writing, and further exploration.

73

Self-Evaluation

One of the most effective ways of having students develop a sense of responsibility, honesty, pride in work, and other personal values is self-evaluation. It is no coincidence that the word *value* is embedded in e*valu*ation. If evaluation is the process of comparing something to a standard of value, then self-evaluation engages students in that task, requiring them to compare themselves and their work to some criteria or standard of value.

In any formal evaluation process, there are four steps. First, someone establishes a goal or objective to be achieved. Second, a method and criteria are established that can be used to measure the degree to which the goal or objective is achieved. Third, someone uses this method and criteria to measure the results of an actual performance. Fourth, someone places a value judgment on the performance that has just been measured, determining just how *good* a job it was or how *well* the objective was achieved. Typically, in schools, evaluation is performed by the teacher. The teacher determines the goal; the teacher decides how the performance will be tested; the teacher measures the performance, and the teacher places a value judgment on how well the student did.

In *self-evaluation*, the student assumes responsibility for the various steps in the evaluation process. The student establishes the goal to be evaluated, figures out how she will know when the goal has been achieved, and then, after a period of time, asks herself, "How well have I done in accomplishing a particular goal or meeting a particular criterion?" Part of that question ("How have I done?") requires an objective assessment. "I ran a mile in twelve minutes." "I turned in all but one of my assignments." The other part ("How *well* have I done?") requires a value judgment. "I'm pleased with my accomplishment; last year I couldn't run a mile at all." "I'm unhappy with my performance; I had set the goal of completing *all* my assignments."

As the following chart suggests, to the extent that the teacher controls the evaluation process in education in general and values education in particular, this is a way of inculcating values. To the extent that the students are engaged in self-evaluation, this is a way of facilitating values development. Therefore, a particular activity can employ a combination of inculcation and facilitation, with the teacher taking responsibility for some aspects of evaluation and the student in charge of other parts of the process (see Table 7-1).

For example, an elementary teacher uses the "mirror strategy" for self-evaluation. The Value-of-the-Month (#16) is honesty. So she has her students look into a mirror and ask themselves, "Was I honest today?" Then they write out and discuss their responses. To the extent that honesty was the teacher's goal or value, this was a method by which she attempted to inculcate that value in her pupils. To the extent she left it to them to determine the criteria for honesty (no doubt influenced by her other teaching on the subject) and how they felt about how honest they were, it was a facilitation activity.

Another teacher might have used the mirror strategy for self-evaluation differently. She might have given her students a list of values and asked them each to select a value that was important to them. Then she could say, "Now take out

TABLE 7-1   Teacher Evaluation or Self-Evaluation

	Inculcation	Facilitation
Who sets the goal or objective to be evaluated?	Teacher	Student
Who determines the method and criteria for assessment?	Teacher	Student
Who measures the extent to which the criteria were achieved?	Teacher	Student
Who places a value judgment on the performance?	Teacher	Student

your mirrors, and look at yourself long and hard, and ask yourself, 'How have I exhibited this value that I think is important, and how do I feel about how I have or have not exhibited this value?'" This example contains even more self-evaluation, because the student is involved in choosing both the goal and the criteria for evaluating it. (In fact, there are few pure cases, because the teacher is inculcating values by introducing the activity and the list of values in the first place.)

The point of this example is not to emphasize the mirror strategy, which is one of many methods, but to distinguish between teacher-centered and student-centered evaluation, between evaluation as a values inculcation and values facilitation activity. This section describes the use of self-evaluation as a tool for facilitating values development; however, many of the ideas here will work equally well when applied in the inculcating mode.

Self-evaluation is the flip side of goal setting. One of the previous methods, What Are Your Purposes? (#56), described how to encourage students to set their own goals and determine their purposes for the day, week, month, semester, or year ahead. Self-evaluation is the natural follow-up activity to help them determine how well they have achieved their goals.

1. *State the goal.*

It follows, then, that the first step in any self-evaluation is to state or re-state the goal or objectives to be evaluated.

- What was your goal for the day?
- Take out the list of goals you wrote at the beginning of the semester.
- I'm handing your lists of five goals we discussed when we began this unit last month. Remember, the first three goals on the list were ones that I set for you, and the fourth and fifth were ones you set for yourselves, based on what you wanted to accomplish or what you wanted to learn.

2. *Assess the level of accomplishment.*

Once students have recalled the goal or objectives, the next question to answer is: To what extent did I achieve it? Here the answers should be as objective as possible. Ask the students to give examples:

- What did you do that shows whether or not you accomplished your goal for the day? ("My goal was not to get in any fights, and I didn't! Johnny called me a name, and I almost decked him, but then I remembered my goal and counted to ten and told him to grow up and walked away.")
- When we started the unit, you said you wanted to learn what foods were good for you or bad for you. Did you learn that? Write down some of the things you learned about that. Write down what you still don't understand about it.

3. *Make a value judgment.*

Once students have determined the degree to which they have or have not achieved their goals, they should evaluate their degree of satisfaction or dissatisfaction. It is time to evaluate *how well* they have done. There are many different ways to do this. One way is to be very subjective about it.

- How do you feel about how you did?
- How well did you do?
- Are you proud of yourself?
- Do you think you did a good job?

Another way is to be both analytical and subjective, for example:

- Rank order the list of goals, putting the goal you think you accomplished the best on the top, the goal you accomplished next best second, and so on, with the goal you think you accomplished the least successfully on the bottom.
- On the list of goals, put a "D" next to those that were difficult to achieve, and an "E" next to those that were easy for you to achieve. Put an "H" next to any you wish you got more help on. Put a "P" next to any where you are proud of how you worked to achieve the goal.

Still another way to have students make a value judgment about their work is *self-grading*, where they are asked to assign themselves a letter or number grade and to justify that grade in writing or when meeting individually with the teacher. Some teachers give students opportunities to grade themselves on anything from specific assignments to the entire semester or year. Some teachers have students determine part of their grade, while they, the teacher, determine another part of the grade. Some teachers combine the student's self-grade and the teacher-assigned grade in some numerical proportion. For every teacher who has tried self-grading and continues to use it, you'll probably find more than one who tried it and abandoned it; nevertheless many do use this method, in some form, and report that it enhances learning goals in academics, values, and morality. Being trusted to participate in grading themselves provides students with a great opportunity for values and moral education, raising many issues about honesty, responsibility, trust, fairness, and pride in work.

4. *Set new goals.*

A final step in a process of self-evaluation, when it is fully used, is to recycle back to goal-setting. Once students have evaluated themselves—either on academic or values, character, or citizenship goals—they are then asked to set new goals for the future.

- What did you learn about achieving your goal for today that you can apply in setting a goal for tomorrow. (Have students pair up.) Each take a minute to discuss this with your partner, and then each of you write down a new goal for tomorrow.
- What did you learn from how you did on this unit that you can apply to the next one? List your new goals for the next three-week unit on electricity.
- Now that we've discussed how you personally did in the last game, both in performance and in sportsmanship, what are your goals for the next game?

As the examples above suggest, self-evaluation can involve anything from a two-minute discussion at the end of a period or school day, to a half-hour activity at the end of a unit, to an essay assignment and several hours of activities and discussions at the end of a semester. It can be used occasionally or as a routine part of classroom learning and extracurricular activities. With the many values and moral issues implicit and explicit in the process, self-evaluation gets to the heart of values and moral education.

SELF-EVALUATION WORKSHEET

Name _____   Date _____

1. What was your goal?

2. In what way(s) did you accomplish or not accomplish your goal?

3. How do you feel about how you did?

4. What new goal(s) will you set for yourself?

74

Study and Debate Controversial Issues

The daily newspaper and magazine periodicals are filled with the controversial issues of the day—health care, the economy, race, school choice, women and gays in the military, abortion, euthanasia, drug testing, guns and violence—the list goes on and on. History, too, is replete with controversy. Was Christopher Columbus a hero or a villain? Was Abraham Lincoln racist? Were Sacco and Vanzetti, the Rosenbergs, and Alger Hiss innocent or guilty? Was it necessary to drop the bombs on Hiroshima and Nagasaki? Who killed President Kennedy?

Studying and debating controversial issues like these is a fertile opportunity for developing and deepening one's own values and moral convictions.[167] It is an opportunity to develop critical thinking and citizenship skills, which are an important part of value education.[131,139] Studying controversial issues also contributes to academic learning goals—both by increasing students' interest in the subject matter and motivating a good deal of reading, writing, and speaking about the subject under consideration. Some publishers, like Greenhaven Press, have entire series of books and booklets presenting opposing viewpoints on controversial issues for other elementary through secondary levels.

Students can be directed to many sources for information about controversial issues, including:

- Newspapers
- Magazines
- Books and articles
- Television and radio
- Parents
- Community members
- You and other teachers
- Themselves

There are also many ways that students can present their reports, analyses, and viewpoints on the issues being studied:

- Classroom discussions
- Oral reports—as individuals or panelists
- Formal classroom debates
- Short writing assignments
- Sentence stems (#64)
- Essays and major papers
- Letters to the school or city newspaper

When dealing with controversy in the classroom, a number of issues inevitably arise:

1. *Depth of study.* Some teachers spend relatively short periods dealing with controversial issues. Others organize their entire curriculum or major units of study around controversial issues. For example, a science or health teacher might organize a unit of study around the controversy over fat and cholesterol: How important is it? Is concern over fat and cholesterol just a fad? How much fat should you have in your diet? How do the benefits of lowering cholesterol compare to the health benefits of exercise, proper weight, and not smoking? To take an intelligent position on these questions, it is necessary to know a good deal of biology, chemistry, research and statistical methods, and other information about human health. Thus, a whole unit of study could be built around the values question What should you do about fat and cholesterol?

2. *Age appropriateness.* The argument is sometimes made that elementary school children are not interested in controversial social issues, do not have the conceptual abilities to handle complex problems, might be upset by being faced with the harsher realities of life, and besides, the time would better be spent inculcating the values we *do* agree upon before introducing them to the controversies that adults cannot agree upon. While acknowledging some truth in all these arguments, this does not necessarily lead to the conclusion that young children should *never* be given the opportunity to learn about and debate difficult or controversial questions.

Children may not be interested in some social and historical controversies before they learn about them, but they may become interested *after* learning about them. (They are not interested in the seven major products of Argentina either; yet *those* are still taught.) They may not be able to handle a lot of complexity, but they can handle a little complexity, and that's a start. They certainly should not be exposed too early to *some* of the realities of life, but unfortunately, in many cases they already are and can use some help in making sense of it all. There are also some controversies that are intellectually challenging, but neither gruesome nor upsetting. And, finally, while it does make sense to use the earlier years primarily to inculcate the values of respect, responsibility, tolerance, and other guiding moral principles that are so important, this does not mean that we must wait until junior high or high school to teach and encourage students to think for themselves. Both efforts can take place simultaneously.

3. *Debate before or after.* Some teachers like to have their students study a controversial issue before taking a position on or debating it. Other teachers like to begin with a debate about an issue as a way of motivating students to get interested in studying the subject. Some like to have students choose and argue a position both before studying the topic and again after they have learned a good deal about it. Each of these approaches has its pros and cons, and each has worked successfully. The important thing is that studying and debating a controversial issue should lead to deeper understanding and reflection about that issue.

4. *Alternatives to strictly adversarial thinking.* There are ways to structure the study and debate of controversial issues that avoid polarization and "win-lose" thinking. As described in Idea #93, it is possible to have the two sides put their best thinking together and arrive at a *new* position which synthesizes the best arguments and solutions from both sides. It is possible, during the course of a debate, to have students understand and acknowledge the valid arguments on the other side, even when they disagree. These approaches to handling controversy not only foster continued critical thinking but teach the sort of civil dialogue and problem solving needed for any society to remain cohesive.

5. *Community sensitivity.* Common sense will lead you to know there are some subjects which are inappropriate for your students. For example, you would never have elementary students debate the pros and cons of abortion. Some people believe this subject is inappropriate for secondary students as well. On a number of controversial issues, thoughtful teachers will draw the line at different points. However, even when you are quite certain that a controversial issue and your approach to dealing with it is a valid addition to your curriculum, it still may be controversial in the community. You must simply use your good judgment here, consult with your principal, parents, or others, and make the best choice you can. When is it wiser to conform to community expectations to better accomplish one's other goals, and when does one take a principled stand and risk the consequences? That's a controversial issue itself. In fact, it might be a good one for your class to study and debate!

75

Class Rule Making

One way many teachers and schools teach character and civic values is by having students create rules for the classroom. This activity helps accomplish many objectives. Students develop a greater understanding and respect for rules and laws in human groups. They understand that rules and laws exist not just for their own sake, but to help achieve mutual respect, fair play, and other values society deems important. The classroom operates more smoothly, because the students have a stake in following and having others follow the rules. And the students feel more empowered, because they helped create the rules under which they will live.

This strategy is employed most often on the elementary school level, with its self-contained classrooms. While it would get rather tedious if every subject-area teacher on the secondary level tried to involve the students in setting classroom rules, this is a problem that is more theoretical than practical, since relatively few actually do it. Therefore, individual secondary teachers in all different subject areas have employed classroom rule making as a way of teaching mutual respect and running a smoother classroom. In other cases, secondary teachers have used class rule making to achieve particular curricular goals. Social studies teachers, for example, have used classroom rule making as a part of teaching about the legal system and how a democratic society determines its rules and laws.

Classroom rule making ideally should begin at the very start of the school year. You can introduce the concept by saying something to the effect of:

> As you know, every classroom has its rules. Usually the teacher sets all the rules. This year, I would like to involve *you* in helping to establish the rules for this classroom. I will still make some of the rules; for example, I would never allow anyone to do something that is unsafe to herself or someone else. But I think you are old enough now to make some of your own rules. First, let's begin by thinking about why we have rules in the first place. Does anyone have any ideas about why we have rules?

You then lead a discussion about rules and why they are necessary in a classroom or in any organization or society. You might list the major reasons for having rules on the board. If you have not done this activity before, you probably will be surprised at the insightful responses students will have, even at the primary level. Of course, every classroom has a few anarchists. If for no other reason than to get your goat, they will try to argue that rules are not necessary; but almost everyone, once they see that you are treating them with respect and trust, will take this responsibility quite seriously and be very thoughtful in their responses about the reasons for having rules. The students will do most of the teaching here; you will probably need only to supplement or clarify and elaborate on their ideas.

Having established the purposes for having classroom rules, you then invite them to suggest classroom rules which they think will help accomplish those purposes. In establishing specific rules, here are some guidelines which may be helpful:

1. *Use positive terms.* As explained in Idea #11, there are two important reasons for trying to state rules in positive terms. The first is that it is better to have students focused on visualizing the desired behavior than the negative behavior. Thus, "Raise your hand before speaking" is preferable to "Don't call out." The second reason is that positively stated rules often do a better job of elucidating a moral principle, while negatively stated rules tend to proscribe only individual behaviors. For example, a negative rule might say "No hitting is allowed," while in positive terms it might translate to "Treat others with respect."

2. *Limit the number of rules.* These are the rules you really want to hold the students accountable for keeping. If there are too many rules, students lose track of them, and it is harder for you to use them as teaching tools. Don't feel as though you need a rule for every possible situation or problem; you can deal with many of those as you would ordinarily.

3. *Add your own rules.* Involving the students in rule making does not mean abdicating your right or responsibility to set and enforce rules of your own (#11). While they learn more about values if they have participated in the rule making, you should also feel free to add one or more rules to the class's list and to explain its importance and meaning to you.

4. *Establish consequences for breaking the rules.* Whenever rules are established, the matter of consequences soon arises. Students are more likely to understand and respect their own rules if they are involved in establishing the consequences for breaking the rules. Surprisingly, the students can be unusually harsh in suggesting punishments or consequences for rule breaking. So, knowing the importance of establishing realistic consequences, you may have to use some persuasion or authority to influence the final determination of what consequences will be employed when rules are broken.

76

Class Meetings

The class meeting is based on the concept that the classroom is like a small community, a society in microcosm. Like any community, a class has goals to achieve, problems to resolve, opportunities to take advantage of, interpersonal conflicts to work out, and decisions to make. All of these issues and concerns can be handled in the context of a class meeting, creating an excellent opportunity for moral education and citizenship education.

Many different kinds of issues can be raised at class meetings. Here are some examples to suggest the wide variety of topics possible:

- The teacher is bothered at how often students are interrupting one another.
- Several students have complained that things have disappeared from their desks.
- One student thinks the class should raise money for famine relief in Africa.
- Some students are concerned about all the cliques forming in the classroom.
- The students who cleaned up the classroom last week are angry because it's messy again this week.
- White students and black students always sit separately in the classroom; the teacher is concerned.
- The class needs to decide what service project it will do for the school.
- The teacher would like some ideas for the next unit she is planning.
- A student thinks the teacher is being unfair in applying one of the class rules.
- Two students want to encourage the other students to attend the play they are in.
- One student has an idea for a class trip.
- Several students feel a new rule is needed.
- The teacher wants the class's feedback on the unit they just completed.
- The solution from a previous class meeting is not working. It needs to be re-examined.

As these examples illustrate, topics for class meetings can range from individual concerns which the whole group can help with to whole-group concerns. Topics may be initiated by single students, groups of students, or the teacher. Topics may be brief and informational in nature or may require lengthy discussions and problem solving.

Class meetings may be called just that—"class meeting"—or go under the names of "circle time," "weekly meeting," "problem solving," "morning meeting," "shared decision making," or other suitable phrases. Many teachers hold class meetings on a regularly scheduled basis. Those who have made the class meeting an important part of their program have generally held weekly class meetings. They can be done on a biweekly or monthly basis as well. Aside from regularly scheduled meetings, class meetings can be called by the teacher on an ad hoc basis. Students who feel the need can request a special class meeting, which the teacher considers and schedules as she deems appropriate. Class meetings typically are ten to thirty minutes long, depending on students' age, interest, and the nature of the problems being discussed.

Some teachers like to chair class meetings themselves. Others prefer a "rotating chair," in which students take turns running the meeting and gaining leadership experience.

Some teachers have students submit ideas for class meeting agenda topics beforehand. Others allow and encourage students to raise issues at the time of the meeting. One teacher has a large manilla envelope taped to her wall, with the words "Next Class Meeting" on the envelope. This allows students who might be too shy to initiate a class meeting topic publicly to safely identify a problem or make a suggestion to be discussed at the next class meeting.

Thomas Lickona has identified six valuable purposes the class meeting can fulfill:

1. Deepen students' sense of shared ownership of the classroom.
2. Improve students' moral reasoning, including their ability to take the perspective of others.
3. Develop their listening skills and ability to express themselves in a group.
4. Develop their self-worth by providing a forum in which their thoughts are valued.
5. Help create a moral community that serves as a "support structure"—calling forth students' best moral selves and hold in place the qualities of good character that students are developing.
6. Teach the skills and attitudes needed to participate effectively in democratic decision making.[121]

Source: Reprinted by permission of the publisher from Benninga, J. S., *Moral, Character and Civic Education in the Elementary School*. New York: Teacher College Press. © 1991 by Teachers College, Columbia University. All rights reserved.P. 80.

Given the variety of worthy outcomes, the class meeting is a particularly valuable strategy in a program of comprehensive values education.

The following section on Community Meetings (#77) contains many ideas and examples that apply to class meetings as well.

77

Community Meetings

When Lawrence Kohlberg and his colleagues at Harvard University were studying moral development, they found that having students engage in discussions of hypothetical moral dilemmas (#70) was helpful, but such hypothetical discussions needed to be supplemented by experiences working on *real* moral dilemmas in real life situations. They developed the idea of the "just community" as a place where students could learn the values of fairness and justice as they solved the everyday problems and conflicts that arise in the life of their school community.[146] Others have viewed the "community meeting" as a forum for teaching students important skills and attitudes for democratic citizenship.

The community meeting is very much like the class meeting, described above (#76), but on a broader scale. It is an occasion for an entire grade, or several grades, or the entire school to come together to discuss issues, solve problems, and make decisions as a community. Modeled on the traditional New England town meeting, most community meetings give every student, teacher, and administrator the opportunity to speak, and decisions are made on a one-person-one-vote basis.

Community meetings have been employed successfully on all levels. High schools such as in Brookline, Massachusetts and Rochester, New York's School Without Walls hold community meetings once a week. The Heath School, a K–8 public school in Brookline has weekly "Family Meetings" for grades 1–3 and "Community Meetings" for grades 4–5, occasional community meetings for grade 6, and weekly class meetings for grades 7–8.[164] This example illustrates that there is no one correct pattern. Each school needs to find its own best approach to community meetings, based on the size of the school, the overall values education or citizenship education program it employs, and many other factors.

The teachers and administrators must be clear about what problems and issues they are willing to allow the community meeting to make decisions on. The principal of Heath School began by having her students write down beforehand the problems they wished to discuss at the Community Meeting, and then she brought a list of appropriate topics to the meeting—for example, saving seats in the lunchroom, breaking into the lunch line, monopolizing playground space, dirty bathrooms, not enough soap in the bathrooms, or no safe place to lock their bicycles. Other teachers and administrators are comfortable having students and teachers raise issues right at the meeting and use that as an opportunity to show students how to set an agenda, keep to time limits, refer some issues to committees, and table other issues. At "School Without Walls," topics at "Decision Making" (their name for the community meeting) have included: planning school social activities, what to do about racism in the community, hiring teachers, how to influence national government policy, and planting a school garden.

When schools begin to use community meetings, the principal or teachers usually lead the meetings. This approach enables them to demonstrate and model effective leadership practices and to teach students how to facilitate broad-based participation, encourage respect for divergent or minority viewpoints, and achieve fair decisions and solutions to problems. At Heath School, for example, the principal helped the students establish four criteria for decisions:

- Is it fair?
- Is it consistent?
- Is it safe?
- Is it necessary?

Once students have learned the pattern for working effectively in the community meeting format, they can be given responsibility for chairing the meeting on a regular or periodic basis.

It is important to remember that a community meeting is just that—a meeting of the *community*. Since we are referring to the school community here, this includes students, teachers, administrators, and where possible, aides, custodians, and others. (It is hard to get the latter groups to attend, but some schools have thought it important enough that they have succeeded, at least some of the time.) This also implies that everyone has a voice. Giving some decisions to the community does not mean having the adults relinquish all their influence. Teachers and administrators can and usually are influential voices at community meetings. Yet, at the same time, the adults often need to hold back, knowing that they have such influence, and allow the students to work through the difficult issues and choices themselves—so they can learn how to do it and because they will feel more responsible for carrying out the community's decision if they feel it really was their decision. *Participating without dominating* is a fine but extremely important line for the adults to walk.

Nor does democracy at the community meeting mean an abdication of adult responsibility. A principal might have to say, "That's a very creative solution. Unfortunately, it's against the law. Try again." A teacher might say, "We (the teachers) can go along with this decision, as long as it is understood that you (the students) will take responsibility for carrying it out. If we see that you are not holding up your end of the bargain, then we will have to take over the responsibility and that means doing it *our* way. Is that understood and agreed to?" Or: "I think we're on the right track here, but the suggestion on the floor would pose a safety problem. We can't have that. Is there a way to do this and still have it be safe?" The principal at School Without Walls has veto power over the decisions at community meeting, although he very rarely uses it.

Decisions reached at community meetings are not always predictable. That is the nature of democracy. They certainly are not always the decisions the adults would have reached by themselves. Sometimes they are better and sometimes they are worse. They are often better, because now the students have a stake in making the solution work—it was, after all, *their* idea. Even when the community makes a poor decision or reaches a solution which does not solve the problem, this can be a valuable learning experience, especially when the problem is re-introduced to the community, the reasons for the faulty solution are analyzed, and a new decision is reached.

The six outcomes listed for class meetings (#76) apply equally well to community meetings. They add up to the community meeting being an extremely powerful vehicle for values education and citizenship education.

78

Meaningful Student Government

Most schools, particularly secondary schools, have some form of student government. Traditionally, the student government has a representative from each class or homeroom, four officers elected either by the representatives or the student body directly, and authority over a limited number of issues, such as school social functions and fundraising activities to support these functions. There are often *two* levels of student government—the student council representatives and officers for *the whole school* and the representatives and officers for *each class*.

For the relatively few students who get to participate actively in student government, it can be a fine experience in citizenship education and leadership skills. However, for most students, even many of the class representatives, student government is typically not a meaningful experience; although it's nice to have the credit next to their name in the school yearbook. Too often, most students' memories of student government consist of being asked to buy tickets to dances, buying brownies at bake sales, and being exhorted to have more school spirit.

Yet, for all its shortcomings, student government is one of the first experiences students have with representative democracy, and it has far more potential than is generally realized. With the goals of values education in mind, here are ways that some schools have found to make student government a more meaningful experience:

1. *More decisions to make.* Give the student government more decisions to make or to participate in making. Some schools have students participate, and in many cases vote, on committees involved with staff hiring, school policy, curriculum, and discipline. Other schools empower student government (or the senior class government) to determine aspects of graduation exercises, to operate a student court which handles certain discipline cases, to develop the program for a number of student assemblies, and to work on solving real problems which the school or the students are facing.

2. *More money to spend.* Give the student government more money to spend. Budget lines may be earmarked for certain purposes, but within those parameters, students are free to decide how to spend the funds. Being able to hire guest speakers themselves, purchase artwork for the school, or contribute to local charities on behalf of the student body, for example, involves very meaningful decisions and considerable learning about responsibility and values.

3. *More issues to consider.* The previous two ideas usually come from student advisors or the administration. This idea and the next one can be initiated by the students themselves, although it often takes a sympathetic advisor or teacher to encourage the students to get started. Many student governments are taking an interest in a wider variety of social issues. They gather information about smoking, alcohol, and illegal drugs or about human sexuality, abstinence, and safer sex, and they disseminate this information by making announcements, setting up literature tables, sponsoring assemblies, or holding after-school groups. They sponsor debates on controversial issues. They organize counseling help or support groups for students with drinking problems, studying problems, family problems, and other common concerns.

4. *More action to take.* Student governments have developed campaigns to fight drug abuse or racism in their schools, to clean up pollution in their local communities, to influence state and national government policies, to boycott the products of a company whose values they oppose, to raise money for famine relief, to turn an empty lot into a children's playground, and to help renovate an old hotel for temporary housing for the homeless. More ideas along these lines are discussed in the sections on Community Service (#21) and Social Action (#80).

5. *More students to involve.* Involve more students in the process. Even traditional student governments have tried to do this, usually by having lots of committees—for the dances, car washes, and the yearbook, for example. With the greater variety of issues and activities for student government described above, there will be the opportunity and the need to involve even more students, extending the benefits of participation to a wider number.

6. *More emphasis on elections.* If all the previous ideas for making student government more meaningful are implemented, the elections for student government representatives and officers will inevitably become more important events. This creates still another fine opportunity for values education and citizenship education, as candidates put more time and thought into their speeches and campaigns, real issues are debated during the campaign period, and more students think about and vote in the election.

7. *Leadership training.* Once students are elected to office, give them the leadership training that will help them to function effectively. Because good leadership training helps students gain self-knowledge, responsibility, and many skills in the areas of goal-setting, decision making, communication, and conflict resolution, this is an excellent opportunity for values education. The Division of Student Activities of the National Association of Secondary School Principals publishes a monthly magazine for high school student leaders, which is an excellent resource on student leadership, student government, extracurricular activities, and values education.[44]

79

Simulated Government Experiences

A number of the previous ideas—the class meeting (#76), community meeting (#77), and meaningful student government (#78)—all involve students in experiencing real democracy within the classroom or school setting. Occasions like these, where students get to practice democracy in structured settings, where teachers and advisors can help students learn the skills and attitudes for democratic participation, are among the most important experiences they can have in moral education and citizenship education.

There are other opportunities for students to learn democracy, values, and morality through *simulated* experiences in government. Unlike the previous examples, where the students' deliberations and decisions actually influence what happens next, where they get to implement the decisions they make, simulated government experiences are pretend situations. They are role-playing opportunities in which students enact very real situations and learn a great deal from the experience; but they do not actually implement their decisions. It is "practicing" democracy in a different but very valuable way.

There are a number of kinds of simulated experiences which the schools can facilitate, both within and beyond the school walls.

1. *Classroom simulations in government.* Students take on the various roles that would be found in different governmental settings, such as:

- Legislative debates
- Mock court trials
- Congressional hearings
- Arbitration sessions
- City council and other public meetings
- Scientific panels
- United Nations Security Council debates
- Cabinet meetings

A good deal of reading, writing, and research can be required as the students prepare to assume these roles. Such experiences are valuable from an academic learning standpoint. By presenting and exploring values and moral issues in these forums, the goals of values education are served as well.

2. *Municipal government for a day.* Students are assigned roles in local government—members of the city council or village board, mayor or supervisor, judges, school board members, police chief, and other roles. For one day, they go out into the community—to the council chambers, courthouse, and the police station—and take on the roles of the public officials. Typically this event is coordinated by the school social studies department or an individual teacher. Some schools have developed quite elaborate programs, involving sixty or more students in various municipal government roles. The students prepare for their day of governing by learning about local government and interviewing or shadowing the local official they will be playing. On the day they take over the "mock government" of the municipality, they are given problems and challenges to work on such as those faced by the actual officials. Thus, the town council debates and votes on a number of policy issues and decisions, the judges decide mock cases, the police officers plan ways to reduce crime and drug abuse, etc. Results and highlights are shared among the participants, with other students, and often in the local newspaper.

3. *Boys State/Girls State.* For decades, the American Legion has sponsored and operated an excellent experience in democratic government for older high school students. Every summer, in each of the fifty states, representatives of schools from across the state come together for a week of educational and recreational activities. Typically, each dormitory of students becomes a "city," elects its mayor, develops a platform on a number of current issues, and sends representatives to the "state convention." On the state level, candidates for governor and lieutenant governor are nominated, state platforms are ironed out, and much campaigning, compromising, and political horse-trading takes place as candidates and their supporters seek to put their platform across and win office. The week culminates in "statewide" elections and acceptance speeches by the victorious candidates. Newspapers around the state, the *real* state, often report the results of the Boys State and Girls State campaigns and platforms, as an indication of what the youth leaders of the state are thinking. For the hundreds of thousands of young people who have participated in this experience over the years, it has been a powerful lesson not only in the mechanics of democracy, government, and parliamentary procedure, but in living side by side and working with students of all different races, religions, and backgrounds from around their state, and developing many positive values.

Beyond these three examples of simulated government experiences which the school organizes or supports, a related, *nonsimulated* experience in self-government should be mentioned.

4. *Youth organizations.* There are numerous youth organizations—Boy Scouts/Girl Scouts, the YMCA/YWCA, 4-H, religious youth groups, and many others—that provide excellent opportunities for young people to govern their own affairs and learn civic, moral, and personal values. Each has a different approach as to how it structures participatory decision making; but almost all of them provide some opportunities for learning and practicing democratic participation and leadership.[58] They also provide other opportunities for the inculcation and modeling of positive values. With the schools being asked to address so many of society's needs and given limited resources to do it, these other youth organizations perform an invaluable service to the nation in the area of values education and moral education.

Never doubt that a small group of thoughtful, committed citizens can change the world. Indeed, it is the only thing that ever has.

MARGARET MEAD

80

Social Action

The several preceding activities help students develop values and learn citizenship skills by making rules, holding meetings, and participating in simulated and limited experiences in self-government. The strategy of social action goes one step further, teaching students to affirm their values and *take action* to create a better world. In so doing, again, they affirm the moral value of helping others and accumulate greater knowledge and skills to become better citizens.

Social action projects typically go a step further than most of the community service projects, described earlier (#21). While charity or community service tends to alleviate particular symptoms of problems or help in individual cases, social action projects try to *solve* a persistent problem in the community or the world. For example, helping some homeless persons get off the streets is an example of charity or community service. Working to eliminate homelessness in the community is an example of social action. *Both are necessary*, and both are worthy activities for values education and moral education. Because there is often a fine line between social action and community service, examples of both are included in this section. Categorizing the activity is less important than engaging students in efforts to improve their world.

Students at all age levels have become involved in social action projects. Examples include:

- Fighting crime by establishing neighborhood watches, working with the police to report drug dealers, and working for a local gun control initiative to reduce teen killings.
- Cleaning up the environment by working for state legislation, planting trees, exposing a local polluter, and raising funds to purchase nature preserves.
- Improving neighborhoods by lobbying local government for better services, getting a traffic light installed at a dangerous corner, and starting a neighborhood beautification campaign.
- Joining national social action efforts for various causes by participating in a boycott, raising money for a national organization, or joining a protest activity.

- Developing interracial harmony, raising money for world famine relief, encouraging a local company to hire more minorities, boycotting a store that sells pornography, opposing censorship, saving energy, working with Amnesty International in writing letters to political prisoners around the globe, and a hundred other ways students have become engaged in improving their world.

Making participation optional and getting parental consent may be needed in some cases. Considerable preparation is also required before engaging in social action. Many academic learning goals as well as values education goals are furthered as students learn to:

- Research the subject.
- Conduct public opinion surveys.
- Understand how the government works.
- Write petitions and resolutions.
- Write letters to editors and legislators.
- Organize and conduct public meetings.
- Conduct peaceful, respectful protests.
- Lobby public officials.
- Work with committees and mailing lists.
- Set up new organizations.

While elementary classes generally engage in less controversial forms of social action, such as planting trees and beautifying the community, this is not always the case. Fourth- through sixth-grade students in the Jackson Elementary School in Salt Lake City, Utah conducted a successful public advocacy campaign to clean up a hazardous waste site three blocks from their school.[117] When fourth-graders visit the mayor's office, with a legitimate concern and the possibility of making the evening news, they get serious attention.

To help students learn the value of and the skills for "sticking their necks out," The Giraffe Project (120 Second Street, Box 759, Langley, Whidbey Island, WA 98260. Phone: 800-344-8255) has developed numerous ideas and publishes a newsletter for teachers at all levels who wish to involve their students in civic improvement and social change projects.

Compassionate humans and concerned citizens often have the impulse to say, "Somebody should do something about that problem." Social action teaches students to say, "*We've* got to do something about that problem." If we want students to feel empowered, to believe they can achieve their values in life, both for themselves and their community and world, then teaching them the attitudes and skills of social action can play an important part.

Activism pays the rent on being alive and being here on the planet . . . If I weren't active politically, I would feel as if I were sitting back eating at the banquet without washing the dishes or preparing the food. It wouldn't feel right.

AUTHOR ALICE WALKER

81

Letter-to-Editor or Public Official

Short of a full-scale social action project (#80), having students write letters-to-the-editor or to public officials is a good way to get them to clarify and affirm their values, to demonstrate caring and concern for their community and world, and to learn more about the democratic process.

Some teachers make writing such a letter a required assignment; others present it as one option among a number of alternative assignments. Sometimes the letters will all be on a particular issue or topic on which the class is focusing; other times the letters can be on any topics the students choose. Depending on the situation, letters can be written to editors of school, local, statewide, or national newspapers or magazines and to local, state, or national government officials.

In all cases, students should be encouraged to express *their own* beliefs, feelings, and suggestions in their letters. This is an opportunity for them to clarify and develop their own thoughts and values and then to act on those beliefs and values by affirming them publicly. The learning is extended by giving students the chance to read or share their letters with one another in class and to discuss the issues further. Before the letters are actually sent, they should be edited and corrected for writing style, spelling, grammar, and punctuation—another case where academic learning and values education go hand-in-hand.

As students' letters are published in the newspapers and they receive replies from the government officials, the newspaper clippings and written replies can be posted on the bulletin board for everyone to see and discuss further.

> *To kids everywhere.*
> *May you be both seen and heard.*
> BARBARA LEWIS, DEDICATION TO
> The Kids Guide to Social Action[117]

82

Election Analysis and Debate

At least every two years, and often every year, there is an election in your community. Whether the races are for local government positions, the U.S. Congress (every two years), state office, or the presidency, candidates are stumping for votes, making speeches, advertising, distributing position papers, and otherwise laying claim to public office and the public trust. These election periods provide an excellent opportunity to further the goals of values education and citizenship education.

This activity is more suited for secondary level students whose cognitive and research skills are more developed; although there are examples of elementary teachers who have used this approach also. The whole class can focus upon one race, or subgroups in the class can look at different races. In either case, there are four steps to the process.

1. *Identify the candidates' positions.* The students read and listen to as many of the candidates' statements as they can find. They list, without evaluation, the candidates' positions on the various issues, and they indicate what issues the candidates have identified as the most important issues in the campaign. Included in this step is noting the key statements the candidates make about their own qualifications for office and the statements they make about the other candidates' lack of qualification for office.

2. *Evaluate the accuracy of their assertions.* Next the students try to determine the accuracy of the candidates' statements, where facts are concerned, and the cogency of the candidates arguments, where reasoning is or should be concerned. In other words, are the candidates telling the truth and are their arguments logical and persuasive?

To complete these first two steps of the process, the students must put aside their own, emerging political views and biases and try to play the role of an objective, investigative reporter. This is an excellent opportunity for the students to learn a good deal about the many issues involved in the campaign and to learn and practice critical thinking skills. The next step gets them involved more personally in making value judgments and defending those judgments.

3. *Take a position.* Once the students have studied and evaluated the candidates' positions, they are asked to decide who they think is the better or best candidate. In addition to their analysis of the candidates' positions and assertions, the students' *own beliefs and values* are now relevant. They can state and explain their choice of best candidate in writing, or small group or whole class discussion, or a combination of these. But, in the end, each student should have her *own position* on the best candidate, because in a democracy, it is individuals and not committees who pull the lever in the voting booth. In writing or verbally, each student will state her preferred candidate and the reasoning behind that choice.

The next step is optional. Depending on the amount of time you wish to devote to this activity, it can stop with the students' presenting their reasoned positions, or it can continue with them arguing and defending their positions as described below:

4. *Promote and defend their position.* In small group discussion, whole class discussion, or a more formal debate, students are then asked to try to convince others of their positions and/or to defend their own positions. You may even give them the opportunity to "campaign" for their candidate or position beyond the classroom. In promoting and defending their positions, students go further in defining and asserting their own beliefs and values, learning from others, and learning how to debate civilly and respectfully with people with opposing views.

I represent the mainstream views and the mainstream values. And they are your values, and my values, and the values of the vast majority of the American people. If I win this election, it will be . . . a confirmation of your belief in these traditional American values.

GEORGE BUSH, 1988

Pass along the values that we learned as children, and that's how we insure the state of the union.

GEORGE BUSH, 1990

We are motivated first and foremost by values.

GEORGE BUSH, 1992
State of the Union address

[We stand for] restoring the basic American values that built this country and will always make it great: personal responsibility, individual liberty, tolerance, faith, family and hard work.

DEMOCRATIC PARTY PLATFORM, 1992

83

Peer Counseling

Peer counseling programs teach young people the skills to encourage healthy development among their fellow students and to reach out and help one another with personal problems and concerns. Such programs foster the values of caring and compassion, teach students the skills to act on those values, and produce a great deal of personal values realization among the participants.* Other names for this approach are "peer helpers," "peer facilitators," "student friends," or local variations, such as the "Madison High Friends."

Some peer counseling programs train students in helping skills and then set them loose as peer counselors at large, keeping an eye out for students who seem isolated or in trouble, reaching out to them, and befriending and supporting them in ways that are appropriate to the situation. Other programs teach counseling and friendship skills to the helpers and then pair them with younger students as tutors or "big brother/big sisters" (#20). Still other peer programs teach students to become group "facilitators" who, in structured situations, work with other

---

*This section could just as easily have been included in Chapter 8 on Skills for Values Development and Moral Literacy. However, because of the great deal of personal growth and values realization experienced by the student helpers in these programs, the method is included in this chapter on facilitative approaches.

classes or groups of younger students, helping them develop more positive self-esteem, healthy attitudes about drugs, skills to resist peer pressure, and other useful learnings. Some programs use a combination of approaches.

Peer counseling can be organized as a special after-school program or as an elective course, often with a psychology credit, for a limited number of secondary students.[83,132] However, other teachers have taken the basic elements of the peer helping concept and involved their entire class, on the elementary as well as secondary level, in learning the skills of empathy and helping. When offered as an after-school or elective program, peer counseling programs almost always share the following five characteristics. (When done in a regular classroom, the program would not involve a selection process, but would incorporate the other four aspects.)

1. *Selection.* Students volunteer to participate. They are screened on: their sincere desire to participate; their willingness to commit themselves to the training sessions and the duration of the program; their recognition of the serious responsibility they are taking on; and the indications they give, or have given in the past, that they can be trusted with this responsibility.

2. *Training.* The teacher, school counselor, or other leader conducts a series of training sessions (ten is a typical number) to teach students the attitudes, skills, and knowledge they will need to be peer counselors. This training usually includes some combination of: typical problems of children and adolescents; recognizing signs of trouble; skills for listening, communicating, helping, and supporting; and knowledge of other helping resources in the school and community.

3. *Peer Helping Opportunities.* These can be cross-age teaching situations, discussion groups, or other structured occasions that the leader helps organize, *or* these can be spontaneous, one-on-one interactions which the peer helpers initiate when they see the need or opportunity. Sometimes peer helpers work in teams, sometimes as individuals.

4. *On-Going Support.* The peer counselors are not simply trained and then left to fend for themselves. Regular meetings are held throughout the program so students can report on how they are doing, get encouragement and ideas from their peers and adult advisor, and receive further training as needed. Peer counselors can often use personal support and self-esteem enhancement themselves, which are provided in both the initial training and the on-going support meetings.

5. *Assessment.* The program should have a distinct end-point. At this time, the students have the opportunity to assess what they learned from the experience, and the adults supervising gather whatever information they need to assess how successful the program was and how in the future it might be improved, expanded, modified, or discontinued. While the activity may be formally coming to an end, hopefully the students will continue to use the lessons they gained from the experience for the rest of their lives.

84

Board of Directors Strategy

This strategy has students examine some of the inculcating and modeling influences in their lives, to better appreciate what those influences have to offer, and to think about how they could develop more mature ways of relating to the inculcators and role models in their lives. It encourages them to appreciate the inculcation and modeling they have received, and to recognize that they are more than the sum of those influences—that ultimately their choices are their own.

Because this activity involves an extended metaphor, it is better suited to older students than younger ones. Elementary teachers have made it work for them by using the same basic metaphor, but simplifying the questions, asking only one question at a time, shortening the time periods, and guiding the discussion more actively.

Begin by asking students to use a whole sheet of paper and to draw the following diagram (Fig. 7-1) in the top half of the page.

FIGURE 7-1.   Your Board of Directors

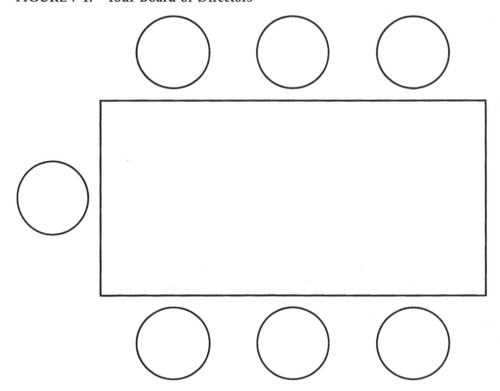

Explain to them the concept of a corporate board of directors—how when a corporation has important choices to make, it calls its board of directors together around a table, and each director contributes her ideas and suggestions, and this helps the corporation make its best decisions. Continue in the following vein:

"In a way, each person is like a corporation with a board of directors. This diagram represents *your* board of directors. Whenever you have an important or difficult decision to make in life, you call together your board of directors. The board consists of all those people who have strongly influenced how you think about life's issues, problems, and decisions. For example *(give an example of your own)*, when I have important or hard choices to make in life, I often hear the voices of my _____ and my friend _____ and my college teacher _____ , all sort of whispering in my ear and telling me what I should do or what they would do in that situation. So I'm going to write their names or initials next to the circles on my diagram here to indicate that these people often sit on *my* board of directors.

"I'd like you to do the same. See if you can think of four or five or six people who sit on *your* board of directors, whose voices you often hear in the back of your head, whose advice or example comes through to you when you are thinking about what to do. When you think of them, put their initials or name next to one of the circles on these two long sides of your boardroom table. . . Keep in mind, you may be glad these people are on your board and welcome their words of wisdom, or you may wish they weren't on your board. But put them down anyway. You may even have someone on your board who is dead, or whom you never met but just read or heard about; but if you carry them around in your mind and you hear from them when life gets difficult or you have important choices to make, then put their names down on your board of directors.

"Now, you see that the one circle at the head of the table here is still blank. This position is reserved for the chairman or chairwoman of the board. That's *you*; you can write your initials next to that circle. You may not always feel like you are in charge of your board of directors; but as you get older, you become increasingly in control. Now I would like to ask you some questions about your board."

Write one, several, or all of these questions on the chalk board or post them on the wall:

1. Who sits on your board of directors?
2. What are one or two things that each member of your board knows about, where you would be wise to listen to their ideas? (Or: In what way(s) are you glad they are on your board? Or: What are their qualifications for being on your board?)
3. Which board members do you hope will always serve on your board of directors? Why?
4. Is there one thing you could suggest to each member of your board that would help him or her be a more effective, better board member?
5. Do you feel you are in control of your board of directors, or are they as a whole, or some of them in control of you? When will you be in charge?

What advice would you give yourself for how you could convince some of your board that you deserve to have more control?

6. Is there anyone else you would like to ask to join your board of directors?

Have students get into small groups—threes or fours, and give each student a fixed amount of time as the focus person (such as two minutes each) to talk about their board of directors and the answers to your questions. Adjust the size of groups or the time limits to fit the students' ages and the number of questions you ask them to consider. Remind them they should feel free to share as much or as little about their board of directors as they wish to.

(Optional) To extend the metaphor and the activity further, you could continue, "You will notice that there is room at the end of the table, opposite the chairperson, left for additional seats. These seats can be occupied by *consultants* to the board. When the board has a particular subject it needs advice and counsel on, it calls in specialists on that subject. Perhaps you have special consultants to *your* board, people other than regular board members who fill these seats when a particular sort of problem is the issue. For example, if you had a problem or decision related to *school* to resolve, are there any other voices you would hear whispering in your ear or you would call upon to help you? Write their initials down at the end of the table. Or if you had a problem or decision related to *dating or sex*, what consultants would or should appear at your board table?" Other examples you could use would be problems or decisions related to drugs, food, clothing, work, family, religion, friendship, or any other values or moral issue you might want the students to consider. Again, allow time for students to discuss their responses in small groups or as a class.

Conclude the activity by having students do "I Learned Statements" (#65), or have them share any ideas they had about how they could work more effectively with their board of directors.

> *Parents can only give good advice or put [their children] on the right paths, but the final forming of a person's character lies in their own hands.*
>
> ANNE FRANK,
> The Diary of a Young Girl

85

I Should

Like the previous idea, this activity invites students to examine some of the inculcation they have been exposed to and to recognize and affirm much of its validity. It helps students morally mature, as they begin to move from unconscious reflection of the inculcators' values and morals to choosing the values and moral guidelines as their own.

Begin by writing the following sentence stem on the chalk board:

I should _____ .

Then ask the students to work alone and complete the sentence with the first words that come to mind. Then ask them to complete the sentence four more times, if they can, just as they did the first time, with whatever words come to mind about how they should be, or what they should do, or what they should not do in life.

When students have individually completed their five statements, develop a class list of "I should" statements by either: (1) having students come to the board and write out one of their sentences, (2) having students read one of their sentences aloud, while you or a student writes it on the board, (3) having the students write out one of their statements anonymously on a separate piece of paper (this elicits some "shoulds" they would be reluctant to say aloud), collecting them, and then writing them on the board, or (4) collecting all five of their statements anonymously, taking the papers home, making a master list (along with a tally of how many students wrote the same "I should"), and distributing copies of the list to them the next day.

Then ask the students the following questions:

1. Which of the "shoulds" on your list and on the class list do you agree with, and which do you disagree with? (They can use the letters SA, AS, NS, DS, SD to indicate for each statement whether they: Strongly Agree, Agree Somewhat, are Not Sure, Disagree Somewhat, or Strongly Disagree. (Numbers +2, +1, 0, −1, −2 can also be used for this purpose.)
2. Whether you agree with it or not, which do you understand, which don't you understand, and which would you like someone to explain to you?
3. Which are the three "I should" statements you agree with the most strongly? Why?

Students should then be given the chance to discuss their answers in small groups and/or as a whole class. In the process, they will be affirming some important values and moral precepts that may have been inculcated to them but they have not yet adopted as their own. You may be surprised to hear how traditional many of the students sound as they explain and justify the importance of some of the "shoulds" they have grown up with. The important thing is that now they are choosing these shoulds as their own, which moves their "I should" statement closer to an "I choose to" or an "I want to" or an "I will" statement.

They may also, at least for the moment, reject the validity of some "I should" statements they have grown up with. In some cases the "shoulds" were inaccurate or frivolous to begin with, such as "I should never wear the same outfit two days in a row" or "I should never say someone *died*; I should say they *passed away*." In other cases, the inculcation may be very wise, but the student is not ready to recognize its validity. That's alright. They are not done growing up. If the inculcation is valid, they will have many more opportunities to recognize and affirm it themselves. Students don't all love poetry the first time we teach it either. Yet we give them another chance and another. We should give them many chances to affirm values and morality as well, and not be discouraged if they don't all jump aboard right away.

This activity can also be used to explore a particular values or moral issue, for example, honesty, friends, money, health, or male-female roles. In that case, you would ask the students to complete the "I should _____" sentence stem in relation to the specific topic. A variation for eliciting their responses, after they have written them down individually, is to have them mill about the classroom, shaking hands and introducing themselves to one another by saying their name and one of their completed sentences. For example, using the male-female roles issue, they would shake each other's hand and say, "I'm Tony and I shouldn't cry." "Hi, I'm Jeannine, and I should take small, lady-like steps." "I'm Jeff and I should support my wife." "I'm Sue and I should be anything I want to be." Doing the activity this way is a provocative and often funny approach to begin exploring serious issues of values and morality.

Chapter *8*

Skills for Value Development and Moral Literacy

86

Critical Thinking

Many of the facilitation activities in Chapter 7 give students the *opportunity* to think for themselves. It is also important, regularly, as young people mature, to teach them the *skills* to think for themselves. Critical thinking skills enable people to make better life decisions and to be more successful in their work, thereby coming closer to realizing their own personal values. Critical thinking skills also enable people to resist undue peer or authoritarian pressure, which sometimes leads people to act immorally.

"Critical thinking" has been defined and described differently by many authors.[39,57,155] Ennis defines it as "reasonable, reflective thinking that is focused on deciding what to believe or do."[40] He lists the important "dispositions" of critical thinking:

- Seek a clear statement of the thesis or question.
- Seek reasons.
- Try to be well informed.
- Use credible sources and mention them.
- Take into account the total situation.
- Try to remain relevant to the main point.
- Keep in mind the original or basic concern.
- Look for alternatives.
- Be open-minded.
- Take (or change) a position when the evidence warrants it.
- Seek as much precision as the subject permits.

- Deal in an orderly manner with the parts of a complex whole.
- Be sensitive to the feelings, levels of knowledge, and degree of sophistication of others.
- Use one's critical thinking abilities.

Others view critical thinking as:

- Thinking on many levels—from simple memorization to organizing, analyzing, generating, integrating, and evaluating.[128]
- The ability to solve problems, using a structured, sequential approach that includes:
  - gathering information,
  - generating alternatives,
  - evaluating consequences,
  - analyzing the pros and cons,
  - choosing, and
  - evaluating the results.
- The ability to think for oneself.
- The ability to analyze arguments, which includes such processes as:
  - distinguishing fact from opinion,
  - recognizing logical fallacies,
  - recognizing propaganda techniques, and
  - analyzing stereotypical thinking .

Clearly one could build an entire curriculum around critical thinking skills, and many teachers employ packaged programs in this area.[39,63,128,138,166] However, there are also many individual activities that foster critical thinking which have proved useful at both the elementary and secondary level. Here are a few, brief examples:

1. *Teach basic logic.* Most dogs are pets; are most pets dogs? Socrates is a man; all men are mortal; therefore, is Socrates mortal? Jane and William love each other; Patty and William love each other; therefore, do Jane and Patty love each other? Is it warmer in the summer or the country?

2. *Encourage thinking on many levels.* Use classroom discussion, questions, assignments, and test questions that require students to organize, analyze, synthesize, and evaluate, as well as memorize.[166]

3. *Bring in newspaper opinion columns.* Have students identify what the columnist is "for" and "against"—what positions, people, beliefs, or values the columnist favors or disagrees with. What support does she offer for her position? Are the arguments logical and cogent?

4. *Have students watch television advertisements* at home, or tape record advertisements and bring them to class for everyone to see. Analyze the advertisements. What information do they give about the products? What are their claims? Are they supported by evidence? What advertising and propaganda techniques are being used to influence the consumer? Do these techniques work? Why or why not? Are the students influenced by these ads? (When they say no, ask them what brand of jeans they are wearing.)

5. *Analyze stereotypes.* List some common stereotypes—such as "women drivers." Describe and ask students to describe examples that don't fit the stereotype. Ask for examples of people from other groups who exhibit the same characteristics as the stereotyped group (such as bad male drivers). Distinguish between generalizations and stereotypes. Ask students why stereotypes are harmful, and give your own thoughts about it. Discuss how generalizations might be accurate or inaccurate and helpful or harmful depending how they are used.

6. *Teach propaganda techniques.* Teach them propaganda methods—for example, repetition, scapegoating, national chauvinism, and crisis creation.[147] Have students go out and find examples of these techniques in the world around them.

7. *Use Socratic questions.* Mortimer Adler and his colleagues advocate the use of Socratic questioning and the "seminar approach" to help students deepen their understanding of important ideas, values, and issues found in readings, art works, and scientific experiments.[2] This approach furthers students's thinking skills as well as their cognitive understanding of the subject under discussion.

8. *Study and debate controversial issues.* A separate section (#74) is devoted to this approach.

87

Creative Thinking

The ability to think creatively helps us find better solutions and alternatives to life's many problems and decisions and, thereby, to better achieve our goals and values. Similarly, creative-thinking ability helps us be more constructive members of the groups and organizations we are part of, helping the group to achieve *its* goals and values in new and better ways.

Many programs and approaches have been developed to teach creative-thinking skills in the classroom.[29,71,75,140,172,173] Of the scores of activities that have been developed, some of the most popular ones mentioned in the literature include:

1. *Brainstorming.* This is possibly the most widely-used and easiest-to-teach creativity technique. For practice, ask students to think of: all the things one could do with an unsharpened pencil; as many ways as possible to decorate, beautify, and make the school more visually interesting and different; all the things a car could be used for other than driving it, or any similar topic. Then explain to them and post the rules of brainstorming:

    a. *Quantity.* Think of as many ideas as possible.

    b. *Record all ideas.* No matter how silly or outrageous.

c. *Don't evaluate.* Don't judge your own or others' ideas; that can come later.

d. *Piggyback.* Build on someone else's idea, free associate.

Guide students through the activity. Write all their ideas on the board, using a few key words. For example, if someone says you can use a pencil "to make a bridge so ants could use it to cross a puddle," you write "Ant bridge" and ask for more ideas. Get lots of ideas, so the students realize the extent of their individual and collective creativity.

Once students have learned the basic skill of brainstorming, use it frequently throughout the year. For example, they might brainstorm all the possible: places to go on a class trip; topics to write a paper about; ways the country would be different if the British won The Revolutionary War; environmental problems that need solutions; things they would like to learn about a particular subject; ways they use math in their lives; and things the school might do to reduce alcohol abuse, to name a few.

2. *Morphological grid.* This strategy shows how creative thinking can involve a combination of analysis, brainstorming, and synthesis to solve a problem. First state a problem. For example, you want to build a better car. First you get the class to list all, or many of, the *attributes* of a car—such as length, passenger capacity, shape, materials, and fuel required. Select four, five, or six attributes to work with and, for each, have the students brainstorm several alternatives for that attribute. The result is a chart like the one below. Then ask them, individually, to choose an example of each attribute and combine them to design a new prototype, for example, a 15-foot long car, for a single passenger, shaped like a cone, with metal ribs and a fabric cover, and fueled by gasoline.

Length	*Capacity*	*Shape*	*Materials*	*Fuel*
10-feet long	One passenger	Conventional	Metal	Gas
15-feet long	Two passenger	Bullet	Plastic	Ethanol
25-feet long	Four passenger	Pencil	Wood	Electric
50-feet long	Six passenger	Cone	Fabric	Nuclear
	Ten passenger	Airplane	Comb.	Wood

Point out to them that many personal, scientific, and social problems can be solved by this method. Again, use it periodically in class to work on other real-life problems or subject matter topics that may arise.

3. *The sense of wonder.* Creative thinking is closely associated with curiosity, wonder, and asking questions. Encourage students to wonder and to ask questions. Do it informally. Respond to their curiosity with pleasure and respect. Structure activities to encourage the sense of wonder. For example, after giving a lecture, or showing a film, or doing a unit, or finishing an activity, write "I wonder _____" on the board, and ask each student to complete the sentence by sharing something she is curious about or wonders about the subject just presented.

4. *Imagining outcomes.* People's creativity is often stifled because they get stuck on short-run details and initial obstacles. Asking people to leap ahead in their imaginations often sets people free to use their creative-thinking capacity. When presenting a problem—for example, better race relations in school—say, "Let's use our imaginations to go beyond the current problem and picture what it would be like in a school where the different groups got along with one another. Forget about the present for a minute; just imagine that ideal future outcome. What would it look like? Can you picture it in your mind? What kinds of images to do you see? Ok, let's give each of you a turn to say one thing that has come to your mind about what a school with tolerance and good will among the races would be like. I'm going to write down your ideas on the board. Alright, who'll begin? What do you see?" Visualizing outcomes is a form of creative thinking, which unleashes a great deal of positive energy and even more creativity as the group then moves on to figuring out how to achieve the imagined outcome.

5. *Free association.* Somewhat akin to brainstorming, but not necessarily in the service of solving a particular problem, free association helps teach students *to trust their own inner thinking process.* Write a word on the board—BASEBALL, FUNERAL, EXPLORING, BEAUTIFUL, FAMILY—almost anything. Ask them to write the word on the top of their paper. Assure them that no one will see what they are about to write; then ask them to write down the first word that comes to mind when they think of "baseball," or whatever word you chose. Then ask them to think of the first word that comes to mind when they think of the word they just wrote and then the first word that comes to mind when they think of *that* word. Explain that this process is called "free association" and that the ability to free associate is an important creative-thinking skill. Tell them they will now have 60 seconds to continue free associating and write down as many words as they can think of that the previous word calls to mind. When the 60 seconds are up, ask the students how it felt, what mental barriers they experienced to freely associating, and how they tried or succeeded in overcoming those barriers.

> *Any activity becomes creative when the doer cares about doing it right, or better.*
> JOHN UPDIKE

88

Communicating Clearly

Good skills for communicating one's ideas and feelings to others are important for both goals of values education. Realizing one's values in life and being a positive contributor to society are both enhanced by the ability to communicate clearly. People with these skills are more likely to get what they want from life and more likely to contribute in group situations.

There are many different skills for communicating clearly. Three sets of skills most frequently taught sets of skills are:

1. *Speaking Skills.* These are skills such as clear pronunciation, eye contact, completing one's sentences, and choosing appropriate language, skills which are necessary to communicate effectively in most settings.

2. *Presentation Skills.* These are the skills for addressing groups and audiences. They include the speaking skills above, as well as additional skills for organizing one's remarks and delivering them to larger audiences.

3. *I-Messages.* This is the term coined by Thomas Gordon[70] for communicating one's feelings to others. An I-Message has three parts; it describes a specific behavior, your feelings about the behavior, and the reason for your feelings. For example: "I feel angry when you arrive 30 minutes after we agreed to meet, because it's important to me to be able to trust you about our agreements." Compared to a "You-Message," which labels and blames the other person ("You are completely unreliable"), I-Messages are more likely to produce successful, non-defensive communication.

These and other skills for communicating clearly to others are taught by a combination of *explanation, demonstration, practice,* and *feedback.* Communication skill training can take place in almost any classroom (through direct instruction, participation in class discussions and activities, presentations in small groups, and speeches to the whole class), student clubs and activities, speech lessons, and elective courses devoted to communication skills.

89

Listening

Empathy—understanding the thoughts, feelings, and experiences of another—is one of the major prerequisites for compassion and morality. Good listening is the most useful means of achieving and demonstrating empathy. Listening also helps a person learn what others think and feel, which is valuable knowledge that enhances one's wisdom and life decisions. Thus, listening skills are important in achieving both goals of values education—better personal decisions and moral outcomes.

Listening skills can be taught as a series of increasingly complex behaviors, such as:

- *Facing the other person.*
- *Non-verbal indications* of listening—eye contact, head nodding, smiling at the appropriate time, etc.
- *Simple guttural or verbal acknowledgements* of listening—"Mmmn," "Uh-huh," "Yup," "Right," "No kidding!" etc.
- *Restating* the speaker's words. Speaker: "When I hear this new argument, it makes me wonder." Listener: "When you hear this new argument, it makes you wonder."
- *Paraphrasing* the speaker's words. Speaker: "When I hear this new argument, it makes me wonder." Listener: "This new argument leaves you wondering."
- *"Active listening"* or *"empathic listening"*—reflecting the speaker's feelings and meanings. Speaker: "When I hear this new argument, it makes me wonder." Listener: "It sounds like you're not feeling so sure of your previous position and are maybe re-evaluating what you think about this issue?" (The tone is tentative, as though asking, "Did I understand you correctly?")

As with speaking skills, entire programs and courses have been developed at all grade levels to teach students listening skills.[22,70] But many teachers find ways to work these skills into their normal teaching. For example, a teacher might say:

> "I'm concerned that people are cutting one another off and not listening well to each other. I'd like to take part of this class to focus on being better listeners. We'll begin by getting into groups of three... In each group, one of you will be the Speaker, one the Listener, and one the Observer. Speaker, you will have one minute to tell the Listener about the most interesting trip you've ever taken. Try to make the Listener understand how special and interesting it was to you. Listener, during that minute, I want you to do your best *not to listen*—to show boredom and disinterest. Observer, I want you to watch them both and to note as many specific behaviors of the Speaker and Listener as you can. Okay, GO... Alright, the minute is up. Now what happened? Observer, what did you see? Speaker, how did you feel? Listener, what were you doing?
>
> Okay, I don't want to leave the Speaker feeling frustrated. Let's try it again. Speaker, take a deep breath, and give the Listener another try and tell your story again. But this time, Listener, I want you to do everything you possibly can to demonstrate *good listening*. Observer, watch what the Listener does. Ready, BEGIN... Time! Alright, what were the Listeners doing this time? Observers, describe what you saw and let's write all the examples of good listening behaviors you saw up on the board here. Speakers, how did it feel to be listened to well?"

A simple exercise like this one is very enjoyable and goes a long way toward teaching some of the most basic listening skills. A similar approach can be used for the next skill levels, having students take turns as speaker, listener, and observer, practicing the more complex forms of listening, which you first explain and demonstrate for them.

Another simple technique to teach good listening is one developed many years ago by Carl Rogers.[106] If you sense students are not listening well to one another in a discussion, or you just want to reinforce good listening skills, institute this rule:

> "For the next part of the discussion, before you make your own point, you must restate or summarize the previous speaker's viewpoint to her satisfaction. If you cannot, then she will say what she said again, and then you can restate or summarize her comments, and if she feels understood, then you can give your own thoughts on the subject."

90

Assertiveness

It is one thing for people to know what they value and have clear beliefs about right and wrong and quite another thing for them to act consistently on those values and moral standards in difficult interpersonal situations. Too often, people remain *nonassertive*, thereby not realizing their own goals or not standing up for their moral beliefs. Or they become *aggressive*, affirming their own values while trampling on the rights and feelings of others. The alternative is to be *assertive*, which is to stand up and act upon one's values and morals, while still respecting the rights and feelings of others in the situation.[55,113]

Values education and moral education is less than comprehensive if it does not help young people learn the skills associated with asserting themselves in situations where their goals, values, and moral and ethical standards are at issue.

Wise and effective assertiveness includes knowing how to:

- *Choose your battles.* Know when it is important to assert yourself and when it is wiser or kinder not to.
- *Find the right time.* Choose the best time and place to be assertive. This is usually right away, in the actual situation; but sometimes it is more appropriate to wait for a time when the other person will be able to listen more carefully or be less defensive.
- *Use nonverbal communication.* Maintain direct eye contact and confident body position and posture. Gestures and facial expressions can also be helpful.
- *Use your voice.* Use an appropriate tone, inflection, and volume.
- *State your position.* Frame the problem in a way that makes the other person sympathetic and not unduly defensive.

- *Propose a solution.* Have a satisfactory, realistic solution in mind and propose it at the right time.
- *Demonstrate respect and reason.* Listen, show understanding, acknowledge valid arguments, and modify your position if warranted.
- *Repeat your position.*   Restate and repeat your position, again and again, if needed.
- *Go to next.*   Have alternative strategies if you do not get satisfaction in the first encounter.

Teaching assertive behavior involves a combination of:

1. *Explanation.* Explain what assertiveness is; the elements of assertive behavior (above); the difference between assertiveness, nonassertiveness, and aggressiveness; and why assertiveness is important. Give examples to illustrate your points.

2. *Demonstration.* Show the class some examples of nonassertive, assertive, and aggressive behavior. Use situations such as these:

> You ordered a school jacket with your name on it and paid for it in advance. When you go to pick it up, the jacket is not quite the one you ordered. You want them to reorder the one you wanted. The manager says he can't, because your name is already sewed on the jacket.
>
> You see one of your classmates picking on a younger student. You don't think it's right. You don't think your classmate will physically harm you, but you know he won't welcome any interference.
>
> Your mother buys clothes for you that you don't like. Your mother thinks the clothes are really neat. You don't want to hurt her feelings, but you don't want this situation to keep happening.

Have a student play the foil (the store clerk, the bully, the parent), while you play the main protagonist and demonstrate how nonassertive, then aggressive, then assertive behavior would look in that situation.

3. *Practice.*

   a. Present a hypothetical situation, such as one of those above, where assertiveness is needed to achieve one's goal or to do the right thing.
   b. Ask students to think to themselves how they would ideally act in this situation (see #29, What Should You Do?).
   c. Divide the class into trios. In each trio, Person A will be the protagonist, the one with the problem; Person B will be the foil, and Person C will be the observer. At your signal, Person A will begin acting out the situation with Person B, trying to act assertively and consistently with her values. When they have finished, Person C should comment, within the trios, which behaviors of Person A they thought were assertive, nonassertive, or aggressive and whether they thought Person A succeeded in realizing his or her values in the situation.

d. Ask for volunteers who were pleased with their assertive behavior, and conduct one or more demonstrations in front of the whole class. If students are not getting the idea, demonstrate some alternative responses for them again, modeling positive assertive behavior yourself in that same situation.

e. Give students another situation, and have them change roles (A becomes B, B becomes C, C becomes A) and practice the skills again.

91

Resisting Peer Pressure

The ability to resist peer pressure is one particular application of assertiveness skills, discussed previously (#90). However, because it is one of the most popular methods in the values education field, particularly as applied to drug abuse prevention, it is described here as a separate strategy for comprehensive values education.

We generally think of peer pressure as a uniformly negative force, responsible for encouraging young people to use popular slang, spend a fortune on designer jeans, refuse to wear hats in the winter, conform to current tastes and fads, and on a more sinister level, join gangs, take drugs, and engage in premature sexual behavior. Unfortunately, all this is often true. However, peer pressure may also encourage young people to do something that would be good for themselves or others, such as join the Scouts, go out for a school activity, or go to college.

Teaching students to resist peer pressure, then, does not mean teaching them to disregard the potentially good advice and example of their peers, but *to think for themselves, to reflect on their actions, to consult authorities and sources other than their peers,* and *to stand up for their own values, morals, and ethical beliefs*. This description of what it means to resist peer pressure provides four useful filters for young people to apply in situations where peer influence is strong. They would ask themselves:

- Are these *my own* thoughts and opinions and justifications I am using, or am I merely repeating and parroting what my friends are saying?
- Have I taken enough time to reflect on what I am about to do—something which my friend(s) would like me to do, or should I think about it and the possible consequence some more before acting?
- What would my parents, teachers, religion, the law, or other respected sources and models say or think about this?
- Is what my friend or peer group advocating truly consistent with my own values, morals, and beliefs about what is right and wrong?

The three steps of explanation, demonstration, and practice used in assertiveness training apply equally well to teaching students to resist peer pressure.

1. *Explanation.* Engage students in a discussion about what peer pressure is. The discussion might include any or all of these questions: When have they experienced peer pressure? What do they like or not like about being pressured to do something? Can they think of any examples of when they submitted to peer pressure; how did it work out? What might they have done differently? Why is it sometimes hard to go against the group's direction? Show students the four questions above. Are these good questions to ask themselves? How might they change or modify them? Make the point that there are three ideal outcomes of a negative peer pressure situation. They may not be able to achieve the third outcome, but it is always in their power to achieve the first and second. The three outcomes are:

   a. Don't engage in the undesirable behavior.
   b. Maintain your self-respect.
   c. Maintain good will with the group or the person pressuring you (if you still want to preserve the relationship).

Discuss the practical aspects of resisting peer pressure. Assuming you want to say "no," how do you do it effectively? You might point out the eight methods the DARE Program teaches:

- Say "No thanks."
- Give an excuse.
- Be a broken record—no thanks, no thanks.
- Walk away.
- Change the subject.
- Avoid the situation.
- Give the cold shoulder.
- There is strength in numbers—hang with safe friends.[49]

2. *Demonstration.* Set up a hypothetical situation in which peer pressure exists. (See the examples that follow.) Ask for volunteers to act out the chosen situation. One student is assigned the role of resisting the peer group's pressure. After the role-play is finished, ask the class what they liked about how the key player tried to resist the pressure. Ask what other steps she might have taken. You might also ask for one or two more volunteers to play the scene again, demonstrating how *they* would resist the peer pressure.

3. *Practice.* Divide the class into groups of five. Give them a hypothetical situation in which peer pressure exists. For example:

- Your friends and you are hanging around outside a candy counter. One friend says he bets you are too chicken to steal a candy bar. The others join in and agree, making fun of you for being a wimp. What do you do?

- You and your friends are leaving the lunch line looking for a table in the cafeteria. One of them spots an unpopular kid sitting by herself and says, "Let's go sit next to her and give her a hard time." The others begin heading toward that table. What do you do?
- Your health education class is discussing teenage sexual practices. Three of the students express an opinion which goes against your own moral beliefs. You suspect that your views will be regarded as stupid and old-fashioned. What do you do?
- You are at a party. A group of kids you would like to know better invites you to join them and begins handing around a marijuana cigarette. What do you do?
- You are alone with your boyfriend. He is pressuring you to have sex with him. He tells you "If you really loved me, you would trust me on this." He tells you lots of your friends are doing it. You fear that if you don't have sex with him you will lose him, and your other friends will think you are silly and immature. What do you do? (This situation is one of the greatest concerns of teenage girls. The inability to handle this dilemma is one of the main reasons for premature sexual behavior.)
- You are a freshman at college and are pledging for a college fraternity or sorority. You really want to get in. Your pledge class is told to paint the fraternity/sorority's Greek letters, 10-feet high, on the huge rock boulders on the lovely parkway adjoining the campus. The other pledges begin making plans for buying the spray paint, and getting the ladder and flashlights. What do you do?

One student is assigned the role of protagonist, one the observer, and the other three are the peer group. Each quintet then acts out the situation, with the protagonist attempting to achieve the ideal outcome, which is to not engage in the undesirable behavior, maintain self-respect, and maintain good will if possible. After the role-play, have the quintets discuss whether the ideal outcome was achieved, and what other alternatives might have been available to achieve a better outcome. Finally, conduct at least one more practice/demonstration round in front of the whole class to be sure the students understand the key concepts and skills related to resisting peer pressure.

4. *Follow-up application.* To extend this activity, ask students to spend the next week observing themselves and their friends and see when and how peer pressure actually occurs in their lives. Then, back in class, ask volunteers to share some real-life examples of peer pressure, and have the class discuss how the situations were handled or might have been handled. Again, you can have the students role-play the different situations.

92

Cooperation and Cooperative Learning

The ability to work cooperatively with others contributes directly to the goals of the four major movements in the field of values education.

Values Realization. Young people must learn to work with others in order to achieve their values and get what they want out of life. The skills they learn in cooperative work groups will serve them well throughout their lives—in future employment, education settings, family, social groups, community organizations, and every other group in which they choose to participate. Unless they choose to be hermits, cooperative skills and attitudes will enhance their relationships, productivity, and satisfaction in all these settings.

Character Education. Some of the most frequent character virtues, which educators today identify as "target values" are: respect, responsibility, tolerance or acceptance of diversity, perseverance, and pride in work. In cooperative learning groups, students learn to respect one another and understand that every person has a useful contribution to make. They learn to take responsibility for their part of the group's task; the group cannot succeed unless they fulfill their responsibility. They learn to work with and appreciate people of different races, religions, classes, abilities and disabilities. And when cooperative learning is effective, the students take pride in their group's successful completion of its task, teaching and reinforcing the values of self-discipline and pride in work. Loyalty and helpfulness are two other character virtues that cooperative learning fosters. In addition, cooperativeness is a valuable character trait in its own right.

Citizenship Education. It is essential in a democracy that citizens be able to work together effectively. Cooperative learning groups teach students to share, to take turns, to listen to one another, to include and value the different contributions which each member has to make—in short, to work cooperatively. Students learn to care not only for their own success but for the common good, an essential democratic value.

Moral Education. The training students receive to work in cooperative groups is moral training. Cooperative learning teaches students to be less egocentric and to respect the rights of others. The ability to listen, to be empathic, and to take another's role contributes to moral thinking and behavior. Understanding and practicing fairness in allocating work assignments, sharing materials, and taking credit for completed work is also a part of moral education.

Cooperation can be taught as a separate skill-building "unit," independent of other curriculum goals. Better yet, cooperation can be integrated into the daily fabric and structure of the classroom, playing a central role in academic learning activities, class meetings and discussions, and just about all aspects of the classroom. The latter approach is called "cooperative learning." Extensive research indicates that cooperative learning not only teaches cooperation skills, but also enhances student self-esteem, attitudes of respect toward others, and academic achievement.[92]

Cooperative learning uses small groups in which students work together on academic learning and other tasks. Teacher lectures, workbooks, individualized instruction, and other learning modes are also used, but the small group is the key to cooperative learning. David and Roger Johnson, leading practitioners and researchers in this area, describe five criteria for effective cooperative learning in the classroom:

1. *Positive interdependence.* Students must perceive that their own success and the success of their group are inextricably connected. "All for one and one for all," "Sink or swim together," and "United we stand/Divided we fall" are slogans that convey this attitude. Positive interdependence is created by structuring learning tasks so that each student's participation is essential to the group's success and by making grades dependent, at least in part, on the whole group's performance.

2. *Face-to-face interaction.* Learning tasks are structured so that students have to communicate directly with one another—talking, listening, explaining, disagreeing, figuring out how they will solve the problem, and working together.

3. *Individual accountability.* Each student is held accountable for learning the material. Working toward a group goal or product does not absolve each member from mastering the task as well.

4. *Interpersonal and small group skills.* Students do not know automatically how to work cooperatively in small groups. They must be taught the skills, given the opportunity to practice them, and then get to use the skills on a regular basis throughout the year(s).

5. *Processing.* Students are given the opportunity to analyze and discuss how well their small groups are functioning, how they are utilizing the cooperation skills they have learned, and how they can enhance their working relationships in their group.[91,94]

There are many ways to actually structure cooperative group tasks. Students can work with a partner, in small groups, or as a whole class working together. Each group can work independently, and/or there can be competition among the groups. Students can be tested and graded individually, and/or grades can be related to group performance.

While there are many ways to assign group tasks, the "jigsaw" method is one of the most popular.[177] The metaphor is that of a jigsaw puzzle in which each student has a different piece; therefore, each student has something essential to contribute for the group to complete the puzzle. Translated to an academic learning situation, the jigsaw method works in the following way:

- Divide the class into small groups. In each group, the following takes place:
- Give each student in the group some of the materials or information needed to complete the task. Or assign each student the job of researching or learning part of the information or one of the skills necessary to complete the task, master the subject, or solve the problem. Or let the students in each group decide which part of the task will be assigned to each member.

- Students then work individually, learning or mastering their part of the task or project or problem.
- (If different groups are working on comparable tasks, students with a particular assignment in one group join with their counterparts from the other groups to share their learnings with one another.)
- Students come together in their original small groups to share their information or skills with their group members, to teach each other what they have learned, in effect, to put their separate pieces of the puzzle together.
- The group demonstrates its learnings—by giving an oral presentation, handing in its group product, taking a written test, or some combination of these or other ways of showing what the students have learned.

Many other examples of cooperative learning are used throughout this book. This is one of the most important, versatile, and useful tools of values education.

93

Conflict Resolution

In the animal kingdom, physical dominance and submission are the primary methods of conflict resolution. As conflicts of all sorts around the world illustrate, human beings are still very much a part of that kingdom. If we wish to have a world based on nobler values than self-serving power and on higher moral principles than "Might makes right," then teaching people to resolve conflicts in constructive ways is essential.

Conflicts begin early—in sibling rivalries at home; disputes over the bigger portion of pie; fights over which preschooler gets to play with which toy; and myriad other conflicts when children get to school—from shoving for a better place on line, to arguing about who gets to use the only black crayon, to serious interracial tensions, to physical violence and even murder over trivial incidents or perceived insults.

As intergroup tensions, violence, and crime have escalated in schools and society, an increasing number of educators have recognized the importance of teaching conflict resolution in schools.[47,93] Roderick reported in 1987 that, in one of New York City's community school districts, over seventy-five elementary teachers and their thousands of students were implementing a Model Peace Education Program, and in Chicago, all sixty-seven public high schools included a six-week unit on dispute resolution in their social studies classes.[158] Teaching students to resolve conflicts in constructive ways includes teaching them to pursue their goals and values without disregarding the rights of others, to treat others with respect, and to settle disputes fairly and justly—all essential objectives of a comprehensive values education program.

> *If civilization is to survive, we must cultivate the science of human relationships—
> the ability of all peoples, of all kinds, to live together, in the same world at peace.*
>
> FRANKLIN D. ROOSEVELT
>
> *We are fighting in Vietnam to prove that violence is not an acceptable means of
> settling our differences.*
>
> LYNDON B. JOHNSON

Many different approaches to teaching conflict resolution in schools have been developed. These include:

Preventative Approaches

1. *A cooperative classroom environment.* One way to teach students how to avoid unnecessary conflict is to establish a classroom norm of cooperation and to regularly utilize cooperative learning structures and methods (#92).

2. *Understanding and appreciating differences/multicultural learning.* Another way to reduce conflict and encourage harmony is to help students understand and appreciate others who may be different from them because of race, culture, physical traits and handicaps, or other individual differences. This can be done by teaching students about the contributions of different groups to the country's history; reading fiction and nonfiction about different cultures and ethnic groups[96,157]; helping students see that cultural diversity is a national strength; and teaching them to recognize and oppose stereotypes in thought, words, and action.

3. *Managing anger.* This is a valuable intrapersonal and interpersonal skill that helps students avoid and reduce conflict in their lives. There are many techniques for taking "time-out," deep breathing, self-talk, and reducing stress, which students can be taught to help them manage their strong feelings productively.[74,79,126]

Skill Approaches

4. *Conflict resolution skills.* Whether these skills are described as "conflict resolution," "win/win problem-solving," "negotiating," "fighting fair,"[169a] or other terms, the idea is to teach students how to resolve conflicts in a constructive manner, a manner in which: (a) both sides' needs are met to a satisfactory degree, and (b) both sides feel the relationship was enhanced and trust was built in the process of working through the conflict. Teaching conflict resolution skills can be simple, as in asking two students in conflict "to come up with one story of what happened."[122] Or it can involve teaching students a multistep conflict resolution or negotiating process, which includes:

- *Defining the conflict.* What are the real issues and concerns?
- *Stating positions and reasons.* Each side states its position on the conflict and its reasons for holding that position. Using "I-messages" (#88) is a helpful skill for this stage of negotiating.

- *Listening.* Each side listens to the other side and restates the other side's position so that both sides feel understood. There may be a number of rounds of this, until both sides feel that their positions and viewpoints have been understood (not necessarily agreed to) by the other side.
- *Finding solutions.* Both sides try to think of solutions to the conflict that meet the goals of both sides. Listing the goals a good outcome would achieve, brainstorming, and creative problem solving are often helpful methods at this stage. The most promising solution is selected.
- *Appreciating.* This is sometimes hard, but it is very helpful to take a minute or two for each side to say something they appreciated about the other side and about how the negotiation just went. It helps repair or enhance the relationship.
- *Renegotiating.* The first solution may not work out. It is often necessary to meet again, analyze what went wrong, renegotiate or recommit to the solution, and try, try again.

5. *Mediation skills and peer mediators.* Sometimes conflict resolution and negotiating skills are not enough, and those in conflict need the help of a third party—a mediator. Knowing when to ask for mediation can be considered a conflict resolution skill in itself. Mediation skills involve helping the parties in conflict to work through the negotiating process just described. Many teachers teach mediation skills right along with negotiating skills.

Many schools also set up "peer mediation" programs. Roderick estimated that over 300 schools around the country had established some kind of student mediation program.[158] Student volunteers (often called peer mediators, conflict managers, peace patrol, or other names) are selected and trained to help reduce interpersonal and intergroup tensions. This may be an informal role where they look for conflict situations in the school and use their skills to try to help reduce the conflict. Or it may be a more structured program in which all students know that, when they are in conflict situations, they can request the help of a peer mediator to help them resolve the problem. Most of the ideas and suggestions associated with selecting and training peer counselors or peer helpers (#83) are applicable to peer mediation programs as well.

Academic Approaches

6. *Using academic controversies.* This approach teaches students to discuss, debate, and constructively resolve controversial issues where they do not have a personal stake. For example: select an academic issue with two opposing positions on that issue; divide students into groups of four; assign two members one side and assign the other two members the other side of the issue; have each pair study and advocate its side to the other pair; have the pairs reverse roles and try to argue the *opposite* side; then have the four of them work together, and try to come up with their own group position that integrates the best and wisest information and viewpoints from both sides.[94]

236   *Chapter 8*

7. *"Peace education" curricula.* In a lesson, unit, or course of study, students learn about peace and peace-making.[61,192] This might include the history of peace-making, famous historical figures who were peace-makers, peace-makers today, the role of law and international law in maintaining peace, literature and poetry about peace, pen pals and cultural exchange programs with students and schools in foreign countries, and other content related to international understanding, peace, and peace-making. Peace education curricula often also include some of the negotiating and conflict resolution skills previously described.

CALVIN AND HOBBES copyright 1986 Watterson. Distributed by UNIVERSAL PRESS SYNDICATE. Reprinted by permission. All rights reserved.

94

Academic Skills and Knowledge

High school drop-outs are three times more likely to be unemployed than high school graduates. This suggests one reason why teaching academic skills and knowledge makes a contribution to values education; if your students can't get a job, they are not going to realize many of their values in life, and they are not likely to be contributing members of society.

Beyond the economic benefits of an education, academic skills, and knowledge can help a person live a richer, fuller life. History, literature, writing, music, art, foreign language—to be skilled and knowledgeable in these areas gives one so many more options for finding enjoyment, meaning, and value in life. They are keys to life-long learning and fulfillment.

How to be an effective teacher of history, language arts, foreign language, and other subjects is, of course, beyond the scope of this work. But it is still important to make it very clear that developing skills, knowledge, and cultural literacy *is* a part of values education and moral education. If there are any suggestions for the type of academic teaching that would be most conducive to values education, they would include:

1. Distinguish between important skills and knowledge and trivial skills and knowledge. Try to teach what is important.
2. When possible, try to show the connection between the subject matter and the real world.
3. Share your enthusiasm for your subject area. Show why *you* value it.
4. Remember, your goal is not just to have the students *know* the subject, but to *value* the subject. The real measure of their academic education is not their test scores, but whether they continue to read history and literature, write letters or poetry, speak the foreign language, and enjoy a variety of the arts throughout their life.
5. In all subject areas, stress the value of craft, of excellence, and of taking pride in one's work. This is a moral as well as a personal value. To have a conscience that does not allow one to be satisfied with mediocre work is not only a sign of self-respect, but of social responsibility. We need to be able to trust one another to deliver the very best effort, whether one is repairing our furnace, caring for our health, or teaching our children. Taking pride in one's work is a habit, which begins in school (or earlier) and continues into the real world of work. It is a value that all teachers can instill in their students, as they foster academic skills and knowledge.

95

Social Skills

Once upon a time, children were taught "manners." To learn manners or "etiquette" meant to learn the behavior appropriate for a lady or gentleman in middle-class and upper-class society. The Victorian concept of social etiquette was imported to America in the later-nineteenth century, as a response to the growing numbers and influence of working-class and immigrant groups, as a way of regaining or achieving a homogeneity of manners and morals in an increasingly diverse society.[12]

Today we recognize the class and cultural bias of the Victorian belief that there is only one proper set of social norms for decent, well-bred men and women to follow. We recognize that all societies have their conventions and their behavioral norms for demonstrating respect, responsibility, and good breeding. For example, to belch aloud at someone's dinner table after a meal would be considered the height of disrespect in most Western countries, while in Japan it would be considered a polite compliment to the host and hostess. To look at people while speaking to them is expected, respectful behavior in most of America, but it is considered a sign of disrespect to a traditional Navajo.

To suggest that a comprehensive values education and moral education include teaching social skills to young people, therefore, does not necessarily mean teaching them only the correct manners for American, white, middle-class society. It means *teaching the conventional manners for the various cultures, ethnic groups, social and economic classes, educational settings, and careers they might wish to participate in or have regular contact with.* "Conventional manners" refers to those behavioral norms which, for that group, communicate good character—respect, responsibility, trustworthiness, and the like.

Learning social skills begins at home and in the community before students ever attend school. It continues on their first day in kindergarten and throughout elementary and secondary school.[45,126] It starts with very basic social skills (saying "Please" and "Thank you," for example) that are common to just about all cultures, classes, and ethnic groups, and it eventually includes more subtle, situational skills for specialized settings, like meeting your date's parents, job interviews, and talking with your employer. Some of the most typical and fruitful areas for teaching social skills include:

1. *Conventions of time.* In some settings, when a meeting is called for 10 A.M., anyone who comes at 10:30 may be viewed as irresponsible and not to be trusted. In other settings, where meetings habitually start late, anyone who arrives at the scheduled 10 A.M. will have people wondering, "Doesn't she have anything better to do than hang around an empty meeting room, when obviously the meeting won't start until around 11 A.M.?"
2. *Dress and appearance.* These skills include knowing what is appropriate clothing for different settings and occasions, when to remove one's hat or coat and how to "dress for success."

3. *Language.* Certain words impress people and others turn people off. Appropriate words, usage, and pronunciation can suggest a good education and increase the likelihood of employment and promotion.
4. *Showing appreciation.* Such skills include saying thank you, writing follow-up notes, and paying compliments in appropriate instances.
5. *Table manners.* Students should know when and where to sit, when to begin eating, correct use of utensils, and gluttonous behaviors to avoid.
6. *Conflict.* A more specific application of conflict resolution skills (#93), these social skills include how to disagree without hurting relationships; diffusing tension; allowing yourself and others to "save face," and handling conflict.

Thomas Lickona described how one fifth-grade teacher "made courtesy-as-respect a high priority. If a student banged a desk top shut, Mrs. Angelini paused to allow the student to say 'Excuse me' to the class (they had discussed the fact that loud noises were an interruption if someone was speaking or a distraction if people were trying to think). Children were expected to apologize if they called someone a name. They were taught to say 'Pardon me?' instead of 'What?' when they wished something repeated. They were taught to say 'Thank you' to the cafeteria workers who served them as they went through the lunch line. And they were taught that all of these behaviors were not mechanical gestures but meaningful ways of respecting other people."[122]

Secondary students need just as much instruction in social skills that convey respect and responsibility in school and in the wider world. Their survival and success may very well depend on how well they learn and practice these skills. Social skills can be taught by explanation and rules, as in the fifth-grade example above, but also by demonstration, practice, role-playing, discussion, and problem solving. Teenagers are quite interested in what it takes to get along and succeed in life, now and in their future. They are quite responsive to learning about social skills, when these are taught through a combination of inculcation, modeling, facilitating, and skill building methods.

Knowing the social conventions of a culture or group does not mean being a prisoner of those conventions. Rather, the reverse is true. Knowledge is power. Knowing the social skills of a culture means having a choice—whether to follow the conventions and succeed within that context, to stretch or transcend the limits, or to try to change the norms of the system. In any case, possessing appropriate social skills increases the likelihood of demonstrating real respect and responsibility within the conventions of that system, therefore, being perceived as a person of good moral character, and therefore, achieving one's own goals and values within that system.

Chapter 9

Developing a Values Education Program

96

The Values Education Committee: Educators, Parents, and Community Working Together

Schools and youth organizations are relative latecomers to the field of values education and moral education. For millennia, it was the family and the religious institutions of the community which had the almost-exclusive responsibility for instilling values and morals in the youth of society. And most people would agree that role is still extremely important today. For any values education program in schools to come close to realizing its full potential, it must have the support and involvement of all segments of society.

Therefore, schools, school districts, and youth organizations who are serious about having a values education or moral education program, which is more than superficial, will involve parents and community members from the beginning. This typically means forming a committee with representatives from various constituencies, such as educators, parents, and religious leaders. Other potential committee members include students, civic leaders, law enforcement officers, or entertainment or sports figures. Values education committees can be formed for the whole school district, for individual schools, or at both levels.

The "values education committee" will develop the list of target values (#1) or, at the very least, refine and endorse the list of target values developed by the professional staff. To help them accomplish this goal, in many instances, *the values education committee will survey all the parents in the school or district to find out their goals for their children.* A survey not only improves the list of target values, but it gives all parents a feeling that they were involved in creating the values education program. The committee also serves to:

- create and review the values education program as it develops;
- solicit feedback and suggestions from the community, which will strengthen and improve the program;
- serve as good will ambassadors for the program in the community—at PTA meetings, civic groups, congregations, and other appropriate settings;
- in the event of misunderstandings or controversy about the program, play an invaluable role in communicating with the public and resolving problems, and
- participate in the on-going evaluation of the program (#100) and in decisions on revising and improving the program.

As with many other controversial topics—such as shared decision-making, drug education, and religion in the schools—educators may be reluctant to share their professional turf and involve parents and community members in the decision-making process. From a strictly political standpoint, this is often a big mistake. If a program has a meaningful impact on students, then parents and community members will soon hear about it, and some misunderstandings, concerns, or controversy will inevitably arise. No matter how good a program may be, some people won't like it and will say so; that's predictable. At that point, community support can make the difference and allow your good program to continue and thrive.

District politics aside, there is an even more important reason to involve parents and the community in a values education and moral education effort. *Values education and moral education always have been, are, and will continue to be a joint responsibility of the family, the school, and all the institutions of the community.* For the schools to go about this task on their own, without the active participation of parents and community members is self-defeating. The only way for any of these groups to succeed in instilling positive values and morality in young people is to work together. It's that simple. If the saying "United we stand/Divided we fall" applies anywhere, it applies to educating our youth in how to be responsible members of the community. We adults don't have to agree on all political, religious, social, and personal values; but we must agree on some very basic ones, such as those "target values" described at the beginning of this book (#1), if we are to succeed in any meaningful program of values education and moral education. While many of the ideas in this book are "optional" for a values education program, this is not one of them. Involving parents and community members from the start is essential for your program.

> *It takes a whole village to raise a child.*
> AFRICAN PROVERB

97

Keep Parents and Community Informed

The previous idea described the values education committee as an important way to involve parents and community in developing and implementing your values education and moral education program. In a sense, this method utilizes a representative form of participation, with the individuals on the committee unofficially representing the viewpoints of their various constituencies. That, however, is just the beginning of parent and community involvement; for each and every parent has a very personal stake in your values education program—his or her child. Therefore, each parent needs and deserves a more personal level of communication than the representative committee can provide. A greater degree of communication can be achieved in a number of ways including:

1. *Informational meeting for parents.* Once the values education committee and the professional staff have drafted a document describing the values education program, invite the parents and community to an informational meeting. If an individual teacher is implementing the program, this meeting can be called just for the parents of her students. If it is a school that is implementing the program, a PTA/PTF meeting can serve the purpose. If it is a district-wide program, then the informational meetings can be held either on the district or individual school level. In any case, the purposes of the meeting are four-fold: (1) to inform the parents, (2) to get their feedback and suggestions to help improve the program, (3) to clear up any misunderstandings and respond to any concerns or problems they may have with the program, and (4) to request their support and active involvement. More will be said about active parental involvement in the next section.

2. *Informational meeting for the community.* Community members can often be invited to the informational meetings for parents, thereby avoiding the need for additional meetings. Sometimes, however, it is appropriate to schedule wider community meetings, as there may be constituencies (senior citizens, for example) who may not feel as comfortable coming to meetings that appear to be aimed primarily at individual school populations. In any case, the purposes of meeting with interested community members are the same as meeting with the parents—to inform, to receive feedback, to respond to questions and concerns, and to invite their support and participation.

3. *Written communications.* Having informed the wider group of parents and community members at the initial meetings described above, it is important to keep them informed—both as a way of encouraging their active support and involvement and as a way of avoiding misunderstandings and misinformation about the program. There are several ways teachers and schools can get written information out to the community, including:

- Letters home from the teacher or school to the parents of students involved in the program. Some schools, for example, send home a monthly letter, describing the values Theme-of-the-Month (#16) and how parents can help reinforce it.
- Newsletters that most schools and districts have for keeping parents and community members informed.
- Letters and newsletters sent to a representative sample of community members, including civic organizations, youth organizations, political leaders, religious leaders, and the media.

4. *Press releases.* This is an easy way for the school district to inform the general public of its programs and activities. Local newspapers readily print stories about interesting programs taking place in the schools. It is a good way to build community support for the schools in general and the values education program in particular.

5. *Work sent home.* In elementary schools, it is common for teachers to have students bring their work home to show their parents. This can be done with some of the activities and assignments done in the values education program as well.

6. *Positive comments sent home.* Let parents know—in letters, notes, "Good-News-A-Grams," or phone calls—some of the good things happening in your class and the positive things you notice about their child's work and character development. Parents will be much more responsive to your requests for help and support if they have already experienced your positive attitude toward their child.

7. *Values education event.* On an evening or weekend, have a "Values Festival," "Values Fair," "Grandparents Day," "Good Citizenship Day," "Drug-Free School Gala," or other event highlighting the school or district's values education program. Use student-created posters and displays, student writings and songs, artwork, or performances by students to show parents and community members the kinds of values being taught and learned in the program.

98

Parent and Community Involvement

It is not enough to simply inform and communicate with parents and community members about the values education program. They should also become actively involved in carrying out the program. The schools can't do the job alone, any more than parents can. Just as the schools encourage parents to read to their children, which not only helps develop reading proficiency but also models *the value of reading*, there are other ways that teachers, parents, and community members can work together to enhance values and morality in the youth of the community.

Parent Involvement

1. *Gain a commitment from parents.* Some schools ask a student's parents to commit themselves to work with the schools on behalf of their child's moral development. This might include agreeing to give their child a responsibility task at home, to withdraw privileges if the student gets in a fight at school, to support the work ethic by being sure their child has a quiet place and time to do her homework, to limit or monitor television viewing, and other specific steps to support the school's academic and values education program. It is also important to gain the parents' commitment to your or the school's discipline plan. At a meeting or by mail, parents can be informed about how discipline problems involving their children will be handled; but it is even better to enlist the parents' *cooperation* in carrying out this plan. A teacher loses much of her moral authority if parents are not willing to cooperate with the school's rules and values about work, promptness, honesty, fighting, and other moral issues. Thus, gaining the active support of the parents on these matters is critical for values education. Some schools simply *request* a commitment and hope parents will cooperate; others try to get *a signed commitment from every parent.* A little extra time spent with parents on this endeavor can go a long way toward helping achieve your values education goals.

2. *Invite parents in to tell their stories.* First, identify parents of your students who have interesting stories that exemplify particular values—like hard work, courage, and concern for others. For example, one parent may have fought against difficult odds to gain a college education. Another may have worked to correct an injustice in the community. Another may have survived a difficult time because of someone else's kindness or friendship. Each of these parents has a real, personal story to tell that could help inculcate and model these values. While some life experiences would be more appropriate for younger or older students, these particular examples could be appropriate for elementary *and* secondary students.

You can identify such parents from your own personal knowledge, if a student happens to mention it, or by sending a letter home telling parents what you have in mind and asking them to let you know if they have any appropriate life experiences they would be willing to share with your class. Parents can speak to the class individually or in a panel format, at a time when it fits in with your particular lesson or unit plan.

3. *Have students interview their parents.* Make it a regular assignment, with a protocol of questions to be asked. Make the questions appropriate to what you are studying or discussing. For example, for an *elementary* class reading stories about friendship, have students ask their parents about their friends—such as who their friends are, what qualities their parents look for in friends, and what their parents have learned about friendship. For a *secondary* class studying health, have them ask their parents questions like: When did you feel healthiest in your life? What is something you'd like to know about health? What could I do to be more healthy? What could you do to be more healthy?

The examples of topics a class might be exploring are myriad, as are the interview questions students could ask their parents about those topics. The idea is to utilize this opportunity for students to listen to their parents and gain a better understanding and appreciation of their parents' experiences and values. Almost all parents will be grateful to any teacher who encourages their children to listen respectfully to them and will feel greater support for the values education program being implemented.

4. *Have students share their work with their parents.* Elementary teachers have done this for years, for example, having students bring home pictures they have drawn. This approach can be adapted to values education on both the elementary and secondary levels. Let's say students have just written a short story, a poem, or an essay or completed a questionnaire dealing with some values issue. They might be asked to read or show their work to their parents and elicit the following feedback from the parent: What is one thing you liked or agreed with in the story? What is one thing you disagreed with or thought could improve it?

5. *Have students do an activity with their parents.* For example, if your elementary class is discussing "altruism"—doing things to help other people—you could ask the students to work with their parent(s) to come up with a list of ten examples of different people who have acted altruistically. The parent should find five examples and the student should find five examples. Then they get together and produce a combined list. For each of the ten examples, they should identify what the act was, who did it, and why they did it. The students then bring their lists back to school, the class discusses them, and the students go back home and tell their parents about the discussion they had. Similarly, a high school class might be discussing a controversial issue and might prepare a public opinion survey about that issue. Each student and her parent would work together to get ten or more survey forms completed—half by the parent and half by the student. Again, the results would be worked into the overall teaching plan and could be shared and discussed further between student and parent.

Unfortunately, teachers know all too well that some parents are unable or unwilling to involve themselves in their children's education. The fact that some students may not be able to enlist their parent's participation or, in some cases, may not even have a parent, should not discourage you from utilizing this valuable learning opportunity. Instead, let your students know:

"I realize that it may be difficult or impossible for some of you to have a parent participate in this activity. If that is the case, I understand that, and here is an alternative way for you to do the assignment. Select another meaningful adult in your life - a grandparent, a guardian, or an adult that you respect, and work with that person in completing the assignment. If that still doesn't work for you, then see me, and we'll figure out another alternative."

"Another alternative" could be yourself or another adult (relative, friend, or a "Big Brother/Big Sister") whom you arrange for the student to work with. If, in fact, a student has no adult in her own life willing or able to become involved in her education, then an intervention in which you pair the student with another responsible, caring adult might be the most important thing that you can do for that young person's values education and well-being.

6. *Form parent support groups.* Many parents are concerned about their children's values and moral development, yet feel powerless or ineffective in helping their children to overcome negative peer, neighborhood, or social influences around them. Some schools have facilitated the formation of peer, self-help groups for parents in which they give one another support and ideas to achieve their mutual, child-rearing goals. When the teacher participates regularly or occasionally in these groups, it can go a long way to developing a school-family alliance that has an enormous positive impact on the students' values education.

7. *Family film night.* Some schools invite parents and students to come to school on an evening or weekend afternoon to enjoy a movie together. One of the film's themes is some value or moral issue. The viewing is followed by a short discussion period with a few good questions provided to help family members talk among themselves and with other families about the issues the film raised. Light refreshments round out the occasion, which helps to enhance students' values and family unity.

Community Involvement

Many of the examples above for parental involvement apply equally well to involving community members in the values education program. You can:

- Invite community members to class or assemblies to tell their stories.
- Have students interview community members.
- Have students do an activity with community members.

In all three instances, you have an even wider array of resource people out in the community than you do with the parents of your students. Community members from the civic, business, religious, governmental, trade, and professional sectors are usually delighted when asked to speak to a school class, to be interviewed by a student on an assignment, or to work with students and schools.

"School-business partnerships" have become more common in recent years to improve the academic education of students. Similarly, the moral education of our youth must be a community-wide effort if it is to be truly successful. In many communities, local businesses have begun to offer free products or services like

*"It's a note from my teacher. You're to go down
to the school and write a hundred times on the chalkboard, 'I'll teach my son to be more respectful.' "*

a free meal or car wash to students who receive school citizenship or service
awards. Some communities have even begun experimenting with the idea of a
student discount card, honored at businesses all around the community, for students who pass a periodic and voluntary "drug-free" test.

Community members and community institutions have a great deal to contribute to a values education program. Often all it takes is someone to ask them to
become involved.

99

Meeting Basic Needs

The viability of values, character, citizenship, and moral education is based on an
assumption—that students' basic physical and emotional needs are being met.
To put it bluntly, a hungry child has little or no attention for most of the activities
in this book. If a child is suffering from physical abuse, emotional trauma, or just
plain hurt feelings that morning, she is going to be less receptive to the best attempts at values education. Therefore, we should recognize, if not for its own
sake, which is justification enough, then for the sake of succeeding with values
education we must help to meet the basic needs of children.

Much of that effort occurs outside the classroom. If it fails to occur at home, then hopefully it takes place in community support systems, social service programs, school lunch programs, and through the best efforts of the school counselors and social workers, which is the justification for including this section in this final chapter of the book. If you are developing a values education program, whatever can be done to coordinate community care for children and to insure that their basic needs are met, both outside and inside the school, will help increase the success of your values education program.

Having said that, meeting the basic needs of children does, can, and should take place in the individual classroom as well. Louis Raths identified eight emotional needs of children and provided examples of scores of "do's and don'ts"—practical ways that teachers can meet these emotional needs.[153] A very brief sampling of those ideas follows. It is not intended that each teacher *should* do each of these things all the time—a teacher can't be everywhere at once—but to suggest the many different ways that teachers sometimes *can* meet some of the basic, emotional needs of students.

1. *The need for belonging.*

- When a student returns from being absent, tell him you missed him.
- Stand at the doorway and personally greet students as they enter the classsroom.

2. *The need for achievement.*

- Give rewards for a variety of achievements—for excellence, creativity, effort, improvement.
- Try to find a variety of media to work in. If the school is only a reading-and-writing school, there will be many students who will not be able to reveal their unusual talents.

3. *The need for economic security.*

- Arrange privately to help those students who need lunch money or additional fees for trips or special assignments.
- Don't praise students for ostentatiousness in their clothes or in their possessions.

4. *The need to be free from fear.*

- Do not threaten students with dire consequences for failing or not meeting your expectations. Let them know that "it won't be the end of the world" if they don't succeed in a particular test or area.
- Give students an opportunity to talk with you, another student, a small group, or the counselor about their fears.

5. *The need for love and affection.*

- Don't reject the attempts of students to do favors for you, or to make gifts for you. If it is something that should not be done, talk to them privately, and do it with great tact and consideration. You probably can do it in a way that

leaves them feeling that you have been touched by their gesture, and it makes you feel awfully good to know that they think this much of you.
- Some students who need love and affection stuff themselves with candy, extra desserts, and extra calories. They are getting "sweetness" through sweet things to eat even if they can't get sweetness in their human relationships. Be sensitive to these obese students. They are particularly in need of friendliness and warmth.

6. *The need to be free from intense feelings of guilt.*

- Help students to see that, when we make mistakes, we can be sorry about them but we mustn't worry too much about them. Instead, we must understand the mistakes so that we won't make them again. Assure them that it isn't necessary to develop feelings of guilt when we make mistakes.
- When students lie, steal, or cheat, don't make a great public ado about it. Don't shame them, humiliate them, or debase them. Try to help them understand their behavior, punish if appropriate, and show confidence that they can and will do better next time.

7. *The need for self-respect.*

- Don't *always* be checking up on students to see if they did their homework, if they did their reading, or if they were talking when they shouldn't, and so on. If they feel you are suspicious of them, their own self-respect is lowered.
- Give students regular opportunities to appraise their own work, and listen to their appraisals. If only teachers do the appraising, students get the impression that the work they do is for the teacher, and not for their own growth and development. If only teachers do the judging, children learn to mistrust their own judgment.

8. *The need for understanding.*

- Don't feel that it is a weakness in your professional preparation if you can't answer all questions students raise. You are probably prepared to answer only the smallest fraction of them. Avoid trying "to give the answer." Try to get students to work on the project; try to get them to recognize authorities, to consult them, to interview them, or to bring them to the classroom.
- When a question occurs at an inappropriate time, don't ignore it. Use one part of the chalkboard for writing down things that are to be addressed later. Or say, "Could you and I talk about that later after school or during a free period?"

There are hundreds of other ideas that have been suggested for meeting the emotional needs of children and youth and many different theories describing emotional needs. Obviously, it is far too great a task for any teacher to accomplish it alone. Yet each teacher can play an important part. To the extent this is done and students' *basic* emotional needs are met, the values education and moral education enterprise will be that much more effective.

Children Learn What They Live

If a child lives with criticism, he learns to condemn.
If a child lives with hostility, he learns to fight.
If a child lives with ridicule, he learns to be shy.
If a child lives with shame, he learns to feel guilty.
If a child lives with tolerance, he learns to be patient.
If a child lives with encouragement, he learns confidence.
If a child lives with praise, he learns to appreciate.
If a child lives with fairness, he learns justice.
If a child lives with security, he learns to have faith.
If a child lives with approval, he learns to like himself.
If a child lives with acceptance and friendship, he learns to find love
   in the world.

ANONYMOUS

100

Evaluate the Results

Any district, school, or individual teacher who is serious about implementing a program of values education and moral education will want to evaluate the results of the program. Broadly speaking, there are two kinds of evaluation. *Formative evaluation* refers to the activities undertaken to develop a program, and *summative evaluation* refers to the activities designed to assess a program's final outcomes. These activities are usually mixed in actual working situations.[82]

Formative Evaluation

Formative evaluation gathers information to help formulate and develop a new program and to improve a program that is underway. One of the most common methods of formative evaluation is to ask the participants in the program (the students and teachers in this case) and observers of the program (parents, counselors, and other teachers) for their perceptions. Although the wording would be different for the different audiences and the different age levels of students, the basic questions include:

- What were the most useful, interesting, helpful, enjoyable, productive, educational, or beneficial aspects of the program?
- What were the least useful, least interesting, or least helpful (or most difficult, confusing, boring, or unproductive) aspects of the program?
- Would you recommend continuing or repeating the program in the future?
- What recommendations would you make to improve the program?

Formative evaluation questions need not all be open-ended. Often the evaluation lists different elements of the program and asks participants in the evaluation to rate each element as having been "Very Helpful," "Somewhat Helpful," "Neutral," or "A Waste of Time," or uses a five-point or seven-point "Likert scale" (numbers representing a positive to negative evaluation) or some other criteria of assessment. These are all still subjective assessments by the participants.

Other, more objective measurements of student performance and behavior are often an important part of formative evaluation. Some examples of these more objective measures are given in the discussion on summative evaluation below and can be very helpful for the purposes of reformulating and improving the program.

Summative Evaluation

Summative evaluation assesses what has been accomplished over a period of time. The data collected in a summative evaluation serves several purposes: (a) It helps the implementers of the program learn if they are accomplishing the goals for which the program was created; (b) it helps decision-makers justify the continuation and funding of the program; (c) it helps respond to potential critics of the program, and (d) it helps improve the program in the future.

The particular questions and activities used in a summative evaluation should be geared to the goals for which the program was established. For example, if a school begins a values education program out of a generalized concern about students' lack of respect for themselves, property, and other students, then the evaluation will seek to ask questions about respect and observe behavior that indicates respect or the lack of respect. Similarly, if rising drug abuse and teen pregnancies were the main concerns that motivated a values education program, the evaluators would certainly want to assess any changes related to drug abuse and pregnancy rates.

There are numerous ways to evaluate the results of a values education and moral education program. These are just a sample:

1. *Ask students.* What have they learned from program? In what ways, if any, has their behavior changed?
2. *Ask parents.* Over the course of the program, has family communication improved, deteriorated, or remained the same? Has their children's behavior become more respectful and responsible, less so, or is it no different than before?
3. *Ask teachers.* Do they see any change in student behavior?
4. *Vandalism.* Have incidents of vandalism and graffiti increased, decreased, or remained the same? Ask the custodian what he or she sees.
5. *Attendance and drop-out rates.* These presumably reflect student perseverance and commitment.
6. *Drug problems.* Any changes in drug arrests, drug confiscations, student attitudes toward drugs on objective paper-and-pencil tests, student estimates

of peer drug use, and correlates of lower drug use such as self-esteem or "locus of control"?

7. *Crime.* What figures do the police have on youth crime and delinquency? Any changes? Have student reports of shakedowns and locker break-ins increased, decreased, or remained the same?

8. *Discipline problems.* Have there been any changes in principal referrals, detention rates, or suspensions, as well as teacher perceptions of student cooperativeness, respect, responsibility, and self-discipline?

9. *Moral reasoning.* Are there any changes in levels of moral reasoning (#70) as measured by paper-and-pencil tests or classroom observations?

10. *Morality test.* Create a paper-and-pencil morality test and administer it before the program and each year thereafter. For example: "A child finds a wallet. What should he do? (a) turn it in, (b) keep the money and throw it away, (c) keep the money and turn in the rest, or (d) don't touch it, pass it by."

11. *Voter participation.* What percentage of 18- to-21-year-olds (the recent graduates of the school's values education or citizenship education program) are voting?

12. *Student achievement.* Are students working harder, persevering, and being more self-disciplined? Are there any changes in grades or test scores?

13. *Student aspirations.* Are there any changes in the kind of goals students are setting for themselves?

14. *Self-esteem.* Are there any changes for better or worse?

15. *Intergroup problems.* Are there any changes or improvements in student behavior toward others who are different in race, ethnic group, religion, age, gender, handicapped status, or other distinctions?

16. *Attitude tests.* Are there any changes on objective, paper-and-pencil tests of tolerance, dogmatism, egocentrism, and other measures of respect, open-mindedness, and concern for others? (The school should not use or maintain individuals' scores on attitude tests. The point is to see if the educational program, on average, is enhancing values and moral attitudes.)

17. *Teen pregnancy rates.* Are they up, down, or no different?

18. *Unobtrusive measures.* There are numerous other ways for assessing the results of a values education program. Some are quite creative and "unobtrusive" and will appeal to even the most "hard-nosed" and objective of evaluators. For example, try scattering wallets around the school and see how many of them are returned. Stand in the hallway and count put-downs-per-minute as students pass one another between classes. Every week have someone drop a tray in the school cafeteria and measure the decibel level of the applause. If that's not enough, you can count seconds of booing at school sporting events, cigarette butts in the parking lot, number of weapons and drugs confiscated per week, or number of teachers or students who, when stopped randomly in the hallway, report that they received a compliment from a student that day.

Such research can be of the *survey* variety, assessing whole groups at different points in time, or *experimental* designs—setting up experimental and control groups, using pre- and post-tests, giving one group the values education program, giving the other group a different treatment, perhaps giving another group no treatment, and analyzing the results with sophisticated statistical procedures. There is no shortage of possibilities for evaluation, other than the shortage of time and money. Nevertheless, any serious values education program will need some evaluation—perhaps brief, perhaps exhaustive—to validate that it is on track and to continue to improve the program.

References and Bibliography

1. Adler, J., Wingert, P., Wingert, L., Houston, P., Manly, H., & Cohen, A. (1992, February 17). Hey, I'm terrific! *Newsweek*.

2. Adler, M. (1982). *The paideia proposal*. New York: Macmillan.

3. Alschuler, A., Tabor, D., & McIntyre, J. (1970). *Teaching achievement motivation*. Middletown, CT: Education Ventures.

4. American Automobile Association. (1991). Traffic safety education posters. Washington, D.C.

5. American Library Association. *Newsletter on Intellectual Freedom*. (Available from 50 East Huron Street, Chicago, IL 60611).

6. Ansley, L., & McCleary, K. (1992, August 21). Do the right thing. *USA Weekend*.

7. Association for Supervision and Curriculum Development. (1986, May). Issue on the teaching of thinking. *Educational Leadership, 43*(8).

8. Association for Supervision and Curriculum Development. (1988). *Moral Education in the life of the school*. p. 19. [A report from the ASCD Panel on Moral Education]. Alexandria, VA: ASCD.

9. Association for Supervision and Curriculum Development. (1988, May). Issue on schools, parents and values. *Educational Leadership, 45*(8).

10. Association for Supervision and Curriculum Development. (1993, November). Issue on character education, with many examples of successful programs around the United States. *Educational Leadership, 51*(3).

11. Baker, M.O. (1989). *What would you do? Developing and/or applying ethical standards. Book A-1*. (p. 6). Pacific Grove, CA: Critical Thinking Press and Software.

12. Baritz, L. (1989). *The good life: The meaning of success for the American middle class*. New York: Alfred Knopf.

13. Battistich, V., Watson, M., Solomon, D., Schaps, E., & Solomon, J. (1990). The Child Development Project: A comprehensive program for the development of prosocial character. In Kurtines, W., & Gewirtz, J. (Eds.). (1990). *Moral behavior and development* (Vol. 1). New York: Lawrence Earlbaum Associates.

14. Bauer, C. (1993). *New handbook for storytellers*. Chicago, IL: American Library Association.

15. Beane, J., & Lipka, R. (1986). *Self-concept, self-esteem, and the curriculum*. New York: Columbia University Press.

16. Bell, T. (1976, May). An interview with Commissioner of Education Terrel H. Bell. *American Education, 12*(4), 26.

17. Benard, B. (1993, November). Fostering resiliency in kids. *Educational Leadership, 51*(3), 44–48

18. Bennett, W.J. (1992). *The de-valuing of America: The fight for our culture and our children.* (pp. 59–60). New York: Summit Books.

19. Benninga, J. (Ed.). (1991). *Moral, character, and civic education in the elementary school.* (p. 170). New York: Teachers College Press.

20. Berg, E. (1992, January 1). Argument grows that teaching of values should rank with lessons. *New York Times,* Education section.

21. Berkowitz, , M., & Oser, F. (Eds.). (1985). *Moral education: Theory and application.* Hillsdale, NJ: Erlbaum.

22. Bolton, R. (1979). *People skills: How to assert yourself, listen to others and resolve conflicts.* New York: Simon and Schuster.

23. Bourman, A. (1990). *Tough decisions: 50 activities in values and character education.* [50 reproducible cards]. Portland, ME: J. Weston Walch.

24. Brandt, R. (1988, May). Knowing when to speak out—and when to listen. *Educational Leadership, 45*(8), 3.

25. Bricker, D.C. (1989). *Classroom life as civic education: Individual achievement and student cooperation in schools.* New York: Teachers College Press.

26. Brown, D.N. (1993, November 21). Virginity is new counterculture among some teens. [Based on a study originally published in 1990]. *Washington Post,* p. A27.

27. Bullard, S. (Ed.). (1993, Spring). *Teaching Tolerance.* [A bi-annual magazine for educators]. Montgomery, AL: Southern Poverty Law Center.

28. Burgess, G. (1968). *Goops and how to be them: A manual of manners for polite infants inculcating many juvenile virtues both by precept and example.* Frederick A. Stokes Company. Reprinted, New York: Dover Publications. (Original work published in 1900).

29. Burns, M. (1976). *The book of think.* Boston: Little, Brown.

30. Butts, R.F. (1980). *The revival of civil learning: A rationale for citizenship education in American schools.* Bloomington, IN: Phi Delta Kappa Educational Foundation.

31. Canfield, J., & Siccone, F. (1993). *101 ways to develop self-esteem and responsibility* (Vol. 1). The teacher as coach. Needham Heights, MA: Allyn and Bacon.

32. Canfield, J., & Wells, H. (1976). *100 ways to enhance self-concept in the classroom.* Englewood Cliffs, NJ: Prentice-Hall.

33. Chamberlin, D., et al. (1942). *Adventures in American education: Did they succeed in college?* New York: Harper and Brothers.

34. Character Education Institute, Dimension II Bldg., 8918 Tesoro, Suite 220, San Antonio, TX 78217. [Distributes one of the most widely used character education programs].

35. Charney, R.S. (1991). *Teaching children to care: Management in the responsive classroom.* Greenfield, MA: Northeast Foundation for Children.

36. Coles, R. (1990). Girl Scouts survey on the beliefs and moral values of America's children: Executive summary. New York: Girl Scouts of the United States of America.

37. Connell, J. (1991, September 24). Public schools 'do the right thing' in stressing the moral path. Newhouse News Service. *Newark Star-Ledger,* p. 3.

38. Consumer Information Center. (1986). *What works: Research about teaching and learning.* Pueblo, CO: U.S. Department of Education.

39. Costa, A.L. (1991). *The school as a home for the mind.* Palatine, IL: Skylight Publishing.

40. Costa, A.L. (Ed.). (1985). *Developing minds: A resource book for Teaching thinking.* (p. 54). Alexandria, VA: Association for Supervision and Curriculum Development.

41. de Bono, E. (1970). *Lateral thinking: Creativity step by step.* New York: Harper and Row.

42. Dees, M. (1993, November 24). Letter to supporters, unpublished. [See also any issue of the Center's newsletter *Intelligence Report*]. Atlanta, GA: Southern Poverty Law Center.

43. Dewey, J. (1963). *Experience and education.* New York: Macmillan.

44. Division of Student Activitites. *Leadership for Student Activities.* [Monthly magazine]. Reston, VA: National Association of Secondary School Principals.

45. Dowd, T., & Tierney, J. (1992). *Teaching social skills to youth.* Boys Town, NE: Boys Town Press.

46. Dreikurs, R., Grunwald, B., & Pepper, F. (1971). *Maintaining sanity in the classroom: Illustrated teaching techniques.* New York: Harper and Row.

47. Drew, N. (1987). *Learning the skills of peace-making: An activity guide for elementary-age children on communicating, cooperating and re-solving conflict.* Rolling Hills Estates, CA: Jalmar Press.

48. Dreyer, S. (1977). *The bookfinder: A guide to children's literature about the needs and problems of youth aged 2–5.* Circle Pines, MN: American Guidance Service.

49. Drug Abuse Resistance Education. (1988). [The "DARE Program" is disseminated nationally through state and local police departments]. Los Angeles, CA: Los Angeles Unified School District.

50. Duff, D., & Woodwell, W. (1989, April/ May). An absence of ballots. [Actually 36.2% *reported* they voted to the U.S. Census; the real figure is estimated at closer to 34%]. *National Voter, 38*(5) 4–9.

51. Edelman, M.W. (1993, November 16). Talk of the nation. Washington, DC: National Public Radio.

52. Elam, S., Rose, L., & Gallup, A. (1993, October). The twenty-fifth annual Phi Delta Kappa/Gallop poll of the public's attitudes toward the public schools. *Phi Delta Kappan, 75*(2), 137–152.

53. Elkins, D. (1977). *Clarifying Jewish values.* Rochester, NY: Growth Associates.

54. Ellis, A., & Harper, R. (1973). *A guide to rational living.* No. Hollywood, CA: Wilshire Book.

55. Emmons, M., & Alberti, R. (1978). *Your perfect right: A guide to assertive behavior* (3rd ed.). San Luis Obispo, CA: Impact Publishers.

56. Engle, S., & Ochoa, A. (1988). *Education for democractic citizenship: Decision making in the social studies.* New York: Teachers College Press.

57. Ennis, R.H. (1987). A taxonomy of critical thinking dispositions and abilities. In Baron, J., & Sternberg, R. (Eds.). *Teaching thinking skills: Theory and practice.* New York: Freeman.

58. Erickson, J. (1990). *Directory of American youth organizations: A guide to over 400 clubs, groups, troops, teams, societies, lodges, and more for young people.* Minneapolis: Free Spirit Publishing.

59. Eskey, K. (1990, June 9). Code blue: A health emergency for American teenagers. [Cited in Reference 116, p. 376]. *The Times Union,* p. 1.

60. Etzioni, A., Berreth, D., & Scherer, M. (1993, November). On transmitting values: A conversation with Amitai Etzioni. *Educational Leadership, 51*(3), 12–15.

61. Fellers, P. (1984). *Peace-ing it together: Peace and justice activites for youth.* Minneapolis: Winston Press.

62. Fleisher, C. (producer). (1989). See Dick and Jane lie, cheat & steal. [A 47-minute video-tape]. (Available by calling Santa Monica, CA: Pyramid Film and Video. 1(800) 421-2304).

63. Fogerty, R., & Bellanca, J. (1986). *Catch them thinking.* Palatine, IN: Skylight Publishing.

64. Fraenkel, J.R. (1977). *How to teach about values.* Englewood Cliffs, NJ: Prentice-Hall.

65. Gallagher, A. (1988). *Living together under the law: An elementary education law guide.* Albany, NY: NYS Bar Association and NYS Education Department. (Available from Bureau of Social Studies Education, NYS Education Department).

66. Gelatt, H.B., Varenhorst, B., Carey, R., & Miller, G. (1973). *Decisions and outcomes: A leader's guide.* Princeton, NJ: College Entrance Examination Board.

67. Gendlin, E. (1978). *Focusing.* New York: Bantam.

68. Gilligan, C. (1982). *In a different voice: Psychological theory and women's development.* Cambridge, MA: Harvard University Press.

69. Goodlad, J.I., Soder, R., & Sirotnik, K. (Eds.). (1990). *The moral dimensions of teaching.* San Francisco: Jossey-Bass.

70. Gordon, T. (1974). *Teacher effectiveness training.* New York: Peter Wyden.

71. Gordon, W.J.J. (1972). *Strange and familiar.* [A series for different age levels]. Cam-

bridge, MA: Synectics Education Systems.

72. Gough, P. (Ed.). (1991, June). Issue on community service. *Phi Delta Kappan, 72*(10).

73. Gray, D. (1989, Fall). Putting minds to work: How to use the seminar approach in the classroom. *American Educator,* 16–23.

74. Greenberg, J. (1984). *Managing stress: A personal guide.* Dubuque, IA: William C. Brown.

75. Hanks, K., & Parry, J. (1991). *Wake up your creative genius.* Los Altos, CA: Crisp Publications.

76. Harmin, M. (1988, May). Value clarity, high morality—Let's go for both. *Educational Leadership, 45*(8), 24–30.

77. Harmin, M. (1990). *How to plan a program for moral education.* (p. 3). Alexandria, VA: Association for Supervision and Curriculum Development.

78. Harmin, M., Kirschenbaum, H., & Simon, S.B. (1973). *Clarifying values through subject matter.* Minneapolis: Winston Press.

79. Harmin, M., & Sax, S. (1977). *A peaceable classroom: Activities to calm and free student energies.* Minneapolis: Winston Press.

80. Harris, T. A. (1969). *I'm OK, you're OK: A practical guide to transactional analysis.* New York: Harper and Row.

81. Hartshorne, H., & May, A. (1928-30). *Studies in the nature of character.* (3 vols.). New York: Macmillan.

82. Hayman, J., & Napier, R. (1975). *Evaluation in the schools: A human process for renewal.* Monterey, CA: Brooks/Cole.

83. Hebeisen, A. (1973). *Peer program for youth: A group interaction plan to develop self-esteem, self-understanding and communication skills.* Minneapolis: Augsberg Publishing House.

84. Holtz, L. (1988). *Do the right thing.* [Half-hour motivational videotape]. Washington, DC: Speakers Bureau Video Corporation.

85. Honig, B. (1992). Teaching values belongs in our public schools. *Ethics: Easier Said Than Done, 19 & 20,* 53–56.

86. Ianni, F., et al. (1984). *Home, school and community in adolescent education.* New York, NY: ERIC Clearinghouse on Urban Education, Teachers College, Columbia University.

87. Isaac, K. (1993). *Civics for democracy.* Washington, DC: Essential Books.

88. Jefferson Center for Character Education, 202 South Lake Avenue, Suite 240, Pasadena, California 91101. [Their "responsibility skills" programs are widely used].

89. Johnson, D.W. (1987). *Human relations and your career* (2nd ed.). Englewood Cliffs, NJ: Prentice-Hall.

90. Johnson, D.W. (1986). *Reaching out: Interpersonal effectiveness and self-actualization* (3rd. ed.). Englewood Cliffs, NJ: Prentice-Hall.

91. Johnson, D.W., and Johnson, R. (1987). *Learning together and alone: Cooperation, competition, and individualization* (2nd ed.). Englewood Cliffs, NJ: Prentice-Hall.

92. Johnson, D.W., & Johnson, R. (1989). *Cooperation and competition: Theory and research.* Edina, MN: Interaction Book.

93. Johnson, D.W., & Johnson, R. (1991). *Teaching children to be peacemakers.* Edina, MN: Interaction Book.

94. Johnson, D.W., Johnson, R., & Holubec, E.J. (1986). *Circles of learning: Cooperation in the classroom* (2nd ed.) pp. 54–56. Edina, MN: Interaction Book.

95. Johnson, D.W., Johnson, R., & Maruyama, G. (1983). Interdependence and interpersonal attraction among hereogeneous and homogeneous individuals: A theoretical formulation and a meta-analysis of the research. *Review of Educational Research, 53,* 5–54.

96. Johnson, L., & Smith, S. (1993). Dealing with diversity through multicultural fiction. Chicago, IL: American Library Association.

97. Josephson, M. (Ed.). (1992). Joint issue on character education. [Includes further discussion and elaboration on the "Aspen Declaration]." *Ethics: Easier Said Than Done, 19 & 20.*

98. Judson, S. (Ed.). (1984). *A manual on nonviolence and children.* Philadelphia: New Society Publishers.

99. Katz, L. (1993, Summer). All about me. Are we developing our children's self-esteem or their narcissism? *American Educator,* 18–23.

100. Kilpatrick, W. (1992). *Why Johnny can't tell right from wrong: Moral illiteracy and the case for character education.* New York: Simon and Schuster.

101. Kilpatrick, W. (1993, Summer). The moral power of good stories. *American Educator, 17*(2), 24–35.

102. Kirschenbaum, H. (1970, February). Sensitivity modules. *Media and Methods, 34,* 36–38

103. Kirschenbaum, H. (1977). *Advanced value clarification.* La Jolla, CA: University Associates.

104. Kirschenbaum, H. (1982, Nov./Dec.). Handling school-community controversies over health education curriculum. *Health Education, 13*(6), 7–10.

105. Kirschenbaum, H. (1992, June). A comprehensive model for values education and moral education. *Phi Delta Kappan, 73*(10), 771–776.

106. Kirschenbaum, H., & Henderson, V. (Eds.). (1989). *The Carl Rogers reader.* (p. 310). Boston: Houghton Mifflin.

107. Kirschenbaum, H., Napier, R., & Simon, S. (1971). *Wad-Ja-Get? The grading game in American education.* New York: Hart Publishing.

108. Kohlberg, L., et al. (1978). *Assessing moral stages: A manual.* Cambridge, MA: Harvard University Press.

109. Kohlberg, L. (1981). *The meaning and measurement of moral development.* Worchester, MA: Clark University Press.

110. Kohlberg, L. (1984). *The psychology of moral development.* New York: Harper and Row.

111. Kohn, A. (1993). *Punished by rewards: The trouble with gold stars, incentive plans, A's, praise, and other bribes.* Boston: Houghton Mifflin.

112. Kohn, A. (1993, September). Choices for children: Why and how to let students decide. *Phi Delta Kappan, 75*(1), 8–20.

113. Lange, A., & Jakubowski, P. (1976). *Responsible assertive behavior: Cognitive/behavioral procedures for trainers.* Champlain, IL: Research Press.

114. Larson, J.W. (1985). *Youth's frontier: Making ethical decisions.* Irving, TX: Boy Scouts of America.

115. Larson, R., & Larson, D. (1976). *Values and faith: Value-clarifying exercises for family and church groups.* Minneapolis: Winston Press.

116. Leming, J. (1993, November). In search of effective character education. (p. 63). *Educational Leadership, 51*(3), 63–71.

117. Lewis, B.A. (1991). *The kid's guide to social action.* Minneapolis: Free Spirit Publishing.

118. Lickona, T. (Ed.). (1976). *Moral development and behavior: Theory, research and social issues.* New York: Holt, Rinehart and Winston.

119. Lickona, T. (1983). *Raising good children.* [Includes a listing in Appendix D of "Books for Kids That Foster Moral Values"]. New York: Bantam Books.

120. Lickona, T. (1988, November). Educating the moral child. *Principal,* 6–10.

121. Lickona, T. (1991). An integrated approach to character development. In J. Benninga (Ed.), *Moral, Character, and Civic Education in the Elementary School* (p. 80). New York: Teachers College Press.

122. Lickona, T. (1992). *Educating for character: How our schools can teach respect and responsibility.* (pp. 44, 238, 251, 296). New York: Bantam Books.

123. Little, R. (1988, September 24). Address to Annual Conference of Nordic Parents Against Drug Abuse, Reykjavik, Iceland. Granville, OH: Quest International.

124. McCullough, D. (1992). *Truman.* (p. 865). New York: Simon and Schuster.

125. McEwan, B. (1991). *Practicing judicious discipline: An educator's guide to a democratic classroom.* Davis, CA: Caddo Gap Press.

126. McGinnis, E., & Goldstein, A. (1984). *Skillstreaming the elementary school child: A guide for teaching prosocial skills.* Champaign, IL: Research Press.

127. McNamee, S. (1977). Moral behavior, moral development and motivation. *Journal of Moral Education, 7*(1), 27–31.

128. Marzano, R.J., Brands, R., Hughes, C., Jones, B., Presselsen, B., Rankin, S., & Suhor, C. (1988). *Dimensions of thinking: A framework for curriculum and instruction.* Alexandria, VA: Association for Supervision and Curriculum Development.

129. Medved, M. (1992). *Hollywood vs. America.* New York: Harper Collins.

130. Metcalf, L.E. (Ed.). (1971). *Values education: Rationale, strategies and procedures.* Washington, DC: National Council for the Social Studies.

131. Meussig, R. (Ed.) (1975). *Controversial issues in the social studies: A contemporary perspective.* Washington, DC: National Council for the Social Studies.

132. Myrick, R., & Erney, T. (1978). *Caring and sharing: Becoming a peer facilitator.* Minneapolis: Educational Media.

133. National Center for Health Statistics. Cited in Bennett, W. (1993). Is our culture in decline? *The Wall Street Journal.*

134. National Council of Teachers of English. (1982). The students' right to read. [16-page booklet]. Urbana, Illinois.

135. National Public Radio. (1993, December 1). Teen sexuality figures included in a report on AIDS and AIDS Awareness Day, on the "All Things Considered" news program.

136. Nazario, S. (1990, April 6). Schoolteachers say it's wrongheaded to try to teach students what's right. *Wall Street Journal*, pp. B1, B8.

137. Nelson, J. (1974). *Introduction to values inquiry: A student process book.* Rochelle Park, NJ: Hayden Book.

138. Nickerson, R., Perkins, D., & Smith, E. (1985). *The teaching of thinking.* Hillsdale, NJ: Lawrence Erlbaum Associates.

139. Oliver, D., & Newman, F. (1967-74). *Public issues series.* (Harvard Social Studies Project). Columbus, OH: Xerox Educational Publications.

140. Parnes, S., Noller, R., & Biondi, A. (1977). *Guide to creative action.* NY: Charles Scribner's Sons.

141. Parr, S. (1982). *The moral of the story: Literature, values, and American education.* New York: Teachers College Press.

142. Paul, R. (1986). Program for the Fourth International Conference on Critical Thinking and Educational Reform. (p. 1). Rohnert Park, CA: Sonoma State University, Center for Critical Thinking and Moral Critique.

143. Paul, R. (1992). *Critical thinking: What every person needs to cope with the modern world.* Rohnert Park, CA: Sonoma State University, Center for Critical Thinking and Moral Critique.

144. Paul, R., Binker, A., Martin, D., & Charbonneau, M. (1987, 1989). *Critical thinking handbooks.* [Student books, for levels K-3, 4-6, 6-9, 9-12]. Rohnert Park, CA: Sonoma State University, Center for Critical Thinking and Moral Critique.

145. Piaget, J. (1965). *The moral judgment of the child.* New York: Free Press.

146. Power, C., Higgins, A., & Kohlberg, L. (1989). *Lawrence Kohlberg's approach to moral education.* New York: Columbia University Press.

147. Pratkanis, A., & Aronson, E. (1992). *Age of propaganda: The everyday use and abuse of persuasion.* New York: Freeman.

148. Prutzman, P. (1988). *The friendly classroom for a small planet: A handbook on creative approaches to living and problem solving for children.* Santa Cruz, CA: New Society Publishers.

149. Purkey, W. (1970). *Self-concept and school achievement.* Englewood Cliffs, NJ: Prentice-Hall.

150. Purpel, D., & Ryan, K. (1976). *Moral education: It comes with the territory.* Berkeley, CA: McCutchan.

151. Quest International, 537 Jones Road, PO Box 566, Granville, OH 43023. [Disseminates some of the most widely-used, comprehensive values education programs for elementary, middle and high school students].

152. Quigley, C. & Bahmueller, C. (Eds.). (1991). *CIVITAS: A framework for civic education.* Calabasas, CA: Center for Civic Education.

153. Raths, L.E. (1972). *Meeting the needs of children: Creating trust and security.* Columbus, OH: Charles Merrill.

154. Raths, L.E., Harmin, M., & Simon, S.B. (1978). *Values and teaching: Working with values in the classroom* (2nd. ed.). Columbus, OH: Charles Merrill.

155. Raths, L.E., Wasserman, S., Jonas, A., and Rothstein, A. (1967). *Teaching for thinking: Theory and application.* Columbus, OH: Charles Merrill.

156. Reichman, H. (1993). *Censorship and selection: Issues and answers for schools* (revised ed.). Chicago, IL: American Library Association and American Association of School Administrators.

157. Rochman, H. (1993). *Against borders: Promoting books for a multicultural world.* Chicago, IL: American Library Association.

158. Roderick, T. (1987/88, Dec./Jan.). Johnny

can learn to negotiate. *Educational Leadership.* 87–90.

159. Rogers, C.R. (1977). *On personal power.* New York: Delacorte Press.

160. Rogers, C.R. (1983). *Freedom to learn for the 80s.* Columbus, OH: Charles Merrill.

161. Rokeach, M. (1973). *The nature of human values.* New York: Free Press.

162. Rokeach, M. (1975). Toward a philosophy of values education. In Meyer, J., Burnham, B., & Cholvat, J. (Eds.). *Values education: theory, practice, problems, prospects.* Waterloo, Ontario: Wilfred Laurier University Press.

163. Ryan, K., & McLean, G. (Eds.). (1987). *Character development in schools and beyond.* New York: Praeger.

164. Sadowsky, E. (1991). Democracy in the elementary school: Learning by doing. In J. Benninga (Ed.). *Moral, Character, and Civic Education in the Elementary School.* New York: Teachers College Press.

165. Saenger, E. (1993). *Exploring ethics through children's literature: Books One and Two.* Pacific Grove, CA: Critical Thinking Press and Software.

166. Sanders, N.M. (1966). *Classroom questions: What kinds?* New York: Harper and Row.

167. Satris, S. (Ed.) (1992). *Taking sides: Clashing views on controversial moral issues,* (3rd ed.). Guilford, CT: Dushkin Publishing Group.

168. Scharf, P. (Ed.). (1978). *Readings in moral education.* Minneapolis: Winston Press.

169. Schimmel, S. (1983). Ethical dimensions of traditional Jewish education. In Chazan, B. *Studies in Jewish education: Volume I.* (p. 94). Jerusalem, Israel: The Magnes Press, The Hebrew University.

169a. Schmidt, F., & Friedman, A. (1985). *Fighting Fair: Dr. Martin Luther King, Jr. For Kids.* Grace Contrino Abrams Peace Education Foundation.

170. Scholz, N., Prince, J., & Miller, G. (1975). *How to decide: A guide for women.* New York: College Entrance Examination Board.

171. Shaftel, F., & Shaftel, G. (1967). *Role-playing for social values: Decision-making in the social studies.* Englewood Cliffs, NJ: Prentice-Hall.

172. Shallcross, D. (1981). *Teaching creative behavior.* Englewood Cliffs, NJ: Prentice Hall.

173. Simon, Sarina. (1989). *101 amusing ways to develop your child's thinking skills and creativity: For pre-school to third grade.* Los Angeles: Lowell House.

174. Simon, S.B. (1973). IALAC: *I am lovable and capable.* Niles, IL: Argus Communications. Hadley, MA: Values Press.

175. Simon, S.B. (1978). *Negative criticism.* Niles, IL: Argus Communications. Hadley, MA: Values Press.

176. Simon, S.B., Howe, L., & Kirschenbaum, H. (1978). *Values clarification: A handbook of practical strategies for teachers and students* (2nd ed.). New York: Hart Publishing. Hadley, MA: Values Press.

177. Slavin, R.G., Sharon, S., Kagan, S., Hertz-Lazarowitz, R., Webb, C., & Schmuck, R. (Eds.). (1985). *Learning to cooperate, cooperating to learn.* New York: Plenum.

178. Smith, G., & Smith, A. (1992.) *You decide!: Applying the Bill of Rights to real cases.* Pacific Grove, CA: Critical Thinking Press and Software.

179. Smolowe, J. (1993, April 5). Sex with a scorecard: A group of high school boys who tallied their conquests ignites a debate over teenage values. *Time.*

180. Sparks, R. (1991). Character development at Ft. Washington Elementary School. In J. Benninga (Ed.). *Moral, Character, and Civic Education in the Elementary School* (pp. 181–182). New York: Teachers College Press.

181. Staub, E. (1972). Instigation to goodness: The role of social norms and interpersonal influence. *Journal of Social Issues, 28,* 131–151.

182. Staub, E. (1978 & 1979). *Positive social behavior and morality,* volumes 1 and 2. New York: Academic Press.

183. Steinfels, P. (1992, May 24). A political movement blends its ideas from left and right [This article discusses the "communitarian" movement. "From kindergarten to college, the communitarians argue, schools should make moral education and character formation leading priorities, rejecting the idea that Americans are so divided over basic values that moral education is impossible"]. *New York Times,* Section D, p. 6.

184. Stone, I.F. (1988). *The trial of Socrates*. (p. 88).Boston: Little Brown.

185. Superka, D. (1975). *Values education: Approaches and materials*. Boulder, CO: ERIC Clearinghouse for Social Studies/Social Science Education and the Social Science Education Consortium.

186. Swisher, J. (1989). *What works?* University Park, PA: Pennsylvania State Univ./Pennsylvania Office of Substance Abuse Prevention.

187. Task Force on Values Education and Ethical Behavior. (1983). *1984 and Beyond: A reaffirmation of values*. (pp. 6–7). Towson, MD: Baltimore County Public Schools.

188. Taylor, D. (1991, September 11). Half-time schools and half-baked education. *Education Week*.

189. Tobias, A. (1991). *Kids say don't smoke: Posters from the New York City smoke-free ad contest*. New York: Workman Publishing.

190. Tobler, N. (1986). Meta-analysis of 143 adolescent drug prevention programs. *Journal of Drug Issues, 16*, 537–567.

191. Tye, J. (Ed.). (1993, Spring). Teen smoking rates increase. [Reporting the results of the annual Parents Resource Institute for Drug Education survey of teenage drug use. "Throughout the 1980's, teen smoking stayed at a stubborn plateau despite all efforts to bring them down. Since about 1988, the number of young people smoking cigarettes has begun to increase." For example, between 1991 and 1992, there was a seven percent increase in smoking among high school students and a 12 percent increase at the junior high level]. *Tobacco Free Youth Reporter, 5*(1), p 1.

192. Valett, R. (1983). *100+ peace strategies for conflict resolution and the prevention of nuclear war*. Fresno, CA: Panorama West.

193. Values Press. (1993). Materials list and workshops on values realization. Old Mountain Road, Hadley, MA 01035.

194. Waitley, D. (1987). *The winning generation: The self-esteem training program for youth*. Cedar Falls, IA: Advanced Learning Consultants.

195. Wallace, J. (Ed.). (1991, Fall). Turning point: Drug users now a minority. *"Just Say No" Newsletter, 4*(1). (Published quarterly by Just Say No" International, 1777 No. California Blvd., Suite 210, Walnut Creek, CA 94596).

196. Wideman, R., and Wood, M. (1983). *Personal and societal values: A resource guide for the primary and junior divisions*. (p. 6). Toronto, Ontario: Ministry of Education.

197. Williams, M. (1993, November). Actions speak louder than words: What students think. *Educational Leadership, 51*(3), 22–23.

198. Whyte, W.H, Jr. (1956). *The organization man*. New York: Simon and Schuster.

199. Wynne, E. (1991). Character and academics in the elementary school. In J. Benninga (Ed.). *Moral, Character, and Civic Education in the Elementary School*. (p. 147). New York: Teachers College Press.

200. Wynne, E., and Ryan, K. (1993, Spring). Curriculum as a moral educator. *American Educator, 20*–23, 44–48.

201. Young, C. (1991, Winter). Alcohol, drugs, driving and you: A comprehensive program to prevent adolescent drinking, drug use, and driving. *Journal of Alcohol and Drug Education, 20*–25.

Index